Vibrant
Health

in the 21st

Vibrant
Health
in the 21st

Editors:

Clemency Mitchell, MB, ChB, MRCGP
Eileen Baildam, MB, ChB, DCH, DRCOG, MRCGP, FRCP, FRCPH
Doreen Bull, MB, BS, DTM and H
Alina Clemonds, MB, ChB
David Marshall, BA, PhD

Design:

Lee Gallaher
Steve Holden

A WORD FROM THE PUBLISHERS

VIBRANT HEALTH is built on the foundations of a hugely successful earlier work.
A GUIDE TO FAMILY HEALTH, launched in 1983, has sold millions of copies.
In 1989 it underwent significant revisions for its Second Edition. More substantial
revisions and a considerable amount of rewriting were undertaken for the Third Edition
in 1993. For the twenty-first century an almost total rewrite, a total makeover and a
new title were felt to be necessary.

Health is everyone's top priority item. Don't settle for half alive. Settle for nothing less than high-level wellness! Regain your good health, feel healthy, and stay healthy. **VIBRANT HEALTH** shows you how.

Vibrant
Health

in the 21st

PRINCIPAL CONTRIBUTOR:
Dr Clemency Mitchell, MB, ChB, MRCGP

CONTRIBUTORS:
Professor Andrew Baildam
FRCS, MD, Consultant Surgeon and Professor of Medicine at Manchester University Hospitals

Dr Eileen Baildam
MB, ChB, DCH, DRCOG, MRCGP, FRCP, FRCPH

G. Martin Bell
MA, MIHE

Dr Doreen Bull
MB, BS, DTM and H

Dr Martin Clee
MD, Consultant in General Medicine with a speciality in Chest (respiratory) Medicine, Conquest Hospital, Hastings

Dr R. W. Emmerson
MB, FRCP, Consultant Dermatologist, Reading

Kristina Hammond
MA, BSc, MCSP, SRP

Dr Drusilla Hertogs
MRCP, DCH, Child Health Doctor

Dr W. M. Huse
MD, FRCS, FACS, Cardiac Consultant

Dr G. A. Jackson
BSc, MB, ChB, MFCM

Dr D. N. Marshall
BA, PhD

Dr J. W. McFarland
MD

Richard J. B. Willis
MA, MSc (Brunel), FRSH, MRIPHH, AITV, MIHE, Health Educator, Executive director
of the UK National Council for Alcohol and Drug Dependency

First edition 1983
Second (Revised) edition 1989
Third (Revised) edition 1993
Vibrant Health 2003

Published by The Stanborough Press Ltd, Alma Park, Grantham,
Lincolnshire, NG31 9SL, England

ISBN 1899505 72 5

Vibrant
Health

in the 21st

Vibrant
Health

in the 21st

Contents

Chapter One

Health or Disease

Health or disease

Disease never comes without a cause. It is not fate or our stars, nor is it often entirely due to factors beyond our control. Most diseases are due to the simple outworking of the laws of cause and effect; they are mainly the results of violations of the laws of health. This is good news because it means that most health problems are preventable, or at least can be postponed. Our own choices can lead to better health and longer life or poor health and early death.

In the rich countries of the industrialised world, the 'diseases of civilisation' prevail and are responsible for most deaths, and for much disability and chronic ill health. Cancer and diseases of the heart and circulation account for around 75% of all deaths in the developed countries, as well as much disability. These diseases are now known to result largely from the 'civilised' lifestyle – the overabundant diet with its high proportion of refined fat, sugar and animal products, the lack of exercise, the use of socially acceptable poisons like alcohol and tobacco, and the high levels of stress in general.

In the past there used to be a very different pattern of disease. Most illnesses and deaths were due to infections. Poor or non-existent sanitation and public health services allowed infections

to spread. Poverty and inadequate food lowered people's resistance, and limited medical understanding meant that there were few effective treatments. All these factors resulted in a high incidence of infectious disease and premature death, as they still do in much of the developing world. Now the picture is changing in the developing countries, but not always for the better. The western diet and lifestyle are becoming more and more popular with everyone who can afford them. Sedentary work and cars are in demand, western style high-fat fast-food outlets are multiplying, the use of tobacco and alcohol is increasing, and with all these changes, so is the incidence of degenerative disease. Thus, the poorest countries now have the double burden of unconquered infectious diseases and rising incidence of degenerative illness.

The poorest countries now have the double burden of unconquered infectious diseases and rising incidence of degenerative illness

Choosing health

The **laws of health** are so simple that children can easily learn and understand them but practising them may be more difficult. It calls for willpower and determination, especially in the face of social and commercial pressures to conform to unhealthy customs. Keeping the laws of health is the route to better health. Ignoring or flouting them sooner or later leads to trouble.

There is one law about which we have no choice, the **law of heredity**. We all inherit our basic constitution from our ancestors. We have certain bodily strengths and weaknesses which influence our resistance and susceptibility to disease. However good or bad this inherited constitution is, good health choices enable us to make the very best of what we have been given. Poor choices will have the opposite effect.

The other laws of health can be summed up under four main headings. These are the laws of activity and rest, the laws of nutrition, the laws of avoidance and the laws of the mind and spirit.

The Laws of Activity and Rest

Our bodies are designed for action. Four hours of vigorous outdoor work each day would be ideal, but unfortunately in the West most people have sedentary jobs that leave little time for exercise. Dr Kenneth Cooper, the father of aerobics, found that his volunteers were relieved of all sorts of symptoms when they followed his exercise

programme. Brisk exercise is, in fact, a major factor in longevity, and in the prevention of heart attacks, stroke, cancer, arthritis and many other problems.

The Laws of Nutrition

There should be an adequate supply of simple, wholesome food, prepared simply and naturally, and an adequate intake of clean, pure water. The type and amount of food should be appropriate to the person's age and occupation, and the climate they live in. They should eat at regular intervals, with the largest meals early in the day, and there should be no between-meal or bedtime snacks. As well as being nutritious, the food should be appetising and should be enjoyed.

The Laws of Abstinence from Poisons

This includes those socially-acceptable poisons: alcohol, tobacco, other varieties of recreational and mind-altering substances, and all unnecessary medications. It also includes avoidance of poisons in the form of pollution, whether from traces of herbicides and pesticides in food, industrial and domestic pollutants or car exhaust. (*A word of explanation here:* no one can possibly remain in this world and avoid all contact with pollution, but there are many choices that one can make to diminish the amount one encounters. People have to make their own decisions about how much they can do and still have time to get on with the rest of their lives!)

The Laws of the Mind and Spirit – Trust in divine power

A peaceful and cheerful frame of mind is necessary for optimum health. Those who have tried it will testify that the best way to achieve such a state is in a close relationship with God. Trust in divine power also builds trust between people – parents and children, teachers and students, colleagues and workmates. When people trust each other, it greatly reduces the interpersonal stress that contributes to disease. One of the ways of building trust in divine power is by studying the Creator's handiwork in the design and working of our own bodies. The complexity of the human body is astounding, and inspired King David to write. 'I will praise you [God], for I am fearfully and wonderfully made.' (Psalm 139:14.) What better motivation could there be for maintaining health, than to keep our bodies fit for our Creator's service?

Fighting disease

Our bodies have a truly amazing **defence system.** When danger threatens, the emergency services of the immune system go into immediate action to ward off the invaders. We, by making right choices, can actually make a great difference to their efficiency and effectiveness.

Although in the West most deaths, disabilities and chronic ill health are due to degenerative diseases, infections still cause many minor, as well as some major, problems and our bodies have a very active defence system to get rid of these foreign invaders. Infections occur when micro-organisms – bacteria, viruses and others – invade, and the defences are mobilised as soon as they enter the body. Because most people in the West are fairly well fed and live in reasonably hygienic surroundings, our immune systems win most of the time, and we have good medical care and powerful antibiotics to take over should they start to lose. The situation is very different where there is too little food, and bad sanitation. Then the invaders win much more often.

> **(!)**
> **When danger threatens, the emergency services of our immune system go into immediate action to ward off the invaders**

Keeping invaders out

First-line defences. Danger threatens at each place where invading organisms could gain entry into the body, and they each have their own specific defences.

The **skin** is perhaps the most obvious line of defence. Invaders can't usually enter if it is clean and intact. The **nose** is well equipped for defence against foreign material that gets breathed in. The hairs filter out larger particles of dust, etc, and the slippery mucus secreted by the cells lining its walls traps germs and small materials including micro-organisms, so they can be blown or sneezed out. The breathing passages in the **lungs** have ciliated surfaces. Cilia are tiny hair-like projections that work together like brushes. They beat rhythmically, moving mucus with its trapped dust and germs up to the throat from where it can be removed by coughing or swallowing. When viruses or bacteria take hold, extra mucus is produced in an attempt to wash them out, hence the running nose or productive cough. Colds, flu, bronchitis and pneumonia all develop from airborne organisms that enter via the nose or throat.

The tears are an important part of the **eyes'** defence system. They contain a mildly antiseptic substance which deals with most invaders. The lids, which close involuntarily when danger threatens, also have a function of washing the tears over the eye every time they blink. Extra tears wash out any dust, dirt or other undesirable substances that get in. The **ears** are self cleaning, and the wax has antibacterial properties.

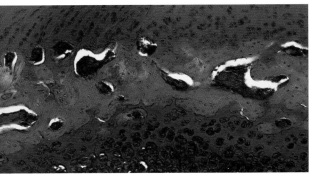

Protection against invaders in food and drink begins in the **mouth**. Saliva is mildly antiseptic. **Stomach** juice sorts out most organisms that get that far. Some very tough bugs survive to cause major problems further on, such as diarrhoea, as the **bowel** does its best to flush the intruders out. The rectum, vagina and urinary passage also have their own specific defensive properties.

Killing invaders

Second-line defences come into action as soon as harmful micro-organisms break through the first line. This is the body's major defence system, with cells stationed in every organ and tissue, and its white blood cells constantly patrolling the bloodstream and tissue fluid. It is an enormous army of cells backed up by complex support services, with huge reserves and highly efficient reinforcement production centres.

These soldiers are permanently on the

alert, instantly ready to go into combat, and can call up vast reserves at short notice. They engage in various types of defensive action, including chemical warfare – they manufacture their own special chemicals to counteract individual invading germs and their poisonous products or toxins.

The most numerous units in this army of white blood cells are usually the neutrophils. We can see their work in boils and other skin infections. Bacteria can get in through a tiny scratch on the skin, and once inside start to multiply. The neutros go into action straight away, each one trapping and ingesting a number of bacteria, killing and digesting them and spitting out the remains. If there are only a few germs and lots of neutros, the neutros will win, and the owner of the skin may not even be aware of what has happened. In fact this is what happens most of the time, when the immune system is working properly. On the other hand, if a large number of germs get in, or if the defence is weakened for some reason, the germs may win

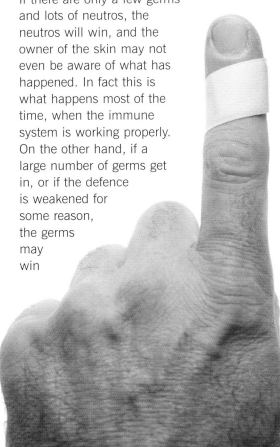

at first. A swollen red painful area will develop in which the neutros are vigorously fighting the invaders. A boil will develop if enough neutros are killed. Their dead bodies will pile up in the form of pus. Fortunately they usually win eventually as reinforcements are sent in, preventing the infection from spreading. The boil bursts, the dead cells are discharged, the germs have been beaten and healing takes place.

Chemical warfare!

There are also chemical warfare units. These are mainly the lymphocytes, which wait in the lymph tissues strategically placed throughout the body, ready for action whenever they are needed. The tonsils and adenoids are part of the lymphatic system guarding the throat, as are the lymph glands in the neck.

The lymphocytes have a number of functions, one of which is to produce **antibodies**. These are chemical weapons specifically designed to attack and neutralise particular germs and their poisons. This antigen-forming process takes longer than the neutros' response. It can be several weeks for infections like chickenpox or measles, but once formed they are designed to stay in the circulation for life, and if a chickenpox or measles virus ever dares to enter again, the circulating antibody immediately attacks and inactivates it.

Increasing the antibody armoury

Immunisation is a method of inducing the immune system to produce antibodies that will stay in the circulation and be ready to deactivate invading organisms before they have time to produce an illness. Unfortunately, they don't always produce the desired immunity, nor is it always very long-lasting, hence the need for booster doses. The idea is to prepare the body to defend itself against specific diseases, for example, diphtheria, tetanus, or polio, by stimulating it to produce appropriate antibodies in advance, so that when the germs strike, the antibody will be available at once and there will be no long time-lag during which the disease could develop. Small doses of organisms which have been modified so that they are too mild to cause disease, but still have their antigens intact, stimulate the lymphocytes to produce antibodies over the next few days. Then if the real germ attacks, the disease is prevented.

Two hundred years ago Dr E. Jenner noticed that milkmaids never got smallpox, a disease that was very common, often fatal, and usually very disfiguring.

A milkmaid told him that it was because they had had cowpox, a mild illness that they caught from their cows. Dr Jenner developed the practice of vaccination, introducing cowpox organisms through scratches on the skin. Thus began the decline of smallpox, the last case of which was recorded in the 1970s.

Since then, vaccines have been developed against many other diseases, and research continues constantly. One of the most commonly used is against **diphtheria**, a dangerous throat infection which was common and frequently fatal in Europe a hundred years ago. The incidence had already greatly declined by the time the vaccine was introduced in the 1940s, and it is now largely unknown in the developed countries of the West, but still occurs in Eastern Europe and some developing countries. **Whooping cough** (pertussis) is a respiratory infection mainly affecting young children. It is an unpleasant illness often causing weeks or months of severe and distressing coughing. It can be fatal in small children, especially if they are undernourished. **Tetanus** is caused by organisms which live in the digestive tracts of farm animals and survive in manure, soil and road dirt. They

Immunisation is a method of preparing the body to defend itself against specific diseases by stimulating the immune system to produce appropriate antibodies in advance

enter the circulation through wounds, especially deep, penetrating ones that have been contaminated. They produce deadly toxins that cause severe and painful muscle spasms that can be fatal if they interfere with breathing. This disease is now very rare indeed in developed countries, partly due to immunisation and partly due to better hygiene and care of wounds, and to improved health and nutrition in general. It is still common in those countries where there are inadequate immunisation programmes, poor hygiene, and where people are frequently in contact with animal dung. This is especially true where

it is used as fuel or in building materials. Tetanus of the newborn occurs in some areas, the organisms entering through the umbilical cord stump.

Polio is a virus passed via the digestive tract, for example by drinking water that is polluted by sewage. It attacks the nervous system and causes muscle paralysis, and death if it paralyses the respiratory muscles.

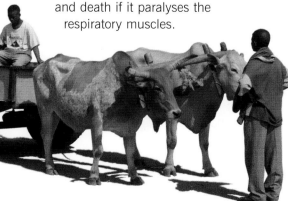

It takes its greatest toll in childhood. It is now extremely rare in developed countries and the Word Health Organisation hopes for its global elimination in the near future.

Meningitis can be caused by several different organisms. It is a dangerous disease that attacks the membranes that surround and protect the brain, and is frequently fatal. Immunisations have been developed against two of the most common and dangerous types.

MMR is a combined vaccine offering protection against measles, mumps and rubella in one shot. **Measles** used to be very common. In developed countries, where children were fairly healthy and well fed, most recovered completely, but in a few rare cases there were serious complications. Some children died or had severely disabling after-effects such as deafness or blindness. In poorer countries, especially where there is inadequate food, and living conditions are poor, serious problems are much more common. **Mumps** is usually a mild illness, but with the possibility of very occasional serious complications, such as sterility if it affects the testicles, or even death if it affects the brain. Fortunately, such disasters are rare, but they are so serious that a vaccine has been developed to prevent this mild disease. **Rubella** (German measles) is usually such a mild disease that it may not even be recognised. However, this is an illness that can have a devastating effect on the unborn child if it affects the mother during the early part of her pregnancy.

Doubts and dilemmas

As effective immunisations are developed and those diseases become rarer, there is eventually a point where the problems due to the disease are fewer than the problems

due to the immunisation. It can also become a problem as to which ones should be given and when, as there is a limit to the number of times parents can be called to bring their children to clinics for jabs, especially if they fear there may be side-

effects. Already in the UK babies are offered immunisations against six different organisms at the age of eight weeks, and boosters at twelve and sixteen weeks. We are assured that there is no danger in this system, and few serious side-effects are ever encountered at the time, but questions have been raised as to whether this is really the best for such young immune systems.

As one group of illnesses is eliminated, another group seems to develop to take its place. In the developed countries there has been an enormous increase in childhood asthma and other allergic problems. These involve the immune system and some have questioned as to whether immunisation programmes could in some mysterious way have contributed to this problem. There has also been a huge increase in the diagnosis of attention-deficit hyperactivity disorder, in children in the developed countries. There may well be multiple causes for this, but some experts are wondering whether some subtle changes caused by immunisation could also contribute to this and to some cases of autism. So far the evidence of a link is considered to be inconclusive. However, it seems sensible to limit child-

Cold water on the feet sends a message of imminent danger and activates the immune system

hood immunisations to diseases that present a danger in their own particular environment, and to the ages when they are likely to encounter them. It is wise to immunise against diseases of which there is a real danger, especially those for which there is no effective treatment. Where malnutrition is a common problem along with over-crowding, poor sanitation and hygiene, the need is even more compelling.

Building resistance naturally

Immunisations can obviously be lifesaving, but resistance to disease depends on much more than the presence of specific anti-bodies. General health and well-being are basic to our resistance to both infections and degenerative disease. There are a number of completely natural ways of boost-ing our defences, about many of which we have choices, either for ourselves or for our families.

Vigorous **exercise** increases the number of white blood cells in the circulation. It speeds up the circulation, so speeding up the process of getting the defence forces to their battle stations, among its many other good effects. Regular hours for **rest** are important too, because the immune system is restored while we sleep. Hormones and body cycles have inbuilt rhythms. Regular hours really are important, especially if there is risk of illness, or if there is actual illness.

You can also boost your white cell count with **cold water.** Cold water on the feet sends a message of imminent danger to the immune system and calls for instant mobilisation of white cells. Dry your feet quickly and put on warm socks after the cold foot bath. You will feel comfortable and your

white cells will remain on the alert. A cold shower or bath has the same effect. This is a good daily practice manoeuvre for the immune battalions. It will also be a pleasant prospect in a warm climate, less so in a European winter! But there is good news: if you take a warm bath or shower, you will get a similar effect if you simply finish off

Cheerfulness stimulates your immunity to disease

with a few seconds of cold water. Be sure to dry quickly and within a few seconds you should feel a warm glow. The cold water will have closed down the superficial blood vessels that throw off heat after the warm bath and you will feel warmer, having had your final cold splash, than you would have done had you stepped straight out of the hot. A word of warning: beware of chilling – too much when you are not used to it will leave you feeling cold and this will have the opposite effect of actually depressing your immune system.

Healthy eating boosts the immune system. All the natural plant foods have helpful properties – the fruit, vegetables, grains, nuts and seeds. There should be a good proportion of fruit and vegetables. Some cooked, some raw. Variety is not only the spice of life, but it is also an important factor in staying well. As well as their quota of vitamins and minerals, the different plant foods each contain their own individual blend of phytochemicals (plant chemicals), each one helping to enhance our defence systems in their own way. Refined foods, especially those high in sugar and fat, have the opposite effect.

Breastfed babies get passive immunity – antibodies from their mothers' blood are passed on in the milk. Breastfed babies have fewer infections of every sort, and they get a head start in preventing future degenerative diseases.

There will be much more about the **laws of avoidance** later in the book. Just to say here that poisons, including socially acceptable ones, all depress the immune system in their own specific ways.

The laws of the mind and spirit. Be happy and cheerful and trust in God for help in meeting the stresses and tensions of everyday life. The mind has an influence on all body systems and their activity. Depression slows down, cheerfulness stimulates. Fortunately, we are not totally at the mercy of our feelings in this matter. We can use our will to think about pleasant topics even if we are feeling terrible. Harness your will-power and if cheerful thoughts are impossible, breathe a prayer of thanks for whatever positive factors you can think of. If possible, say it aloud. Read a psalm of praise, will yourself to sing a cheering hymn or song. As you make this effort, it actually alters the chemistry of your brain. Endorphins help to lift our spirits *and* they boost the immune system too. Cheerful thoughts *do* help to heal the body as well as the soul.

Chapter Two

HIV, AIDS, STDs

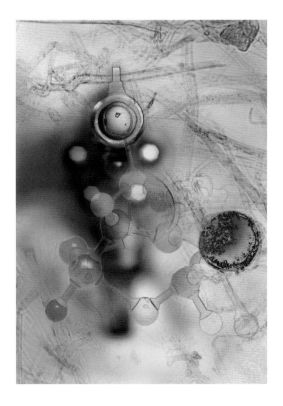

The Human Immunodeficiency Virus (HIV), the causative factor of the Acquired Immune Deficiency Syndrome (AIDS), has been variously described as The Global Epidemic[1] and in particular as An African Crisis.[2] One scientist stated, 'We've learnt to think of HIV as a simple-minded mass murderer at loose in the immune system.'[3] Another writer says, 'Fifteen years into the AIDS epidemic, optimism is a foreign state.'[4]

As these introductory remarks indicate, there is present a disease of the immune system that not only plays havoc with all the body systems but which has affected so many people worldwide that it is considered epidemic if not pandemic. Statistics are outdated as soon as they are written. New cases are recorded at an alarming rate. The total number of HIV cases worldwide has reached 47,000,000 of which 34,000,000 live in Sub-Saharan Africa. To date, those who have gone on to develop AIDS worldwide and to die of the conditions associated with the virus amount to 13,000,000 people of whom again 11,000,000 were citizens of Sub-Saharan countries.[5] As yet no remedy has been found which will halt the increase of new cases and deaths.

HTLV–III Virus

The organism responsible for the development of AIDS in the body is a virus belonging to a family of viruses called retroviruses which has been isolated from peripheral blood cells, bonemarrow, lymph nodes, saliva, plasma and semen. This virus has been named HTLV-III/LAV. There are also divergent strains of HTLV-III.

The origin of the virus is unknown, first being observed as recently as 1981. Isolated but unrecognised

> **As yet no remedy has been found which will halt the increase of new AIDS cases and deaths**

cases of HIV/AIDS may have been observed even earlier.

HTLV-III is so potent an invader of the body that the normal reaction of the body to produce antibodies is overcome, thus rendering the immune system 'deficient' or unable to cope. The virus lives in the host cells until sufficiently replicated to damage or destroy the CD4 or T-helper cells which are part of the body's defence mechanism.

The syndrome

A syndrome is a cluster of symptoms and signs of a disease or condition which if observed individually may indicate some other condition as may be seen from their description. The following symptoms become obvious over varying time-spans:

* swollen glands, particularly in the neck and armpits;
* extensive fatigue with no obvious cause and lasting for several weeks;
* unexpected weight loss, in excess of 4.5kg/10lb over a two-month period;
* fever and night sweats which might last for a number of weeks;
* persistent diarrhoea, again with no obvious cause;

* persistent shortness of breath and a dry cough;
* skin disease showing itself as hard pink/purple/dark blotches appearing particularly on the mouth or eyelids and closely resembling blood blisters or bruises.

Persons infected by the HIV frequently develop serious diseases associated with the lungs, digestive and central nervous systems. Two illnesses which are commonly found in AIDS patients are Kaposi's sarcoma which is a rare form of cancer affecting the

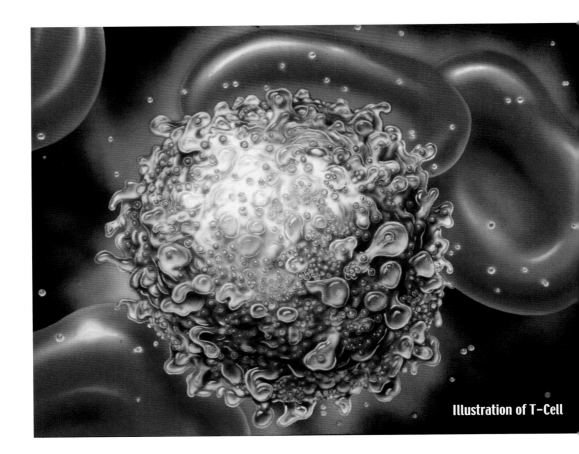

Illustration of T-Cell

skin and, to some extent, other parts of the body; and *pneumocystic carinii pneumonia*.

That the symptoms and conditions started by and associated with HTV-III do take time to develop – if at all – can be seen from the fact that, of the total number of cases of HIV infection worldwide, about one third of these will develop

as a result of AIDS.[6] Sadly, many of the children are born with the HIV infection or acquire it in their early teens.[7] One report notes that teenage girls and women in Africa are up to six times as likely to be infected with HIV as males of the same age. The same report, speaking of the worst-affected regions of Central and East Africa, says that about

into the range of symptoms, or syndrome, normally regarded at AIDS. Approximately two thirds of these AIDS cases will die of the condition. So it does not follow automatically that an HTLV-III carrier will succumb to AIDS. Two thirds will remain relatively fit and well. Still, these figures should not be regarded too complacently. Currently nearly two million children in Rwanda, Uganda, Kenya and Zambia are losing their parents

half of all pregnant women are now infected with HIV, which is twice the incidence in the general population.[8] In one of the states of South Africa the HIV prevalence rates in pregnant women rose from 4-11%.[9] Little wonder that babies are born HIV positive. Health promoters have suggested that Africa's safe-sex advice should be targeted at girls and older men – the former because of their vulnerability, and the latter because of their choice of unprotected sex with underage prostitutes – although people of all ages need to be made aware of the risks.[10]

Few societies are as fortunate as Saudi Arabia where it appears that an as yet undiscovered mechanism fortifies the immune system thus reducing the number of AIDS cases by about 91% compared with the USA. Initial research has shown that one in one-hundred Caucasians have a specific genetic mutation that makes them highly resistant to HIV.[11]

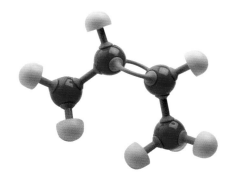

HIV/AIDS transmission

As we have already seen, HIV can be transmitted to the developing foetus through the circulating blood of the infected pregnant mother, and at a significantly alarming rate. About one in seven HIV-free babies are infected with the virus through breast milk.

More generally HIV infection is acquired through hetero-, bi-, or homosexual contact, with heterosexual encounters accounting for three-quarters of all transmission worldwide. Five to 10% of transmission is related to homosexual activity, a figure that roughly parallels intravenous drug use although not related for the most part. HIV-infected blood transfusions contribute 3-5% of cases, while various other sources may infect up to 17% of those affected. Since the recognition of the existence and prevalence of AIDS and its possible transmission via blood and blood products, the preparation of blood for patient use has undergone change. A heat process kills the virus in dry blood products and blood screening techniques have been introduced as part of the donor procedure.

Detecting HIV infection

On the basis of the various symptoms listed above, the presence of HIV infection will be strongly suspected and an HIV antibody test arranged. Since the virus is not detectable

because of its size, the test simply reflects antibodies present in the blood which have been produced by the body's defence system. It is to be emphasised that this is not an AIDS test. There is no test for AIDS. AIDS is a clinical diagnosis based on the syndrome or cluster of symptoms and the presence of antibodies in the blood.

In 2000 the World Health Organisation estimated that, globally, there were 36.1 million adults and children living with HIV/AIDS

The production of the antibodies may develop within a few weeks or take some months. Interim tests showing negative results may, therefore, be misleading and, indeed, a small percentage of infected people may lack the antibodies, thus giving the wrong conclusion that they are free of the infection.

In any case, both the test and subsequent reporting of the results need to be very sensitively handled, along with good long-term counselling and support where the results are positive.

Dealing with the problem

Desperate situations have called for desperate remedies. In the search for a drug response to HIV infection and the various

symptomology of AIDS a number of approaches have been explored.

Drug use has centred on drugs used to boost the immune system in the treatment of cancer and, while not meeting with universal success, they have helped to make life a little easier for a great number of people. The drugs of choice up to now have been zidovudine (AZT), didanosine and zalcitabine, singly in the early days of AIDS treatment and more latterly as a cocktail of antiviral drugs. A new drug, nevirapine, field tested in Uganda, turned out to be better than AZT in a group of six-hundred women with HIV. At around fifteen weks after birth 25.1% of babies whose mothers had received AZT were infected with the virus, in the group of babies whose mothers had received nevirapine 13.1% had the virus. It is thought that with nevirapine being the most effective and cheapest option – around $4 per baby – hundreds of thousands of babies could be spared from starting life with HIV.[12] Coupled with the intense AIDS education given in Uganda, and a consistent fall in new cases over a few years, there might after all be some hope.[13] In other places research

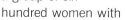

has shown a drop in maternal transmission rates of HIV to 50-70% if mothers are treated with AZT.[14]
It has been

estimated that by 2005, sixty-one out of every one thousand babies born in South Africa will die before reaching their first birthday. If AIDS were taken out of the mortality figures the death rate would drop to thirty-eight babies per one thousand.[15] One attempt to make this drop a reality has

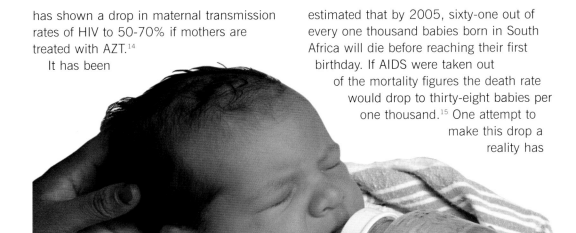

HIU and AIDS - the facts

HIV stands for **H**uman **I**mmunodeficiency **V**irus. This virus was isolated in Paris in May 1983 by Luc Montagnier and has peculiar characteristics. It is a retrovirus and is spread in three clearly defined ways:
1) Through unprotected vaginal or anal sex;
2) Through blood-to-blood contact especially where needles are shared by drug users or through unsafe transfusion techniques;
3) Maternally from mother to baby during pregnancy.
HIV is unique in that it fights the CD4 or T-helper cells which co-ordinate the immune system's fight against infection. Most of the

CD4 cells are damaged rather than destroyed by the viral attack, consequently they do not work properly and the immune system's response to HIV is dampened down.

AIDS results from being infected by HIV, and the initials stand for **A**cquired **I**mmune **D**eficiency **S**yndrome. Acquired means that it is caught; Immune Deficiency means the body has lost the ability to fight against infection; Syndrome means a collection of physical signs.

focused on the production of an HIV vaccine. Early attempts to use dead forms of the virus or mutated forms held out good hope, especially since the majority of the people vaccinated have had good health for about a decade. Now these hopefuls have finally started to develop signs of AIDS, so an effective vaccine is ruled out for the time being, although experiments with genes still aim at vaccine production.[16]

It is ironic that research for an HIV vaccine is still a main goal in HIV/AIDS reduction since a controversial theory has it that the tremendous leap in HIV cases coincided with the testing of a polio vaccine in Africa during the 1950s.[17]

When the body's immune system is damaged by the HIV, serious infections may take hold. These infections are said to be opportunistic and are the ones that cause the symptoms of AIDS which may lead to the person's death.

Pneumocystic Carinii Pneumonia (PCP) and **Kaposi's sarcoma** (KS) are two particular opportunistic infections:

PCP
* caused by a fungus, pneumocystic carinii;
* slow, insidious onset; increasing shortness of breath, dry cough, occasional chest pains;
* treatable with antibiotics.

KS
* growth of blood vessel walls, beginning as a red/purple nodule which is thickened but not painful;
* such growths may be found subsequently in the mouth, gut and lungs;
* treatment will vary on site of growth.

AIDS patients who develop pneumocystic pneumonia will, along with the cocktail of antiviral drugs already listed, be treated with the antibiotics pentamidine and co-trimoxazole. Complications can arise from the side-effects of any or all of these drugs, thus adding to the sickness of the individual concerned.

Mental turmoil

The attention of media interest had focused on the medical aspects of AIDS sufferers. The death of famous people following har-rowing illness is all too well documented. The psychological turmoil for all concerned is only just now being realised. Investigators have listed the following fears of those who have been diagnosed as having a positive HTLV-III serology:

* personal distress;
* loss of insurability;
* loss of employment;
* loss of a 'lover' (with all that the word 'lover' might imply morally or immorally).

As the virus is often transmitted through sociably unacceptable practices, those affected are subject to the usual stigmas of prejudice, suspicion and isolation, causing acute personal distress. Although the virus **cannot** be passed on through the normal contact of individuals, sufferers have been treated as if they were contagious lepers.

It has been suggested by some that HIV/AIDS is God's wrath since many of the unsocial modes of transmission are con-demned in the Scriptures. The somewhat mysterious origin of the virus and lack of cure confirms in some minds the supernat-ural element. Clearly the HIV/AIDS sufferer has enough to contend with without bigoted judgement being added to the burden. It would be difficult to see why God, after thousands of years of vastly differing sins, should suddenly decide to settle his score with, among others, homosexuals, drug addicts, and babies, rather than other 'offending' segments of society. It is com-passion that is required, not condemnation.

Illustration of the AIDS Virus

Other sexually-transmitted diseases

Sexually-transmitted diseases (STDs or venereal diseases) are diseases caught by sexual contact with an infected person. Today doctors refer to these diseases as Genito Urinary Infections and these are usually treated in GU clinics. These infections include:

* **syphilis** (often referred to as pox);
* **gonorrhoea** (common name – clap);
* **hepatitis B**;
* **herpes**;
* **thrush** (Candidiasis);
* **genital warts**;
* **AIDS** (see details on pages 26, 27).

The more sexual contacts a person has, the greater the risk of personal infection and of spreading disease in the community. These sexual contacts include, along with vaginal intercourse, anal and oral sex, the latter leading to infections of the mouth and throat.

Syphilis

Next to HIV/AIDS infection syphilis has the most dangerous consequences to a person's health and is caused by an organism called a *spirochaete* because of its shape. Specifically the *spirochaete treponima pallidum* (pale corkscrew). The organism thrives in the warmth and moisture of the mucous membranes of the vagina, anus, or mouth and is present in the blood and tissue fluids of a person who has been exposed to the infection.

STAGE 1: PRIMARY SYPHILIS

* painless, clean, serum-filled sore appears on penis or vagina; can also appear on lips, anal region, or fingers;
* sore appears 1-12 weeks after sexual contact;
* sore disappears without treatment after about 2-3 weeks, thus creating a false sense of security.

> **A community where denial flourishes is a community whose members are vulnerable to the silent spread of HIV and will be unprepared for its devastating effects**

STAGE 2: SECONDARY SYPHILIS

* indistinct rash appears all over the body from 2-6 months after contact;
* low-grade fever, headaches, flu-like sore throat;
* symptoms last (if untreated) for 2-6 weeks;
* DO NOT ADOPT A WAIT-AND-SEE ATTITUDE, SERIOUS AND PERMANENT DAMAGE MAY OCCUR.

STAGE 3: TERTIARY SYPHILIS

* takes many years to arrive at this stage during which severe damage will occur to heart, brain and other vital organs.
* Treatment should be obtained as early as possible and will usually consist of antibiotics given for specific periods of time. Advanced cases of syphilis will be monitored for life.
* There is no immunity from the infection and reinfection is always a possibility.

Safe Sex

Limit your partners	→	the more you have, the greater the risk of infection.
Think before you have sex	→	obvious signs of disease or infection may be present. It is not worth the risk.
Use a condom or diaphragm	→	these do not confer absolute protection against genital infection but may help reduce risk.
Practise good hygiene	→	pass urine and wash your genital area as soon as possible after intercourse using soap and water.
Tell your partner	→	if you know you have an infection, You may have recieved your infection from your partner or transmit it to him or her.

Prevention really is better than cure. Limiting one's sexual activity to a single faithful partner will do more to reduce STD risk than most other factors. Prevention is firmly rooted in lifestyle. Changes at this level are fundamental to the total health and well-being of the individual and society. However, where treatment has been prescribed for existing conditions these should be firmly followed and all necessary checks undertaken.

Prevention

Gonorrhoea

* Caused by the *gonococcus* germ;
* Incubation period of infection 2-10 days (average 3-5 days);
* creamy discharge from penis or vagina (this sympton may be missing in women) examined with microscope slide;
* urine cloudy and burning.

   Complications may include:
* pelvic inflammatory disease [PID] in women (*gonococcal salpingitis*): where the tubes down which the eggs pass to the womb become blocked and the eggs made infertile;

* pregnant woman with gonorrhoea may transmit the infection to the eyes of her newly-born baby (*gonococcal ophthalmia neonatorum*);
* *epididymitis*, a painful swelling of the scrotum;
* gonococcal prostitis;
* gonococcal arthritis;
* fibrous urethral strictures (may need surgical correction).

All of the above complications are treatable with antibiotics.

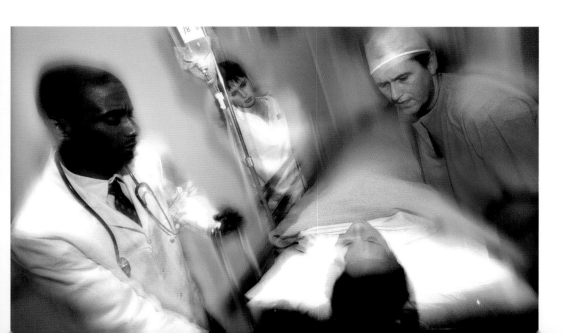

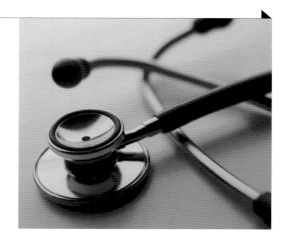

Candida albicans
* caused by a fungus-type germ
  – *candidiasis*;
* often called *thrush* or *Manilla*;
* produces a thick white discharge
  accompanied by soreness and itching
  in the genital area.

Warts
* caused by a virus – *condylomata
  acuminata* and produced in and around
  the genital area.

Herpes genitalis
* a virus of the same family as that which
  causes cold sores on the lips producing a
  crop of minute blisters on the genitals;
* may be accompanied by swelling in
  nearby glands.

Balanitis
* inflamed tip of penis usually found in
  unhygienic, uncircumcised males.

Trichomoniasis
* caused by the organism *trichomonas
  vaginalis*;
* vaginal discharge develops 7-12 days
  after infection (has an unpleasant odour);
* men may be symptomless or have a
  slight discharge and soreness of the
  penis.

Lymphogranuloma venereum
* caused by a virus and resulting in
  enlargement of the glands in the groin.

Non-specific genital infections
As the name suggests, a variety of
infections, sexually transmitted, affecting the
genitalia in different ways:
* cystitis   inflammation of the bladder;
* vaginitis   inflammation of the vagina;
* urethritis   inflammation of the urethra
                 (water tubes);
* proctitis   inflammation of the rectum
                 (anus).

Chlamydia
* a minute parasitic bacterium which if left
  untreated can cause serious infection in
  women – pelvic inflammatory disease [PID]
  with resulting infertility;
* abnormal discharge from vagina, urethra,
  penis, or anus;
* desire to pass water frequently, with pain
  and burning sensation on doing so.

Treatment for all of the above is usually
by antibiotic or antifungal preparations and
should be commenced as early as possible
to avoid any serious complications. It is also
important that sexual partners be checked
at the same time, for peace of mind if
nothing else.

Interfaith Declaration on HIV/AIDS

AIDS is an affliction of the whole human family, a condition in which we all participate. It is a scandal that many people suffer and grieve in secret. We seek hope amid the moral and medical tragedies of this pandemic in order to pass on hope for generations to come.

We recognise the fact that there have been barriers among us based on religion, race, class, age, nationality, physical ability, gender and sexual orientation which have generated fear, persecution and even violence. We call upon all sectors of our society, particularly our faith communities, to adopt as highest priority the confrontation of racism, classism, ageism, sexism.

As long as one member of the human family is afflicted, we all suffer. In that spirit, we declare our response to the AIDS pandemic:

1. We are called to love: God does not punish with sickness or disease but is present together with us as the source of our strength, courage and hope. The God of our understanding is, in fact, greater than AIDS.

2. We are called to compassionate care: We must assure that all who are affected by the pandemic (regardless of religion, race, class, age, nationality, physical ability, gender or sexual orientation) will have access to compassionate, non-judgemental care, respect, support and assistance.

3. We are called to witness and do justice: We are committed to transforming public attitudes and policies, and supporting the enforcement of all local and federal laws to protect the civil liberties of all persons with AIDS and other disabilities. We further commit to speak publicly about AIDS prevention and compassion for all people.

4. We promote prevention: Within the context of our respective faiths, we encourage accurate and comprehensive information for the public regarding HIV transmission and means of prevention. We vow to develop comprehensive AIDS prevention programmes for our youth and adults.

5. We acknowledge that we are a global community: AIDS is devastating certain parts of the world community. We recognise our responsibility to encourage AIDS education and prevention policies, especially in the global religious programmes we support.

6. We deplore the sins of intolerance and bigotry: AIDS is not a 'gay' disease. It affects men, women and children of all races.

7. We challenge our society: Because economic disparity and poverty are major contributing factors in the AIDS pandemic and barriers to prevention and treatment, we call upon all sectors of society to seek ways of eliminating poverty in a commitment to a future of hope and security.

8. We are committed to action: We will seek ways, individually and within our faith communities, to respond to the needs around us.

This document can be found under the heading 'Council Call' on the ANIN website: *www.anin.org*

References:

[1]PURVIS, Andrew (1997), 'The global epidemic', *TIME*, 30 December-6 January, page 46.

[2]DAY, Michael (1999), 'Delivering a disaster?' *New Scientist*, 30 January, page 20,

[3]DAY, Michael (1998), 'Guerilla warfare', *New Scientist*, 28 November, page 42.

[4]LACAYO, Richard (1997), 'Hope with an asterisk', *TIME*, 30 January-6 January, page 50.

[5]DAY, 'Guerilla warfare', ibid.

[6]PURVIS, op cit, page 48.

[7]SPINNEY, Laura (1999), 'A dangerous age', *New Scientist*, 25 September, page 14.

[8]ibid.

[9]PURVIS, op cit, page 47.

[10]SPINNEY, op cit, page 14.

[11]DAY, Michael (1999), 'Arab resistance to HIV remains a riddle', *New Scientist*, 20 February, page 17.

[12]JOHNSTON, Nicole (1999), 'Bargain lifesaver', *New Scientist*, 24 July, page 4.

[13]MACAULEY, Pat (1998), 'AIDS across the world', *Triple Helix*, Spring, page 12.

[14]DAY, 'Delivering a disaster?', op cit, page 20.

[15]ibid.

[16]DAY, Michael (1998), 'Against the tide', *New Scientist*, 28 November, page 5; DAY, Michael (2000), 'Kenyan Setback', *New Scientist*, 29 January, page 5; BOYCE, Neil (1999), 'End of the line?', *New Scientist*, 30 January, page 11.

[17]EDITORIAL (1999), 'The cruellest irony', *New Scientist*, 4 September, page 3; GILKS, Charles (1999), 'Blame me', *New Scientist*, 13 November, page 45.

Chapter Three

Heart Saving

Heart disease is the world's number one killer.

In the developed countries diseases of the heart and circulation cause more than 50% of all deaths.

In the developing world these diseases will soon overtake infectious diseases as the main cause of death.

At the same time, in some developed countries, although heart disease is still the number one killer, the incidence is actually going down. Finland is a notable example. In the 1960s this cold northern country, with its many dairy farms and high animal fat diet, led the world in heart disease deaths. Government policy was changed to encourage fruit farming instead of dairy farming, and to promote a better diet with more fruit and less milk.

There was also a strong emphasis on exercise and on stopping smoking. Since then, premature deaths (in men and women under 64) due to heart disease have decreased by 75%. In the USA the incidence has also fallen with this sort of programme, but not to the same extent. The incidence of heart disease varies from country to country, and between different parts of the same country. It is considerably higher in Scotland and the north of England than it is in the south east, and the highest UK incidence is in Northern Ireland.

At the same time that the incidence seems to be falling, if only slightly, in

Western Europe, it is rising steeply in Eastern Europe. France remains a mystery. Why should it have a much lower incidence than the rest of Europe? Some have put it down to red wine, others to more sunlight, or the higher intake of fresh fruit and vegetables.

As far as the rest of the world is concerned, the more westernised the diet and lifestyle become, the higher the incidence of cardiovascular disease. This is a very serious problem to those developing countries that have not yet overcome the problems of infectious disease. They now have the double burden of the diseases of wealth in one half of the population and the diseases of poverty in the other half.

Heredity - age - lifestyle

Many different factors contribute to the incidence of cardiovascular disease. Heredity is important. Those with a family history of

heart attacks, stroke and other diseases of the heart and circulation, are more at risk. The risk increases with age, and is higher in males, though after the menopause women start to catch up. The rest of the risks concern lifestyle factors which can be changed and about which most people can make choices.

Risk factors

There are four very important and well-known medical risk factors, that were first widely demonstrated by the famous study, still going on, which started in 1949 in the small American town of Framingham. By the late 1970s it became clear that the people of that town who had these conditions were at a much higher risk

The World Health Organisation states that 50% of cardiovascular disease could be prevented if people could be persuaded to adopt healthier lifestyles

of coronary heart disease than those who did not. These conditions that predispose to heart disease are • high blood cholesterol, • high blood pressure, • obesity and • diabetes.

✱ They are all very much affected by lifestyle factors, especially diet. Any one of them alone will increase the risk, and the more factors present, the higher the risk.

✳ Smoking alone actually raises the risk of cardiovascular disease more than any single one of these factors and compounds the risk when other factors are present.

✳ Physical inactivity and stress are also important.

These findings suggested that factors that would lower blood cholesterol, blood pressure, blood sugar and weight would reduce the incidence of heart disease.

The World Health Organisation Cardiovascular Disease Prevention Programme states that 50% of cardiovascular disease could easily be prevented if people could be persuaded to adopt healthier lifestyles. Those working in lifestyle medicine are convinced that an optimal

programme will prevent 90%. Such a programme is one that includes healthy eating, vigorous exercise, freedom from poisons, and freedom from harmful stress.

Risks in reverse

Not only can cardiovascular disease be prevented, it can be reversed. Nathan Pritikin, who was not a medical man but an engineer, set up a programme in the 1970s in Southern California which worked wonders in relieving the symptoms of cardiovascular disease. Similar methods are used at Weimar Institute, also in California, and a number of other places, with outstanding results. But it was only when Dean Ornish, at the University of Sacramento, in the early 1990s, published a paper demonstrating that coronary artery blockages actually decreased on his programme, that the medical profession began to accept that the disease could be reversed. His programme included • very low fat, very low cholesterol diet, • regular exercise and • stress control. His patients had angiograms (special imaging techniques that measure the

diameter of the coronary
arteries) at the begin-
ning and end of the
programme. He also
had a 'control group' of
patients with similar
problems, but who were
not on the programme.

The angiograms
showed that over 80%
of those on the pro-
gramme had *regression*
of their arterial disease:
that means that their
arteries were less
blocked. Over 80% of
the *control group's* arteries were more blocked at
the end of the yearlong
research programme.

How the heart works

The heart is quite simply
a pump with extraordi-
nary powers of self serv-
icing and self repairing.

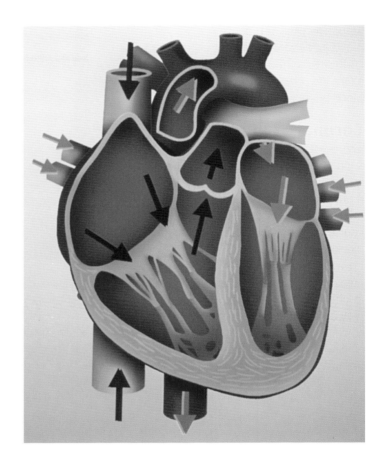

It is built of a unique type of muscle fibre
with a built-in electrical conducting system
to co-ordinate its action. It beats around
seventy times a minute, totalling 100,000
beats a day, never stopping as long as life
lasts, and only resting in the fraction of a
second between beats. If it should stop for
more than a few seconds we would lose
consciousness, and if it was not started
within a few minutes, irreversible brain
damage would occur, and soon after that
death.

The heart is actually two pumps, joined
side by side, and working together in com-

plete harmony, pumping the average adult's
five litres of blood round the entire circulation every five minutes. The pumps each
consist of two chambers separated by
valves. The upper chambers receive the
blood and the lower chambers pump it out.
The right atrium or upper chamber receives
the dark blood that is low in oxygen and
high in carbon dioxide as it comes back
from the rest of the body, and the right ventricle pumps it to the lungs. In the lungs the
blood gives up its load of carbon dioxide
and takes on a new supply of oxygen,
which gives it a bright red colour. The left

atrium receives the bright red oxygen-rich blood and the left ventricle pumps it round all the rest of the body, where it reaches every tissue by way of the 100,000 miles of blood vessels.

Coronary arteries

The heart has its own special circulation to supply the blood to its muscle tissue. These are the coronary arteries. By far the commonest cardiovascular problem is coronary artery disease. In this disease, over the course of many years these arteries get blocked by fatty material, just as pipes fur up with calcium deposits in hard water areas. It's a gradual process, often starting in childhood, and appreciable fatty streaks may be visible in the arteries by age twenty. By forty, the arteries may be 50% blocked. Usually there are no symptoms at all until an advanced stage is reached, for example a 70% blockage at age sixty. By now the heart is unable to get enough oxygen for the extra work involved in physical exertion like going up stairs or walking uphill, or with emotional stress.

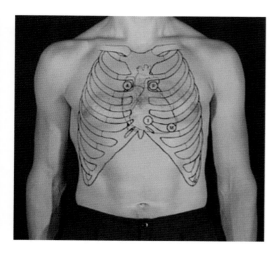

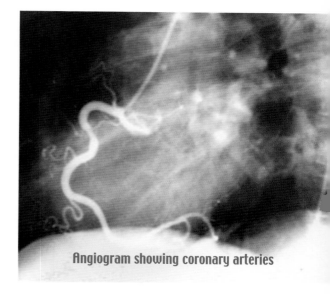

Angiogram showing coronary arteries

Angina

The first sign of trouble may be angina: pain or tightness in the chest in these situations. Other people are less fortunate, and their first symptom of trouble may be a heart attack, possibly a fatal one. A blockage can be due to a sudden spasm of an artery, or to a breakdown in the fatty lining causing a blood clot to form. If only a small area loses its blood supply, complete recovery is possible, but a larger area will take longer to heal and the heart may be left permanently weakened. A really large area of damage will prevent the heart from working at all and death will result.

Causes

• High blood cholesterol • high blood pressure and • obesity are three related factors that all promote cardiovascular disease.

If the cholesterol level is high, other fats are likely to be high as well, and that means

Most disease processes can be shown to be attempts by the body to overcome abnormal situations

that the blood is relatively thick, sticky and viscous. This sort of blood needs more pressure to get it around the circulation, so the blood pressure tends to rise. Fatty deposits get left in the walls of the arteries and over the years they become narrower, and this also needs a high pressure to keep the blood circulating. Sticky blood at high pressure going through narrow clogged up vessels is a recipe for disaster. In addition, the overfilled fat storage tissues need extra blood vessels, making another demand on the heart and blood pressure.

Why does the fatty material stick to the artery walls in the first place? Evolutionary theory might tell us that it is due to a design fault in the human organism. Actually, most disease processes can be shown to be attempts by the body to overcome abnormal situations. Atherosclerosis (*athero* means soggy and describes the fatty material, *sclerosis* means hardening, referring to the fibrous material) begins with a healing process.

Although coronary artery disease is the most well known, the process can affect large and medium sized blood vessels throughout the body. A tiny break in the lining of an artery is quickly repaired with a very thin layer of fatty material, which is then

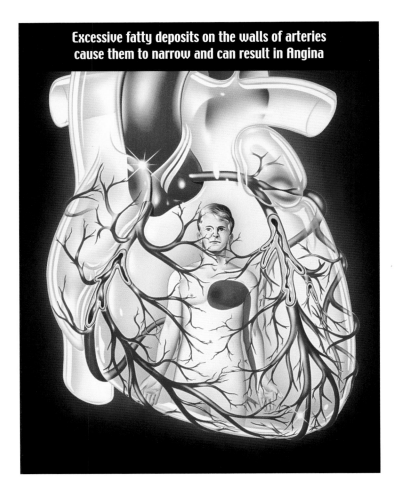

Excessive fatty deposits on the walls of arteries cause them to narrow and can result in Angina

sealed in place with a very thin layer of fibre. The original damage to the artery wall could be due to some harmful chemicals in the circulating blood. This could be compounded by lack of vitamin C, as one of the well-known effects of vitamin C deficiency is leaky blood vessel walls, and it could be that the cholesterol fibrous patch is a temporary repair job to maintain the wall until the conditions are right for removing it. If the conditions are not improved, the process continues repeatedly until the artery is almost completely blocked up. If, however, the wrong conditions are reversed, the arterial blockage can begin to reverse too.

In the last half century enough research papers to fill a warehouse have been published linking atherosclerosis to dietary fat and cholesterol. The conclusions of these papers consistently link coronary artery disease and the other degenerative arterial diseases with cholesterol and saturated fat intake.

Cholesterol occurs in all animals but does not occur in any plants. It is present in every animal cell and is present in every animal food product except egg white. (Eggs are enormous single cells and the cholesterol is in the yolk.) Saturated fat is the prominent fat in mammals, including, of course, cows, sheep and pigs. The saturated fat is also present in their milk, which is one reason why ovolacto vegetarians are still prone to

heart disease. When saturated fat is present with cholesterol in the food, the blood level and arterial damage is worse than it is if the cholesterol is associated with unsaturated fat as it is in fish and poultry.

The standard cholesterol-lowering diets emphasise limiting red meat and using chicken and fish, and skimmed milk. These diets were worked out before it was understood that animal protein raises cholesterol levels, even in the absence of fat, which goes some way to explain why these diets have not been very successful. It is important to understand that fish and poultry do not, as many think, lower cholesterol levels; they actually raise them, but less so than red meat does.

Plant foods

Plant foods are the obvious choice for preventing
and reversing arterial disease. They contain
no cholesterol and the fats they contain are
pre-dominantly
unsaturated. They
also contain fibre
which acts as a
trap to remove
cholesterol from
the digestive tract
before it is
absorbed. A plant
food diet is ideal
in every way. It
adds no cholest-

erol and little saturated fat to the blood, making it thinner
and less likely to clot. This blood is much easier to pump
around the system, so the blood pressure can be lower.
As a plant food diet tends to be bulkier and more filling, it
is lower in calories and, if there is an increase in exercise
as well, the fat stores can be reduced along with the extra
blood vessels they needed. This type of diet is also likely
to be high in vitamin C, which is necessary for healthy
arteries.

An unrefined plant food
diet will help to prevent
cardiovascular disease by
• lowering blood cholest-
erol and • blood pressure,
and • by helping to reduce
weight. In fact it is the only
permanent way to reduce
weight for many people.

As it brings down the
weight it brings non insulin
dependent diabetes (much the
commonest type) under control
as well. In fact, you just can't
lose with a natural unrefined
plant food diet.

**Tobacco is a major
factor in cardio-
vascular disease.
Smokers are ten
times more likely
to die before 60
than non-smokers,
and many of these
deaths will be due
to cardiovascular
disease**

Exercise

However, diet alone is not enough. In the UK, a sedentary lifestyle, though not the most serious, is probably the commonest cardiovascular risk factor. Most people just don't get enough exercise, and in the UK physically inactive people have about double the risk of a heart attack of those who are moderately or vigorously active. There is good evidence that regular and frequent moderately intense exercise protects against heart attacks. Thirty minutes of moderate activity on at least five days each week is recommended. People who already have

Thirty minutes of moderate exercise five days a week can help prevent heart attacks

heart problems need to exercise too, but of course within the limits of their symptoms. Walking is the best and safest all-round form of exercise, except for those who absolutely hate walking. Exercise is most helpful when it is enjoyed, and also when it has a purpose like gardening and other forms of active work.

Smoking

Tobacco is a major factor in cardiovascular disease. Smokers are ten times more likely to die before age sixty than non-smokers, and many of these deaths will be due to cardiovascular disease. The effects of tobacco smoking on the heart deserve a large section in this chapter, but to save repetition, as there is a separate chapter on smoking, here is a summary: Among the

numerous poisons in tobacco smoke, nicotine seems to be the main culprit where the heart and blood vessels are concerned. Nicotine causes the blood vessels to contract which in turn causes the blood

pressure to rise. It makes the heart muscle more irritable and more likely to beat irregularly. Smoking promotes the development of atherosclerosis and also increases the tendency of the blood to clot. In addition to all this the carbon monoxide in tobacco smoke reduces the oxygen-carrying capacity of the blood by up to 10%. This combination of effects is ideal for promoting coronary artery disease and other cardiovascular problems and explains why smokers are so much more at risk than non-smokers.

Alcohol

Alcohol poses some tricky questions. Some researchers claim that it helps to prevent coronary artery disease, and many research projects have been done, some of which do suggest that there is a contribution. This is

It is vital to cultivate a peaceful and contented frame of mind
!

puzzling, because alcohol is a very potent cell poison with a special affinity for the cells of the nervous system, and it seems unlikely that such a poison would actually have a protective effect on the heart. Seventh-day Adventists, who by and large are total abstainers, have an appreciably lower incidence of coronary artery disease than the general public. This is especially true of the totally vegetarian ones, who avoid all animal food. They certainly don't seem to miss the supposed protective effect of alcohol. Some of the research relates to the good effects of red wine, and it is true that red wine does contain some phyto-chemicals that protect the heart. They come from the skins of the red grapes, and can be obtained by eating red grapes or drinking red grape juice, without the harmful effects of alcohol.

Caffeine

Caffeine is also controversial, with experts able to quote research supporting both sides. Some have found links between caffeine and high blood pressure, and coronary artery disease. Optimal health programmes avoid caffeine because of its ability to increase stress in general and insomnia in particular. Although there may be little hard evidence about caffeine and the heart, there is plenty of evidence about other harmful effects of this popular substance.

Social, psychological and spiritual factors

Social, psychological and spiritual factors are of course very important in preventing cardiovascular disease too. Psychologists have described two different types of personality with regard to heart disease.

The type A person is aggressive, ambitious, intolerant, pushy, impatient and stressed. This is the type who is likely to have a heart attack.

Type B is calm, contented and laid back, and unlikely to have a heart attack.

These descriptions are caricatures but they do illustrate the fact that unhealthily stressed people do tend to have worse health than contented people, and many a man, and quite a few women too, have succumbed to heart attacks or strokes that have been precipitated by a fit of rage or other severe emotional stress. Psychological factors are perhaps the most important of all the factors in both prevention and cure of cardiovascular problems.

Apart from eating well, exercising well and avoiding poisons, it is vital to cultivate a peaceful and contented frame of mind. The most successful way to do this in today's stressful world, is to develop trust in divine power. In the gospel according to Matthew, chapter 11, verses 28 to 30, is Jesus' invitation to all who are stressed: ' "Come to me, all you who are weary and burdened, and I will give you rest. . . . learn from me, . . . and you will find rest for your souls." ' The Bible is a treasure chest of divine wisdom and comfort, and, believe it or not, there is now scientific evidence that religion is good for your health!

Clearing blocked arteries

✳ **Angioplasty.** There is more than one way to do this. Angioplasty is a method where a tube is actually passed into the blocked artery, under the guidance of ultrasound scanning. When the tube reaches the blocked area, it is inflated, clearing the blockage by squashing it flat against the artery wall. If this doesn't work, a stent (a tiny tube) can be inserted to keep the formerly blocked part open. Angioplasty can give immediate symptom relief, but because the cause of the atherosclerosis hasn't been removed, the arteries almost always reblock,

often within a year or so.

✳ **Bypass surgery.** Coronary artery bypass surgery is a very major and common operation in the Western world. Veins taken from the patient's leg are used to bypass the blocked areas of the coronary arteries. Between one and five grafts can be done. The immediate effects are very good, and many patients will feel better than they have done for years. Certainly the cardiac symptoms will be relieved, but this surgery can have serious side-effects, including strokes and other forms of brain damage, fortunately usually minor ones, but still enough to prevent the patient from resuming all his former activities. Even when the immediate results are excellent, unless the factors that caused the problem are changed, the grafts themselves are liable to block up within a few

> ## Diet plays an important part in cardiovascular disease control, but not all diets are equally good

years. On the other hand, with an optimal health programme, the grafts can be expected to give many years of useful life.

❋ **Lifestyle.** A much more satisfactory form of treatment is to remove the factors that caused the problem, and so start to reverse the disease process. As the disease may take a lifetime to develop, we should not be surprised that it takes a few years to reverse. The encouraging thing is that the benefits of disease reversal are felt long before the process is complete. In fact, symptoms of angina normally start to improve almost as soon as an optimal programme is started, and certainly the patient can expect to feel noticeably better after ten days.

Diet plays an important part in cardiovascular disease control, but not all diets are equally good. The standard heart diet, approved by the American and British heart foundations, could be described as a modified ordinary diet. Cholesterol is limited to 200mg a day, and fat is limited to 20% of the total calories, as opposed to the normal diet with over 200mg of cholesterol, and nearer 40% of the calories from fat. This diet is no doubt better than the average one, but it doesn't go far enough to be really effective. It may slow down the disease process, but it certainly does not stop it. In one ten-year study, the arterial blockage had increased in 41% after three years, and in 85% after ten years, in patients following the Heart Foundation's guidelines.

The diet Dean Ornish used for his

Lifestyle Heart Trial was very similar to the diet Nathan Pritikin used at his Longevity Research Institute. It consists mainly of unrefined plant food: fruit, vegetables, whole grain cereals and pulses, and a very small amount of skimmed milk products and egg white, adding up to 5mg of cholesterol a day and under 15% of the calories from fat. After one year on the Lifestyle Heart Trial diet, 84% of patients showed a measurable improvement, according to their angiograms. Their total cholesterol levels came down, the good HDL level rose, and the bad LDL level fell. Additional factors in the programme were stress management train-

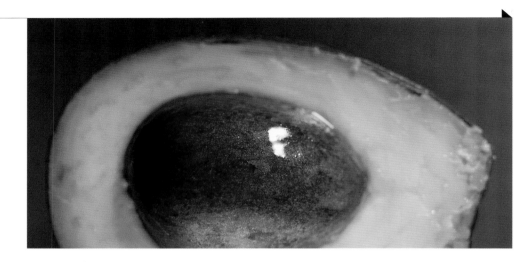

ing, avoiding smoking, alcohol and caffeine, the latter not so much because of any direct effects on the heart, but because stress control was also an important factor in the programme.

The diet at Weimar Institute and its sister institutions goes further. It is 100% plant food, and therefore 100% cholesterol free. As it is almost completely unrefined, a wide variety of seeds and nuts can be included, and even olives and avocados, without fear of there being too much fat. The average unrefined plant food diet provides most of its calories from carbohydrate (mainly as starch) and 10-15% each from protein and fat. This programme also produces very good results. It gives rapid relief of symptoms including angina, normalisation of blood pressure, blood cholesterol and blood sugar levels, and weight loss in the overweight. There are also good results with many other degenerative problems, such as diabetes and arthritis. This programme includes vigorous exercise, encourages the use of water and sunlight as treatments, excludes the social poisons and has an optional Bible-based stress-relief pro-

gramme with daily prayer and praise.

All really successful heart programmes include strong social and emotional support. Having a support network of caring friends or relatives can make all the difference between recovery and invalidism. Let's support our harassed and overworked friends, neighbours and family members. Our encouraging input might even prevent some heart attacks. Nearly 200 scientific studies have been made of Seventh-day Adventists, to find the secret of their longer, healthier lives, and lower incidence of heart disease, strokes and cancer. One of the most important factors may well be the strong social support that belonging to a comparatively small denomination gives; but the strongest support they have comes from their belief in the kind and loving Heavenly Father who is in control of time and eternity.

We have linked the following factors with early death and heart disease: • Stress • Smoking • Alcohol • Weight • The need to exercise • Diet. Each of these factors will now be dealt with, in turn, in separate chapters.

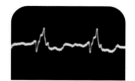

Chapter Four

How to Cope with Stress

A medical student was shown the way into a huge cylinder. It was twenty feet long and sixteen feet in diameter. It was made of seven-inch armour plate. Inside he found a beautiful little furnished apartment where he would live for the next few days.

The apartment was carpeted throughout, with a small kitchen, a bed, a settee, chair, desk and reading lamp. The whole environment inside the sealed-off room could be controlled at the will of white-coated scientists – temperature, humidity, light and sound.

The volunteer understood that the experiment he, and others, would participate in would demonstrate how we cope with changes in our environment. But it was much more than that. *It would demonstrate dramatically that the thoughts of our minds affect the health of our bodies.* Special mirrors allowed observers to look in unnoticed and elaborate sensors and wires monitored the responses in various parts of the young man's body.

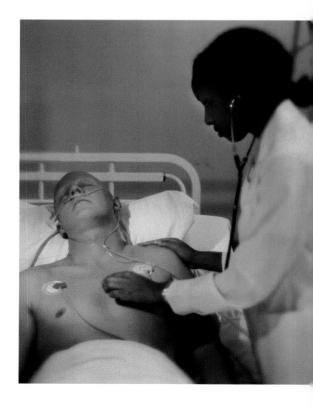

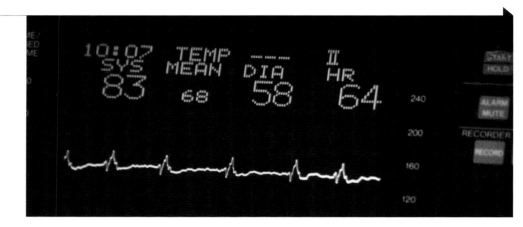

After the individual had settled into his new 'home' tests began. Information was noted from electrical tests on the brain, heart and muscles. Not a twitch or an alteration in body temperature, nor the slightest tension of muscle, went unnoticed.

The loudspeaker made it possible for the student to listen to the conversation of the staff outside the chamber. What he did not realise was that much of what seemed to be idle conversation was deliberately planned. One day, for instance, as he was lying in bed, his eyes closed, a doctor was chatting to another doctor and said something like, 'Did you write that letter you promised your wife?' Immediately the muscles that would hold a pen tightened in the student's hand. Later, when the conversation was about walking, the muscles of ambulation tensed.

The doctors went from one part of the body to another with similar responses, knowing that the student was listening to every word they said though, to look at him, it appeared he was sound asleep.

On another occasion they chatted outside the chamber and one of the men asked the other: 'How did the medical students do in the examination?' This student had taken the examination referred to and, immediate-

ly, there was generalised tension. 'Oh, they did terribly,' came the reply, and suddenly the student's blood pressure rose, his heart beat faster and his respiration rhythm changed. The doctors went on to talk about another subject – and then came in with the *coup de gráce*. They discussed a certain young lady that this boy was courting, or trying to court, and as soon as her name was mentioned his blood pressure rose significantly, his heart rate changed, his breathing became uneven and shallow and, when the doctor said, 'Yes, I met her last evening, she was out with so and so' . . . he hit the jackpot!

Scientists who have conducted this and many similar experiments have found that every thought and fancy is reflected in the physical organism. On your way to the shops or to work tomorrow morning look at the people around you. How many of them look tense and drawn, how many over the age of 25 are smiling and really happy? Most of them will have developed an unnecessary sense of urgency. Rushing around when they could walk and driving as if on a race track. You've heard of road rage. Our lives were never meant to be lived in the constant state of tension that is so common today.

We have entered a world of mobile phones, laptops and credit cards. The pace is fast-forward. Life is exacting. With all the advantages of westernised, urban living, comes stress and almost everyone suffers from it at some time.

Stress is simply the body's reaction to the wear and tear of life. Every single activity in which we engage and emotion we feel – whether it's asking the boss for a rise, getting badly sunburned or suffering loss of sleep – sets up stress. And the way your body reacts to such stress agents or *stressors* has much to do with your immediate health and your potential for a long life.

We must remember, however, that individual vulnerability to stress varies widely, and whereas one person can adjust to changes in his lifestyle, others will crumble under the same circumstances. Indeed, we should remember that stress is a very essential part of life. In its simplest form it means 'stimulation' and therefore it can

Our lives were never meant to be lived in the constant state of tension that is so common today

be perfectly true that many people work better 'under pressure', as we say.

Stress can often be the spice of life. Our bodies and our minds were built to take stress and to thrive on it and the occasional shock of adrenalin is a great cure for boredom and indifference. When handled well, stress gives us added motivation to overcome obstacles and brings us strength to handle threatening situations which might damage or destroy our happiness, our homes, our safety or our self-esteem. The problem comes with overload.

Beyond a certain level, which is different for every individual, stress becomes destructive. Intense and persistent anger, fear, frustration or worry can threaten health. It is this build-up of stress without release of tension which leads to trouble. We need to know the limits of our abilities beyond which we reap negative and harmful results.

Actually, it is not the stress itself that is so important and dangerous as the mental and physical response that we make to what Hamlet called 'the thousand natural shocks that flesh is heir to'. Recently, biochemists have come to the fore in this research on stress and have established its importance in connection with coronary heart disease. The adrenalin that is pumped into the system by all our shocks, worries and anxieties would have been used up naturally years ago by sheer hard work. In civilised society we stifle our impulses, and we take very little exercise. Our adrenalin increases the heart rate and blood pressure, increases the output of blood fats, and increases blood concentration. Lack of exercise and hard work to burn off the chemical effects of our tensions and worries is one of the major reasons why coronary heart disease is the number one killer in society today.

> **Stress is a friend or foe according to the personality of the one experiencing it**

In a similar way, we often realise that when Uncle Harry is in hospital with his ulcers it is largely due to the excessive pressures of work at his office, or to worries about his family. The more mechanised and 'up-tight' we have become, the greater the problem.

A suitable definition of stress has still to be formulated. What one person finds stressful others enjoy and there are among the population 'stress seekers' as well as 'stress copers'. Some prefer a peaceful, untroubled routine life, while others seek out problems to solve and challenges to meet. Most of us are extremely fearful of heights but there are those 'stress seekers' who like to climb

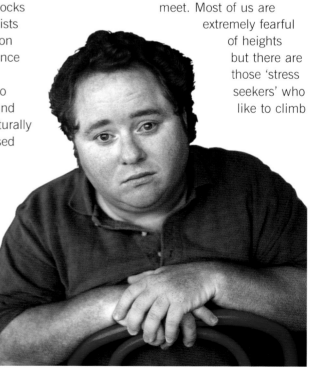

mountains or take part in free-fall parachuting or bungee jumping. To them this is exhilarating. It's unlikely, however, that the same group would want to go potholing. Stress is a friend or foe according to the personality of the one experiencing it. The overall facts are, however, that the effects of population explosion with the development of a techno-logical society, computer-isation and mass media, take their toll. Add to this the enormous increase of marital breakdown, the ever-widening generation gaps, economic crises and job dissatisfaction or loss, and you have a recipe for stress. In these circumstances most of us are stress copers doing our best to keep our heads above water.

The first signs of stress can be excessive tiredness, irritability, inefficiency at work or at home and depression, after which the body will break down at its weakest point. Some people get severe headaches, others backaches, skin rashes, bowel disorders or severe indigestion. Even these are only warning signs. But if disregarded they can lead to serious problems like the stomach ulcers and coronary disease already mentioned. Chronic hypertension, chronic fatigue syndrome, burnout/breakdowns and heart attacks follow.

Dr John Tomlinson, who prepared a television documentary on stress, said: 'The problem is getting people to recognise that these symptoms are caused by mental strain and not some mysterious "bug".'

One of the first times these harmful effects were appreci-ated was when a young Canadian hunter was injured in a shooting accident and taken to a nearby army post where his wounds were tended. The shotgun blast left a hole in his side that never healed. This fis-tula made it possible for the doctor who attended him to observe the digestive process in his stom-ach. For a number of years a Dr Beaumont fed pieces of food into the patient's stomach and watched digestion in action. By and large his patient was co-operative and, while he was in a placid state of mind, the doctor noticed that his stomach lining was a fresh pink colour. On the other hand, when he was fearful or shocked, his internal organ became pale and starved of blood. At times of anger it would appear red and inflamed and would even break out in tiny haemorrhages. This was the beginning of a

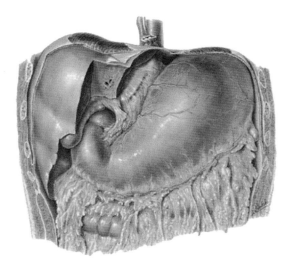

new area of medical science which some would claim points out the possible underlying reason for as much as nine-tenths of our illnesses.

Many years ago it was said, 'The relation that exists between the body and the mind is very intimate. When one is affected the other sympathises. The condition of the mind affects the health to a far greater degree than many realise. Many of the diseases from which men suffer are the result of mental depression. Grief, anxiety, discontent, remorse, guilt, distrust, all tend to break down the life forces and to invite decay and death.' – E. G. White, *Ministry of Healing*, page 241.

In Britain a counselling service exists for teachers, as for the members of many other professions. However, it would appear that teachers require far more counselling than other professionals. Their counselling service is used far more. In addition, there is a greater degree of absenteeism through illness among teachers than among any other professional group. It is accepted that the stress levels in teaching are higher than those in most, if not all, other professions.

Studies have been done on the effects of stress in a variety of social contexts. Phenomena as diverse as road rage, child abuse, and high rates of drug and alcohol abuse have been linked with stress levels.

Enough of the nature and dangers of stress; what we really want to know is how to cope with it.

Life's bank account

One of the most important discoveries in recent years is that each person is born with a certain amount of vital force which must last him all his life. The amount varies from person to person. Professor Hans Selye, a pioneer in stress research, has gathered together tens of thousands of pieces of medical study which describe the body's reaction to just about every conceivable type of

stress. He describes this bank account of nervous energy like this: 'It is as though at birth each individual inherits a certain amount of adaptation energy, the magnitude of which is determined by his genetic background. There is just so much of it and we must budget accordingly.' – *The*

Stress of Life, page 15.

In other words, we can make withdrawals of nervous energy at will but we can never increase the vital force we receive at birth by making deposits. The only control we have over this precious treasure is the rate at which we make our withdrawals.

Those who tend to be spendthrifts will soon find themselves in difficulty. Many people believe that after they have exposed themselves to stressful activities a rest can restore them to where they were before, but this is false. Experiments on animals have shown clearly that each exposure to stress leaves an indelible scar and uses up reserves of vital force that cannot be replaced. However, there is much we can do to improve our situation and maintain our bank balance.

Get away from it all

If you recognise that you are a stress sufferer, one of the best things you can do is to take a complete break from normal. There are differing opinions as to how long that 'complete break' should be. Some advocate frequent short breaks while others advocate a minimum of two- or three-week holidays at one time. If you are the kind of person who worries about packing, crowded airports and overbooked package holidays, don't

It is not the outward storms and stresses of life that disrupt and defeat personality, but its inner conflicts and miseries

plan your three weeks overseas, even if it is in the sun. Learn, too, from those people who come back from their holidays looking like dishcloths – because they have travelled thousands of miles in the car 'doing' this place or that, and have spent every night at a rave or a disco.

The whole purpose of a holiday is to relax and get away from the stresses and strains of life. This year why not plan to find a small hotel or caravan in some beauty spot where you can *really* unwind or take a boat and cruise gently up a canal or river? You will be surprised what a difference it will make. And, come to think of it, you might save some extra stress that could result from overspending on a luxury holiday.

But holidays come just once or twice a year. Try to build into your diary other days out or weekends with friends and family that can be looked forward to and enjoyed.

It took a war to teach us that we need to balance our work with relaxation

Learn to loaf a little

It took a war to teach us that we need to balance our work with relaxation. During the Battle of Britain military production was given the highest priority, and in one aircraft factory employees were scheduled to work seventy-four hours a week – they were pressed to the limit. In fact, the management, aware of high absenteeism and deteriorating morale, decided that they would try lowering the required time by ten hours from seventy-four hours to sixty-four hours a week. They were pleasantly surprised to find that production levels remained exactly the

same as before. This made them decide to experiment. After a few weeks the required work load was reduced by a further ten hours to fifty-four hours a week and as a result production – which was previously thought to be 100% – went up by 15%, and along with it the morale of the workers improved. There was less spoiled work, fewer accidents and less absenteeism.

We have the war to thank for our traditional tea break. It was found that workers improved in efficiency when in-troduced to a ten-minute break in the morn-ings and the afternoons. In some factories workers were even provided with a roll of paper on which to lie down and catnap as well. This may sound 'way out', but many businessmen today are finding this to be the answer to their stress problems, and are not ashamed to put their heads down once in a while or even stretch full length on a carpet-ed floor. Ten minutes later they are ready for anything!

Rest is the stuff of which long life is made. It can be gained in any quiet place. Give your self *cushions of time*. Stress diseases are the so-called hurry-worry ills resulting from too tight a schedule. Such pressure leads to slip-ups, accidents and injuries. Take time for yourself, lean back on your bed, prop up on two pillows and read a good book. Forget clocks, calendars, appointments, problems and debts. This time is just for you – and your body – to help you unwind and make your day a nicer one and your life a longer one.

Get plenty of sleep

It has been shown that animals die more quickly from lack of sleep than from lack of food. Sufficient sleep is vital for nervous

stability. The amount recommended by doctors varies with age, ranging from fifteen hours between three and five years, to seven or eight hours for an adult. To get a good night's sleep one should go to bed regularly at the same time and not too late. Don't let the attractions of television or other excitement shorten the time when you ought to be asleep. Nothing will age you faster, or burn up the reserves in your energy bank more quickly, than loss of sleep.

Sleep is one of nature's most effective restorers, not only physically, but mentally. It sweeps away fatigue and helps us retain our mental balance.

This short explanation may help you to understand why stress appears when there is sleep deprivation due to alteration in shift duties and other commitments, or when the family, and particularly the mother, is disturbed night after night by the nocturnal activities of babies or children.

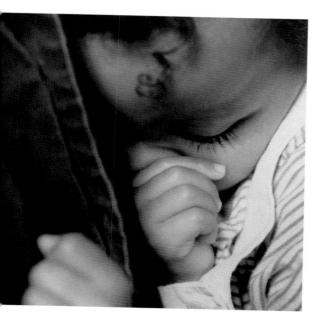

Exercise with care

For many people it doesn't help to suggest that they get plenty of sleep if insomnia is part of their problem. This too could be due to the build-up of adrenalin in their systems, and a little regular exercise which stretches the big muscles could be the answer to a good night's sleep as well as breaking the vicious chain of stress. If you have felt tension building up at the office or in the home, you owe it to yourself to balance work with play.
Sports centres have become popular places to spend a lunch hour or evening. Choose

an exercise or a sport that you will enjoy, and preferably something that you can continue in good or bad weather. Badminton, bowling, gardening, hiking, climbing, walking and swimming, all have their benefits as adrenalin-discharging activities.

Talk about troubles

You've heard it a score of times, 'A trouble shared is a trouble halved.' It always helps

Sports centres have become popular places to spend a lunch hour or evening

to get worries off your chest by confiding in a sympathetic friend. When serious problems start to get you down, don't be afraid to discuss them with your family doctor, your pastor, minister or priest, or an understanding member of your family. Gloomy, angry, unkind and selfish thoughts bottled in your mind cause the neurons in the area of the brain called the *hypothalamus* to fire nervous impulses to the pituitary glands that lie just below the brain, helping it to produce the hormone called STH. It is STH circulating in the blood that triggers the adrenal glands located slightly above the kidneys to produce special hormones that cause the blood pressure to rise, the heart to beat faster and the muscles to tune up in order to escape danger from without the body or attack infection or toxin within. When the outpouring of these hormones is caused by continuous negative thinking their effect is very harmful.

On the other hand, when our thoughts are calm and tender, the hypothalamus send forth impulses that cause the pituitary gland to secrete a chemical called ACTH, which, in turn, causes the adrenals to secrete cortisone and other substances. These substances have the effect of returning blood pressure and heart rate to normal.

An improved blood supply aids the processes of digestion, elimination and assimilation, and, as a result, we have a feeling of peace, relaxation and optimism.

If we are Christians we are able to talk out our troubles with God, who always hears and cares.

Hobbies and pastimes

Before the days of television and other forms of mass entertainment – which tend to increase our stress factors –

people spent their evenings and leisure hours in conversation, music and reading. A good creative hobby is an extremely effective prescription against stress. People who can lose their day-to-day worries and responsibilities in art, model-building, stamps, embroidery, basketry, candle-making and a host of other pastimes are fortunate indeed. One wonders, however, how many other potential sculptors, potters, flautists and dressmakers there might be among those who carry their troubles home with them in a briefcase or long for peace of mind night after night in front of the 'box'?

Hydrotherapy and massage

There is nothing like a warm bath, foaming with pine essence, to relax you at the end of a long day. Water can be used both to stimulate and relax the body. A cold mitten friction can tone up the system in the morning and a warm bath or shower prepare you for bed at night. A warm hot water bottle behind the neck will complete your comfort.

Another very effective procedure is the hot foot bath. This is valuable because of its effect on the entire circulation of the body. By dilating the blood vessels in the feet and legs it relieves congestion in other parts of the body.

Habits and an orderly way of life

By the time a child knows how to cycle, the movements necessary to maintain his balance have become reflexes. He no longer makes the conscious effort that caused his nerves to become tired and tense

in order to maintain his balance. Reflex actions take far less nervous energy than those requiring a conscious effort. For repeated actions to become automatic you must have orderliness. For example, if a working man is to do his job automatically his hand must always be able to find the same tool available in the same place. Whatever your task, orderliness and planned actions will help calm your nerves.

Seek some peace and quiet

The constant noise of machines, cars, lorries and trains, ringing of telephones and the noise of the radio, fray the nerves. Many people sleep through noises that they have become accustomed to but the brain still registers them. This is proved by the fact that if a noise to which we are accustomed, such as a ticking

clock, stops we suddenly wake up.

A British government committee on noise reported that there was no doubt that noise affects our health and is responsible for tension and speedy fatigue. Noise is measured in decibels from 0, which is the point at which hearing begins, to 120, which is the level at which the human body feels pain. The rustling of leaves may register at 10 decibels, while a noisy motor cycle or scooter 80-90 decibels. Have you thought that noise could contribute to your tensions? If you cannot avoid it at work, at least balance your life with intervals of peace and quiet in the countryside or at home, and if you live by a noisy road or railway line, double or triple glazing may be a very valuable investment for your health's sake.

Eat well

Even our diet can affect the stress that we suffer. Processed food, especially refined carbohydrates in the form of white flour products, and too much sugar, rob the body of essential vitamins of the B complex, which are the basic ingredients for a healthy nervous system.

Almost everyone who is suffering from nervous exhaustion is deficient in the vitamin B complex. For most people today who eat peeled, boiled and fried packaged convenience foods in a hurry, there is need to build up on the B complex vitamins. This can be done out of a bottle in such preparations as Brewers' Yeast tablets or, better still, by eating wholewheat bread and cereals rich in B vitamins, fruit and vegetables.

Relaxation techniques

Finally, here are a few relaxation techniques.

For a loosening exercise sit on an armless chair or stool and lean slightly forward so that your arms dangle. Shake your hands hard as though shaking off water. Pretend you are a string puppet and your shoulders are being pulled as high as possible – then cut the strings and allow them to fall. Pretend that you are carrying two heavy suitcases and feel your shoulders being pulled down then drop the cases and relax. Afterwards roll your shoulders gently forwards six times and then backwards six times. Pretend that your neck is broken and let your head drop forward. Imagine it becoming heavier. Then slowly raise it. Repeat several times.

To relax muscles deliberately is more difficult than to contract them and it can seem almost impossible for a beginner. However, there is a law of the

The proper function of the nerves is dependent upon the balancing of the load, just as with an electrical system

Gradually work through the body, trunk, shoulders, arms, neck and head, deliberately tensing and straining each part in turn, concentrating on the feel of tension, then relaxing and registering the effect of this part of your body at rest.

From a study of anatomy it is clear that there is an intricate system of conductive fibres called nerves which serve, largely through the intermediation of the brain, to integrate the various organs of the body. These nerves carry impulses by a mechanism similar to that by which electric wires carry electrical impulses.

The proper function of the nerves is dependent in great measure upon the balancing of the load which is placed upon them, just as is the case with an electrical system. When an overload is encountered, such as is produced through plugging two heavy users of electricity such as an

body whereby, when one muscle group is deliberately tensed, the subconscious mind simultaneously relaxes the opposite group of muscles to permit the contraction to occur. We can use this law to our advantage by voluntarily contracting an opposing group of muscles so that those muscles and nerves that are commonly tensed become relaxed. To do this either lie down, preferably with a low pillow and a pad or cushion under the hollow of your back, and under your thighs, or sit straight in a chair. When you are comfortable, concentrate first of all on your feet and ankles and, as far as possible, tense them up by screwing in the toes and lifting the foot. After a few moments, stop and relax, registering the feelings of your relaxed feet in your brain. In the same way, tense your calf muscles, followed by those in your upper legs and buttocks.

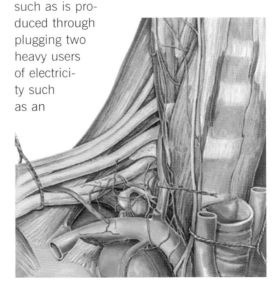

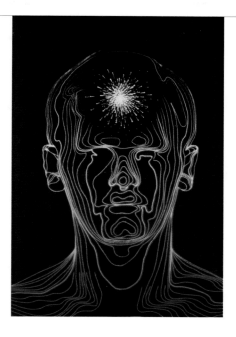

electric heater and an electric iron into the same line, the outcome may well be the burning out of the fuse. Similarly, when the nervous system which intermediates emotional and sensory impulses of the human body, becomes overloaded, a fuse has to go, or at least the superabundant nervous impulses must be sidetracked. These accumulate as bodily manifestations of disturbed emotional patterns, usually referable to emotional tensions.

These emotional patterns are somewhat diversified, but the symptom patterns are as recognisable by the experienced physician as the symptom patterns of pneumonia or appendicitis. While in any case the diagnosis cannot be made definite without confirmatory physical examination and laboratory findings, the definiteness of these emotional patterns cannot be denied.

At the risk of being guilty of oversimplification, we are listing three of the most common symptom patterns, not with the idea of affording a diagnosis from those suffering from emotional tensions, for diagnosis is not as simple as that, but in order that there may be some comprehension as to the type of symptoms produced. If overloading the nervous system can be recognised early and corrected, there is hope that the burned-out fuses, as it were, and the accumulation of emotional tensions, can be prevented before

deep ruts are worked in the road to permanent damage.

Three of the more common tension patterns suggest themselves:

1) The stiff-neck tension pattern is characterised by painfully contracted muscles in the back of the neck. From here the pain may extend upwards to the top of the head and the forehead, in the form of headache, downward into the trapezius muscles which are located above and between the shoulder blades, and/or forward to produce a tense feeling in the throat. Often it appears that this muscular tension is an attempt at compensation of 'lack of backbone' in dealing with problems. The person becomes tense and apprehensive and often there is sleep disturbance. Paradoxically this, which may have started as a manifestation of a lack of backbone, may eventually lead to a stubborn, unbending attitude such as characterised the Israelites under Moses, who were called 'a stiff-necked people'. For this reason, these sufferers often become especially hard to help because they cannot see their way clear to accepting the explanations of their symptom pattern, nor can they readily alter their ways once the pattern becomes firmly established.

2) The chest-tension pattern consists of complaints referable to the chest such as conscious (and sometimes rapid) beating of the heart, discomfort over the heart region which may even be described as pain, a sense of squeezing of the chest as in a vice, and laboured breathing even when no exertion factors have preceded it. Physiologists point out that this is largely due to an imbalance of the nerves of the heart, the nerves which put the brakes on the heart being understimulated and the nerves which speed the heart being overstimulated. Perhaps the term 'losing heart' best expresses this, for the heart is running away with itself as it were, as the driver's foot presses more firmly on the accelerator. Once the driver's foot is transferred from the accelerator to the brake, almost instantaneously relief follows. These sufferers are often fairly easily relieved of their complaints, once the nature of their source is pointed out, even though up to this time the patient is quite convinced that he has organic heart trouble. This relief is often accomplished by the resolution of an anxiety through getting it 'off the chest'.

3) The stomach-tension pattern, often referred to as 'nervous indigestion', is characterised by a feeling of bloating after eating, a sensation of inward tension in the abdomen. These symptoms correspond to what happens when the stomach is filled beyond its functional capacity. Interestingly enough, they are produced in the stomach when the emotions reach a state and type of tension such as we might describe by the term 'fed up'. Often, emotional tensions which affect the stomach are those of resentfulness and bitterness. These tensions may at times be rather tenacious. On the other hand, very frequently, temporary relief of symptoms is obtained through medicines which tend to re-establish the nervous balance of the stomach. If permanent relief is to be obtained, it is usually necessary to deal with the resentful and unforgiving spirit. Otherwise a peptic ulcer will eventually result in some cases.

Admittedly, this description of tension patterns is an over-simplification. These patterns may coexist or may change from one into the other. There are also other possible tension patterns, for instance those involving the skin, the lower bowel (colon), or the bladder. Our purpose in describing the tension patterns has been largely to emphasise that there must be forthright dealing with the causes of emotional tensions. Otherwise disease symptoms may continue to impair health and be conducive to the contracting of even more serious disease. (Paul E. Randolph, MD, FACS, *Release From Tension*, pages 19-23.)

Rhythmic breathing also calms and

God is one source of peace that we neglect at our peril

soothes mind and body. The in-breath is a sign of tension as, also, is breath holding. Think of the gasp of fear or pain. On the other hand the out-breath is relaxing. Think of a sigh or the second half of a yawn. Breathing exercises are another aid to overcoming stress. Simply sit or lie completely relaxed and, without any strain or effort, take six leisurely, pleasurable breaths. Imagine that someone is pouring air into you and fill your chest just comfortably full, no more. Keep the breathing pattern rhythmic with the accent on the relaxing outward breath. Ladies who practise psycho-prophylaxis, which is largely based on breathing patterns, have found it possible to come through one of the most stressful experiences of their lives, childbirth, without the need of gas and air or other anaesthetics, completely conscious and completely relaxed.

We hope that this chapter will help those people who find themselves tense and tired and unable to relax. You may have become aware at work or home that you feel contin-

ually tired and edgy and that you are losing your temper more often – that, in fact, you are becoming stressed. Possibly you have tried many methods of relaxation before, without success, and have wearied of the search for relief. We hope, however, that you will find what you seek in this chapter. When our minds are ill at ease we also suffer physically, spiritually, and socially, but, with change for the better in our mental attitudes, as we learn to cope with stress, all the other sides of life that make us whole beings are equally strengthened.

There is one source of peace that we neglect at our peril. One Bible writer says this about the peace that comes from perfect trust in God; 'You will keep in perfect peace all who trust in you, whose thoughts are fixed on you!' (Isaiah 26:3, NLT.) Jesus promised all his followers 'peace in me'. He continued, ' "Here on earth you will have many trials and sorrows. But take heart, because I have overcome the world." ' (John 16:33, NLT.)

Chapter Five

How to
Stop Smoking

People smoke for a variety of reasons, mostly social and psychological, and have reinforced their habits over varying periods of time. The intense physical desire to smoke in association with the range of life events and personal experiences leads to psychological addiction to tobacco. Were it not for the latter, and the medical problems that it causes, smoking really would be the pleasure that smokers claim.

Nobody sets out to become physically addicted. It is a subtle process. As the Chinese proverb has it, 'Habits are cobwebs at first, cables at last.' Medical writer Thomas McKowen hit the nail on the head when he stated: 'Our habits commonly begin as pleasures of which we have no need and end as necessities in which we have no pleasure. Nevertheless, we tend to resent the suggestion that anyone should try to change them, even on the disarming grounds that they do so for our own good.

. . . It is said that the individual must be free to choose whether or not he wishes to smoke. But he is not free; with a drug of addiction the option is open only at the beginning, so that the critical decision to smoke is taken, not by consenting adults but by children below the age of consent.'

Stopping smoking means that the would-be quitter has to attack the psychological and physical addictions simultaneously. Choice is part of the equation for success. Smokers have to choose not to smoke and then work through strategies that will enable them to break their habits.

Few people today can be ignorant of the ill-effects of smoking. Right from their school days people have learned that smoking harms their lungs, heart, arteries, brain, kidneys, bladder, skin and eyes. They know that smoking: raises blood pressure, harms the unborn baby directly and by lowering birth weight and increasing disease susceptibility, speeds up the ageing process, and that heart disease and cancers lead to disability and premature death.

For some people facts and statistics alone will be sufficient motivation to quit, but others will not be moved by the data concerning these diseases and conditions. Disease and death is associated with old age rather than youth. Waiting for the signs and

symptoms of health problems to appear before action to quit is taken may have disastrous consequences.

A clean break

Although many smoking cessation plans advise cutting down, with a particular quit-date in mind (and psychologically more bearable), the evidence suggests that it is in fact better to make a clean break.

This has been demonstrated most dramatically in studies with pregnant women who smoke. Researchers concluded that there was a direct correlation between the number of cigarettes smoked and decrease in the baby's weight. The data showed that a baby's weight decreased sharply for every cigarette the mother smoked and levelled off at a low weight around eight cigarettes a day, so just cutting down was no help. Men or women smoking even one cigarette raise their blood pressure for up to nine hours and make their lungs work harder. Making a

clean break allows all the body systems to get back to something approaching normality faster.

> **Sticking at the elimination process for ten days will bring a positive change physically and emotionally**

Eliminating nicotine

The good news about quitting smoking is that the physical addiction (but not necessarily its effects) is not such a hard matter to deal with as one might suspect. In fact it will go almost as quickly as it takes the body to be rid of nicotine, usually within 36-72 hours providing the following advice is followed. Nicotine has one redeeming feature, it is soluble in water. Assuming, of course, no more nicotine is introduced to the body, the body would eliminate nicotine quite naturally via the urinary system, by sweating and during the normal course of breathing.

The process can be speeded up by drinking lots of water and by perspiring more. Extra baths or showers will keep the skin pores open and able to work efficiently at elimination. The use of a well-wrung warm flannel mitten rub over the body extremities and torso will help to improve circulation and elimination

common to see quitters drinking tea or coffee as if it were going out of fashion, and then wondering why they return quickly to their smoking habit. Avoiding caffeine-containing drinks for at least a couple of weeks will help to break the dependency and the psychological associations.

Recent advice to quitters, from a range of stop-smoking agencies, has included the use of nicotine replacement in the form of chewing gum or patches. While these have been popular and a psychological support, in the light of what has been said about nicotine, this may not be a wise route to take. Users of these items have frequently complained of nausea and disturbed sleep patterns. At some stage even this nicotine has to be eliminated from the body, so making a clean break really is best.

Will-power

'Use it or lose it' is the slogan when it comes to physical exercise. The same is true of the use of will-power. If you thought that will-power was some kind of philosophical motivational thinking inhabiting your mind, you would be wrong.

Will-power is the ability to make decisions and to see them through. To put it another way, the ability to choose. It has a physical basis. The frontal lobes of the brain are the regions responsible for such thinking. Keeping one's brain in as good a running order as possible will help in making choices and seeing

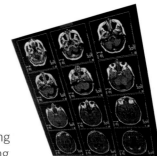

of the nicotine residues.

Since nicotine is a stimulant, the fact that the smoker is not getting his or her regular daily dose, and is eliminating residual amounts, will leave the person feeling very tired. The first three or four days are the worst, leaving the individual emotionally drained and sometimes depressed. However, sticking at the elimination process for about ten days will bring a positive change physically and emotionally.

Try to avoid quick pick-me-ups. There is good reason for this as frequently the nicotine habit has been reinforced (both physically and psychologically) by the use of drinks containing caffeine. Caffeine has a similar molecular make-up to nicotine, so using caffeine can act as a very powerful trigger for the urge to smoke. Unless the nicotine/caffeine link is recognised it is quite

them carried out. The chemistry of the brain is crucial to good mental functioning.

The brain requires one fifth of all the oxygen that is inhaled. Smoking, either directly or through passive smoking, robs the brain of the necessary oxygen and replaces large amounts of it with the exhaust gases carbon monoxide and carbon dioxide. Not only that, smoking constricts blood vessels, so hindering the supply of whatever oxygen is available. The area of choice, among others, is weakened. Anything which encourages a good intake of oxygen, such as deep breathing and exercise activities, will help the brain to function at its best. The exercise enhances the circulation and enables the brain to think more efficiently.

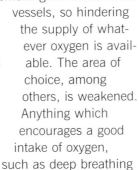

Another important aspect of brain chemistry is its use of vitamins, minerals and trace elements. The nervous system is serviced in particular by the whole range of B vitamins, each with a specific role to play. A diet rich in these vitamins will help the brain to function well. Wholewheat, wholegrains, bran, wheat-germ, and yeast extracts (such as Marmite) will provide the optimum amounts of B vitamins as part of the regular daily diet.

Where the diet has been lacking B vitamins the deficiency can be remedied by adding these to the diet or by taking a B complex tablet or Brewers' Yeast tablet (not the one with caffeine added!) as recommended on the manufacturer's label. [If you have been prescribed drugs by your doctor described as MAOs then avoid yeast products.]

Supplementation may be useful for people who show signs of physical stress and/or are not able to think clearly while quitting. Once the immediate need is passed, the diet should be able to meet one's normal requirements. If there is no obvious positive response to either the use of B supplements or the inclusion of B vitamin items in the diet the reason may be found in the amount of sugar used. As sugar metabolises (breaks down for use in the body) it burns B vitamins, so robbing the nervous system of its supplies. Cutting down on sugar may help to restore the vita-min B supply-line to the nervous system.

Will-power, then, has a physical basis which can be helped by exercise and careful attention to specific components of the diet. With the thinking apparatus working at its best, choices will be easier to make and to carry through, and will-power will become stronger with use.

All habits make chemical pathways using

What's in a cigarette?

Tobacco smoke contains over 4,000 chemicals, the vast majority of which are present either naturally in the tobacco and transfer into the smoke, or are formed when the tobacco is burnt. Below are just some of the more menacing ones:

Acetone	Solvent used as nail polish remover
Arsenic	Commonly used as rat poison
Ammonia	Added to cigarettes to enhance the addictive elements of nicotine
Benzene	Used as solvent in fuel. Also in dyes and rubber
Cadmium	Highly poisonous metal used to make batteries
Carbon Monoxide	Poisonous gas that is lethal in large doses
Formaldehyde	Used to preserve dead bodies
Lead	Highly toxic metal, capable of causing serious damage to the brain, kidneys and nervous system
Nicotine	The chemical that makes cigarettes as addictive as they are – a very powerful drug
Tar	Substance that actually transports many of the other chemicals contained in cigarette smoke directly into the body

Of the list of chemicals named above (just a few of the thousands contained in every cigarette), many are known carcinogens (cancer causing).

Few people today can be ignorant of the ill-effects of smoking

various routes through the nervous system. The advantage of this is that we do not have to keep making the same conscious choices over and over again. As we think and enact our choices the brain and

the body work together. We call this co-operation a neuromuscular action. A ten-a-day smoker will go through the same (or similar) smoking operation 3,640 times a year, deeply engraining the smoking habit and doing it automatically year after year. Smoking is a neuromuscular habit.

When we choose to make changes, we establish a new habit pathway which pro-duces chemical inhibitory substances at the nerve connections, junctions and terminals. The smoking habit is gradually replaced by the new non-smoking habit with its own pathways. Although habits can be changed, the old habit pathways do not go away, they lie dormant. In the event that someone who has stopped smoking decides (chooses) to smoke a cigarette the old habit pathways

are reactivated. This phenomenon accounts for the lapsing smoker smoking more the second or third time round than previously. One similar habit is superimposed, laid on top of another; not one smoking habit but two! Continually choosing not to smoke makes it increasingly unlikely that the old habit pathway will be called back into use. However, the risk of returning to smoking is there (although evermore distant), that is why it is said that ex-smokers are only one cigarette away from smoking.

Secondary habits

Neuromuscular habits vary from smoker to smoker. How the cigarette is smoked, the kind of personal rituals involved, how and where the cigarettes are carried, the times and circumstances under which they are

used, are called collectively the secondary habits of smoking.

To achieve success in quitting a smoker will need to identify his or her secondary habits and devise strategies to deal with them. In identifying this cluster of habits it is likely that a number of clear patterns will emerge. Whether or not this happens, an underlying strategic principle is that all these habits require a range of small counter-habits that will help to break-up the old pattern structures.

If, for example, a smoker uses the ciga-rette for creativity or stimulation before start-ing a job, or for relaxation when finishing a job, it will be necessary to find some new and non-harmful way of achieving these ends. It is best not to rely on one particular counter-habit, overused it might become a new obsession! People soon become addic-ted to boiled sweets or other substitutes.

Sweets and dummy cigarettes can pro-vide something for the mouth and hands to play with during the quitting period. How-ever, if these or other items or activities are thought of as substitutes there is a negative psychology at work. The concept of substitute is such that the word car-ries the connotation of being second best, not the real thing, and makes it easier to revert to smok-ing, the real thing.

Activities that are extrovert and distracting, keeping both the mind and body busy, especially in the early days of quitting, will help to while away the seem-

ingly longer days. Avoiding, as far as possi-ble, the usual meeting venues will also help to break smoking associations. Try a range of new and exciting options, but remember that the secondary habits of smoking will take longer than the physical addiction to shake off. It really is a change of lifestyle.

Weight control

One fear that keeps many people smoking is that by stopping they will put on a lot of weight. This is not an inevitable consequence, especially if measures are taken early enough. Nevertheless smok-ing and weight are connected.

For many people in a hurry, smoking becomes a substitute for eating,

with breakfast being the most missed meal. Smoking also acts as an appetite suppressant. When the individual stops smoking two things happen: the appetite returns and food tastes better; and people tend to eat more to satisfy the oral vacuum. Even if no extra food was eaten there still might be a tendency to weight gain as the food is digested and utilised more efficiently.

The trick is not necessarily to eat less, but rather to eat sensibly. Diets low in fats and sugars will help the body not only to maintain its ideal weight but also to protect it against such conditions as heart disease and cancer, and for that reason are part of the recommended diet of the cancer and heart disease agencies.

Their further recommendation to increase fruit and vegetable intakes will help to provide the vitamins, minerals and trace elements referred to earlier. The vitamins will boost both the nervous and immune systems. Complex carbohydrates such as legumes, wholemeal pastas, brown rice, and potatoes are of major importance in weight control and provide slow-release energy for the body's needs.

There are some foods that lessen withdrawal symptoms and these are largely fruits and vegetables. Other foods increase withdrawal symptoms and are mainly animal proteins. Use of these can increase the urge to smoke. Fortunately, the fruits and vegetables, especially if eaten raw in salads, are not going to contribute to a weight problem so can be eaten in fairly large amounts. It is not necessary to starve to control weight.

Being careful about what one eats has a number of advantages for the quitter. A selection of the right foods can take away the desire to smoke as well as provide all-round health benefits and an ideal weight. Balanced with exercise, which provides the extra oxygen, weight and fitness levels will soon contribute to a fine sense of well-being.

This sense of well-being might be sabotaged if alcohol is used. Not only does it provide 'empty calories' which may upset the weight control efforts, it also affects adversely the frontal lobes of the brain where the will-power is centred. It is important not to let down one's guard when trying to exercise will-power. It would help the quitter if he avoided alcohol (and places where alcohol is consumed) while working through the quitting time.

Outside help

Surprising as it may seem, most people who stop smoking do so without any kind of problem. While that is no consolation to those who do experience difficulties, having withdrawal symptoms or interpersonal problems is no shame; people and their circumstances are all different. Some people are happy to go it alone and would prefer emerging victorious without any kind of help.

Diet Strategy

With all of the above in mind, the following tips will be of help in planning the dietary strategy:

* Eat a good breakfast, including unrefined cereals.
* Eliminate between-meal snacks.
* As far as possible remove empty and refined calories from the diet.
* Reduce or avoid the use of free sugar and cut down on the hidden sugars in:
    - desserts (ice cream, chocolate, cake, pie)
    - jam or jellies
    - sweetened cereals or sugar on breakfast cereals (use raisins instead)
    - soft drinks or fruit drinks (use pure fruit juices)
    - tinned fruit (rather use fresh fruit)
    - tinned foods generally (often unnecessarily sweetened).
* Use brown rice rather than white rice.
* Use wholewheat bread rather than white bread (even though enriched).
* Avoid alcoholic drinks.
* Cut down drastically (or avoid) all visible and hidden fats in:
    - cooking oil, margarine, usual salad dressings (use virgin olive oil)
    - fatty meats
    - milk and dairy products (where milk is used try skimmed milk or switch to soya milk). Use non-fattening spreads in small quantities to replace margarine/butter
    - baking preparations (high in fat and sugar).
* Use at most two eggs a week.
* Eat a light fruit supper or none at all.

The statistics show that many can give up if they know that there are other people sharing their problems. To these, group quitting sessions have been a valuable source of support. However, it is not necessary to have the formal structure of a cessation programme to have a similar level of support. Besides, usually, there is never one around when you need it most.

Family members or friends can be either the best support or the worst of enemies in helping one to stop smoking. 'Friends' who encourage 'just one cigarette' can be a constant pain! With so many people now *not* smoking it has become easier to surround oneself with non-smokers who can give moral and practical support. Indeed, one of the main reasons for quitting may be that the individual is the only person in the work/social group still smoking. In any case, seeking the company of non-smokers during the quitting period may be of great help.

It should not be forgotten that divine help is also available. People of faith everywhere testify to the power that comes to the individual through prayer. So having a faith and being able to draw on it during what might be a time of crisis makes sound sense. Research amply demonstrates the power of prayer in overcoming problems associated with health difficulties and has been recognised as a powerful motivating and healing force by the World Health Organisation in connection with smoking cessation.

Emergency situations call for emergency reserves, so using whatever helpful resources are to hand will supply the necessary support, whether individually or as part of a group. Let *God* do your worrying!

Stress free

People who start smoking again give stress as the number one reason for doing so. Smoking is, however, an inappropriate response to stress. There is a false sense of security that comes from believing that a cigarette relaxes.

Identifying the causes of stress and devising workable strategies for dealing with them without using cigarettes is a must. The chapter *How To Cope With Stress* will help you here. Then, when the stress comes along, it can be handled appropriately. Where possible, learning specific stress coping techniques and finding a suitable relaxation method will help to minimise the effects of stress. Add to these the dietary stress-proofing and exercise programme referred to earlier and even the hardest craving smoker should be able to survive!

Most of the anxieties that ex-smokers experience come from anticipating situations where previously cigarettes would have been used. As these cannot be avoided, in many instances, meet these situations with a coping plan in mind. Do not panic. Whatever happens do not find excuses for going back to smoking.

Some of the difficulties can be avoided by keeping some basic **DO**s and **DON'T**s:

✳ Get the support of someone you can rely on generally and when things get tough.
✳ Never offer cigarettes to anybody, not even the cigarettes you have left over.
✳ Do not buy or carry cigarettes for anybody else.
✳ Do not keep cigarettes around the house for that 'just in case' excuse.
✳ Never light a cigarette for anybody.
✳ Have only non-smoking passengers in your car.
✳ Use only non-smoking accommodation and compartments while travelling.
✳ Do not give smoking equipment as gifts (ashtrays, lighters, cigarette cases, etc).
✳ Put away your ashtrays.

To summarise:

- *Choose* not to smoke.
- Do not give in to peaks of craving. Although intense, these do not last long, gradually spacing out and diminishing in intensity.
- Follow the dietary advice.
- Start a rewarding exercise programme either alone or with others. Whatever happens, keep active but do not overtire.
- Get plenty of fresh air.
- Learn a suitable relaxation technique.
- Trust in God.
- Have regular medical checkups for peace of mind and if any symptoms related to smoking persist.

Giving up smoking for most people will be relatively easy if the above pointers are kept in mind. Your motivation for quitting is important. The more reasons for stopping that can be included in the mental list, the better. Try to encourage others not to smoke, it will reinforce your choice and give them support. Do not overdo it though, 'There is none so righteous as the newly converted'!

Chapter Six

Alcohol and You

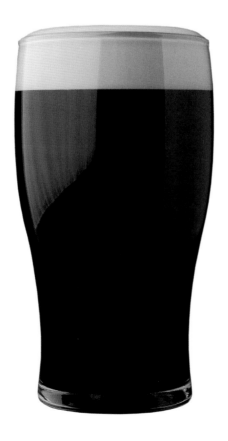

If the advertisements are to be believed, various brands of alcohol will enable the drinker • to appeal to the opposite sex, • change their social strata and status, and • add glamour to otherwise colourless lives. Whatever we might think about its use, alcohol is used to mark the introduction of the newborn child to the world, recognise particular social landmarks along life's way, and as a way of showing respect for the deceased. Many people drink for the sheer 'pleasure' of it.

The flip-side of the coin shows a different picture as alcohol is implicated in 50% of all murders; one in four sexual offences; 88% of criminal damage; 78% of assault cases; and 83% of disturbances of the peace.

• Some 20,000 to 650,000 (estimates vary) domestic accidents are related to alcohol use. • Alcohol is a factor in 1 in 5 work accidents, and 2 in 5 fires. • 200 deaths from drowning have alcohol as a major factor.

What is alcohol?

What is there about this substance that wields so much power and has such a wide ranging effect? There are a number of alcohol solutions which are used in domestic, commercial or manufacturing processes. The one that is used as a drink is *ethyl alcohol* (C_2H_5OH) and, depending on the drink used, is found in varying concentrations. It is made by either fermentation (as in beer) or by distillation (as in whisky). The ethyl alcohol produced is a central nervous system depressant, contrary to the opinion of many that alcohol is a stimulant. When ethyl alcohol is drunk the body breaks it down (as part of the digestive process) first into *acetaldehyde*, then

> ### Alcohol is implicated in fifty per cent of all murders
> (!)

acetate, and finally into the waste products of *carbon dioxide* (CO_2) and *water* (H_2O). It takes approximately one hour to load the system with alcohol, and about 10-12 hours for it to be broken down into CO_2 and H_2O and eliminated from the body by exhalation and urination (passing water).

The calories (or units of energy) provided by alcohol ingestion are often referred to as 'empty calories' in that they do not provide any nutritional value to the body. They are stored in the body fat, hence the joking reference to beer-drinker's belly.

Effects of alcohol

It is socially acceptable to drink alcohol in most countries worldwide, the exceptions being those countries which see alcohol use as contrary to the prevailing religious belief. While it may be a matter of personal choice and taste to drink alcohol, we should be aware that it does have adverse effects. These occur literally from the moment of use and, as might be expected, increase with the amount and/or particular alcoholic drink chosen. Since many of the changes that take place are incremental and are not noticed immediately, the continued use of alcohol may lead to a false sense of security in matters regarding health risks.

The effects of alcohol as it goes through the body include the following:

mouth

- an increasing thickening of the tissues that line the mouth.
- a gradual loss of taste, compensated for by an increase in condiment use, particulaly pepper and mustard.
- recent research has shown that the changes to the tissues may predispose to cancers of the mouth.[1]

pancreas

- the cells of the pancreas become irritated, swell, and bleed (*haemorrhagic pancreatitis*).
- blocks the flow of digestive enzymes.
- when the cells are damaged or destroyed the individual will become diabetic.

heart

alcohol inflames and damages heart muscle (*cardiomyopathy*), leads to fatty degeneration, and (along with the effect on the liver) an increased risk of *atherosclerosis* (hardening of the arteries).

stomach and intestines

- alcoholic gastritis is found in around 30% of alcohol users to some degree.
- causes stomach and duodenal ulcers which heal when alcohol is not used.
- 95% of the alcohol used is absorbed into the bloodstream through the stomach and intestines.
- nutrition interfered with: in particular – thiamine (B_1), B_{12}, folic acid, fat, and some amino acids.
- stomach lining shrinks.

- the superficial blood vessels dilate causing the individual to feel warm while actually experiencing heat loss, so leading to a chilling of the body.
- *white cells:* the alcohol slows down the circulation and the action of the cells, thus delaying the process of resistance to infection. This greatly increases the susceptibility of alcohol users to various diseases.
- *red cells:* alcohol causes the cells to clump together, this increases the risk of blood clotting, and it inhibits oxygen transportation to the tissues (*anaemia*).

circulatory system

liver

- when the tissue cells are inflamed they block the tiny canals to the small intestine, bile is not filtered properly and jaundice results.
- tissue cells are destroyed with each drink taken, leading to cirrhosis of the liver (a condition eight times more common in the alcohol dependent), and fatty degeneration of the tissue.
- nutritional deficiencies are experienced due to the person taking alcohol in preference to nourishing food.

It has been widely publicised that a little alcohol is good for the heart. Strictly speaking this is unlikely to be true. The research which led to this media conclusion was the British Regional Heart Study[2] in which abstainers' heart conditions were compared with those of moderate and heavy drinkers. The results appeared to show that the moderate drinkers had better heart health than either abstainers or heavy drinkers.

What was not known at the time was that the abstainers studied were people who had been told to quit drinking because of an existing heart condition. The results might have been quite different if lifetime abstainers had been used in the study. However, an abstaining person is not necessarily a fit person. Moderate drinkers may be careful in other aspects of their health. The author of the study says that on the basis of the report no one should start drinking to protect their heart as the amount of alcohol said to confer benefit would still harm the liver and the brain. Other studies have shown that it was not necessarily alcohol that protected but rather an ingredient (*flavanoid*) found in the skin of red grapes (and, incidentally, in the skins of all red fruits and vegetables).

- alcohol causes swelling of the prostate gland, and interferes with sexual performance.
- 1-2 units (see chart) daily during the first three months of pregnancy may lead to spontaneous abortion.
- 10+ units daily during pregnancy may result in *Foetal Alcohol Syndrome* (FAS) in which physical injury is caused to the developing foetus.

kidneys and bladder

- alcohol increases fluid loss and extra water is expelled.
- the bladder becomes inflamed, making it difficult to stretch and accommodate the extra fluid.

Many of the above changes (which are by no means exhaustively described) occur even in the presence of adequate nutrition and are accelerated where good nutrition is lacking.

Blood alcohol levels and effects

Blood alcohol concentration levels cause measurable changes in behaviour, reactions and responses which increase usually with quantity of alcohol imbibed. But a person not used to drinking alcohol may experience similar effects at much lower levels.

- we have already noted that alcohol is a depressant, it also has anaesthetic and analgesic (pain relieving) properties.
- alcohol causes a gradual destruction of the cells of the cortex of the brain (the outer area) with shrinkage of the surface of the brain. Cells lost are never renewed.
- loss of control and of reflex actions occur (half a drop of alcohol per thousand drops of blood – 0.05% – slows reflexes by 10%) (approximately 2 cocktails).
- alcohol has an affinity with nerve cells with a high lipid (fat) content, so higher concentrations of alcohol are found in nervous tissue.

brain and spinal cord

Cause and Effect

These amounts of alcohol per 100 mls of blood and effects include:

30 mg/100 mls   an increased risk of an accident, and amounts to 1 pint of beer; 2 glasses of wine; or a double whisky.

50 mg/100 mls   a loosening of inhibitions, impaired judgement and increased cheerfulness. This state is often mistakenly thought to arise from a stimulant effect of alcohol. It is produced by 1½ pints of beer; 3 whiskies; or a half bottle of wine.

80 mg/100 mls   loss of driving licence in most countries if caught driving under the influence of alcohol. An intake of 2½ pints of beer; 5 whiskies; or 5 glasses of wine would put one in this state.

150 mg/100 mls   loss of self-control, exuberance or quarrelsomeness, slurred speech, caused by 5 pints of beer; 10 whiskies; or 1 litre of wine.

200 mg/100 mls   double vision, staggering walk, loss of memory, achieved through 6 pints of beer; ½ bottle of spirits; or 2 bottles of wine.

400 mg/100 mls   sleepiness, coma, oblivion, at ¾ bottle of spirits, etc. This and the following in any amounts above those already indicated:

500 mg/100 mls   death possible.

600 mg/100 mls   death virtually assured.

½ pint of beer   1 glass of table wine   1 glass of sherry   1 single whisky   = 8g alcohol 1 unit

Clearly, some people may be drinking at higher rates of usage than some of the levels and their effects indicated, without necessarily displaying the effects. This is because their drinking pattern has become established at various levels (a process known as *toleration*), so they use more alcohol before the same effects are observed. This is a dangerous practice, especially if deliberately entered into, because of the serious physical effects of the

alcohol. In the light of the damage sustained there is really no such thing as sensible drinking.

Acute and chronic effects of alcohol

The effects of alcohol on society can be seen in the opening statistics. These effects, while having some overlap, are classified as being *acute* or *chronic*:

Acute effects include drunkenness, crime, drinking and driving, hooliganism, and family violence. Alcohol is reckoned to be a factor in 1 in 3 child cruelty cases, and 50% of physical abuse against women is alcohol related. In one UK study, 1 in 3 women attending a women's aid hostel claimed that violence occurred regularly when their husbands were drunk.

Chronic effects include alcohol dependence, physical and mental illnesses, social problems, unemployment and suicide. These effects also carry over into the lives of family members, friends and communities.

Recovering from alcohol dependency

Some people's personal circumstances are so depressing as to be overwhelming, and these factors need careful attention if the individual is to benefit long-term. Alcohol dependence should be seen as part of a wider lifestyle picture, and often includes other addictions.

A first step in dealing with any problem is to acknowledge that it exists, and then outline steps to deal with it.

Once the person with the dependency has recognised his or her problem they can be encouraged to find the motivation to change their harmful behaviour and seek treatment and help. In fact, at all stages in the process of recovery the individual's

motivation needs to be supported.

Depending on the severity of the problem, clinical help may be necessary and a long-term course of treatment outlined. Individuals should follow, carefully, instruction for immediate treatment and any subsequent steps that need to be taken, and be surrounded with the necessary emotional and spiritual support that will enable them to gain strength in their decision and maintenance of a changed lifestyle. Practical support may also be necessary for some individuals until they are able fully to play their part at various levels of involvement in the home and work environment.

Sadly, some of the physical damage done may not be repaired, but a healthy lifestyle

may offset any further deterioration in the person's condition. Sobriety can be maintained if the motivation and support is, and remains, strong. Keeping clear of drinking opportunities and cultivating the friendship of non-drinkers will help to provide the conditions for the individual to flourish. This may be achieved best in an accepting faith community where the spiritual input adds an extra dimension of support. The World Health Organisation recognises that spiritual motivation for health behaviour change is potent and more long-lasting than many other motivations.

The advertisements tell us nothing of the problems listed above. We should not be fooled by the superficial glamour portrayed. Many millions of people worldwide enjoy the things that the ads picture without the use of alcohol. Indeed, without the alcohol many enjoy these things even more by having *real* quality of life.

References
[1]Donaldson, David (1998), *Alcohol consumption worldwide – and the relationship with cancer*, Journal of the Royal Society for Health, vol 118, No 2, page 75.
[2]Editorial (1991), *Heart Disease and Drink – the health message remains clear*, Alcohol Alert, Nov/Dec, page 3.

Chapter Seven

The Use and Abuse of Drugs

'Respectable' drugs

Alcoholism is the world's third major disease, killing one million people a year in Europe alone. And all alcoholics begin as 'moderate drinkers'. Cigarette smoking kills over 100,000 people in Britain each year. Alcohol and smoking are, more or less, socially acceptable drugs. Nonetheless, they are killers. They are dealt with in separate chapters.

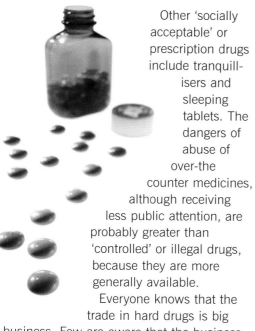

Other 'socially acceptable' or prescription drugs include tranquillisers and sleeping tablets. The dangers of abuse of over-the counter medicines, although receiving less public attention, are probably greater than 'controlled' or illegal drugs, because they are more generally available.

Everyone knows that the trade in hard drugs is big business. Few are aware that the business involved in prescription drugs is even bigger. The pharmaceutical industry is one of the fastest growing in the world. Millions of pounds are spent on advertising, and the promotion of brand names to doctors has a great influence on what product will be eventually prescribed to patients. The pharmaceutical industry spends on average over twice as much on advertising as it does on research and development of new products. In many Western countries there is one drug company representative for every eight doctors.

Around thirty million prescriptions for tranquillisers are issued annually in England alone. 'Minor' tranquillisers, such as Valium and sleeping pills are the most common drugs on repeat prescription and taken in prolonged use. They will control the *initial* symptoms of anxiety, but simply used on their own they cannot control an emotional or spiritual problem. Used over a long period these drugs can hinder rather than help because they prevent the patient discovering the root of the problem and coming to terms with the real issue. It has been estimated that between one third and one half of all those who take these 'minor' tranquillisers regularly each day for three months or more are likely to become psychologically dependent on them.

Tackling the causes

We should seriously consider tackling the stresses of everyday life by making a

supreme effort to get at the cause of the situation rather than dealing with the symptoms.

Drugs can be used to *control* and *treat* some illnesses. These should always be used under medical supervision. *Many of the conditions for which patients consult*

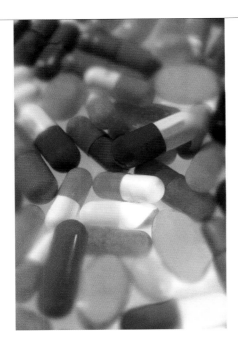

doctors these days could be better treated in ways other than by drugs. Many illnesses have a mental component which can be helped considerably by sympathetic understanding and explanation of the disease process.

Worries concerning financial, social and marital problems loom large these days. The problems of housing and overcrowding can make tempers brittle when children play up. Often a brief consultation with a general practitioner is not the best answer to the many stress-related problems that arise. One is likely to come away with a prescription for tranquilliser pills given by the doctor as a temporary measure until he can see his patient on several subsequent occasions to try to understand the underlying problem

and find an answer. These may help temporarily, but it is far better to try to get help with the root *cause* than smother the symptoms with drugs.

Here are a few suggestions:

✳ Be honest with yourself; don't complain of some bizarre symptom if the real trouble is disharmony at home, etc.

✳ Share the problem with a reliable relative or friend who would respect your confidence. This could well be someone other than the best friend with whom you often associate. You will be surprised how anxious people are to help, if you give them the chance and approach them sensibly.

✳ If more professional advice is needed you might get this from your doctor, health visitor, the local minister or social worker – depending on the particular difficulty.

If it proves impossible to resolve the situation your doctor may refer you to a consultant or prescribe medication. Any drugs taken should only be used under the medical supervision of one person. Otherwise confusion may result.

Finally, why not consult the Great Physician? Prayer is a two-way communication and is available free, anywhere, any time. To a believer the therapeutic value of this is profound.

Drug history

From man's earliest days various plants and crude chemicals have been used to treat illnesses.

The foxglove was found to help certain

Why not consult the Great Physician? Prayer is a two-way communication and is available free, anywhere, any time.

What drugs do to the body

PHARYNX

Cocaine constricts the arteries of the nasal passages and blocks the supply of oxygen to these delicate tissues, causing many cells to die. With time, enough cells can slough off to cause irreparable damage to the pharynx.

VOCAL CORDS

Cigarette smoke can cause changes in the elasticity of the cords, producing changes in the voice. A multitude of malignant cancers of the respiratory system – from the mouth to the lungs – can be linked to smoking.

LUNGS

For smokers, cigarette smoke destroys the cilia lining the trachea, causing bronchitis or 'smoker's cough'. Continued smoking will eventually rupture the tiny air sacs of the lungs, leading to emphysema. Talcum powder, used to cut heroin and other intravenous drugs, can clog the tiny arteries of the air sacs, causing the lungs to fill with fluid.

PANCREAS

Alcohol is considered the number-one cause of pancreatitis in the United States. Its toxic effects can extensively damage the cells which then release digestive enzymes into the surrounding tissues – in effect, digesting itself. Continued alcohol consumption can lead to gastritis, diabetes, and complete loss of pancreatic function.

DIGESTIVE SYSTEM

Drugs taken by mouth, such as narcotics, can cause nausea and vomiting. Heavy use of alcohol can erode the stomach lining, cause diarrhoea, and induce massive internal bleeding. On the other hand, stimulants such as cocaine and amphetamines reduce bowel function and cause constipation.

BRAIN

Most abused drugs in some way modify the functions of the brain or the perceptions of the mind. Extended use of such intoxicants and stimulants can cause loss of brain tissue, decreased mental acuity, and a wide variety of psychological disorders. Over-stimulation of the brain, as with high doses of a form of cocaine known as 'crack', can lead to seizures, or even death.

CIRCULATORY SYSTEM

People who smoke have a greatly increased risk for atherosclerosis – a condition where the arteries become 'crunchy', clogged with brittle deposits of cholesterol. Nicotine, a stimulant from cigarette smoke, raises the blood pressure, which aggravates circulatory problems brought on by clogged arteries, and sometimes causing peripheral vascular disease. Aside from accidents and diabetes, this condition is the single leading cause of amputation.

HEART

Stimulants, such as cocaine and amphetamines, speed up the heart rate and raise blood pressure. Such stimulation, especially when coupled with heart disease or other cardiac insufficiency, can lead to chest pains or, in severe cases, heart attack.

LIVER

Here complex molecules – some of which may be toxic – are metabolised to simpler, less harmful components. Some drugs, such as alcohol, produce toxic by-products when metabolised, and these products can cause extensive cellular damage to the liver. Dead cells are replaced with scar tissue, which over time causes the liver to become hard and fibrous – a condition known as cirrhosis. A cirrhotic liver loses its capacity to detoxify the blood, causing jaundice, fatigue, mental disorders and death.

types of heart disease and the juice of the poppy pod to relieve pain and have a tranquillising effect. Highly refined extracts of these plants are still used today as Digoxin and Morphine. Many useful drugs have side-effects and if these give pleasurable sensations or affect the mind there is a danger of misuse which can damage the human body. Morphine is such an example.

Opium and cocaine have been both used and abused for centuries. Other mind-altering or psychotropic substances have been used, including hashish (pot), peyotyl, etc. Some of these were originally used as part of heathen religious rites. Others induced an unnatural state of intoxication but had their side-effect in lethargy. Barbiturates came along in the early 1900s. At first they were hailed as the answer to insomnia, among other things, but it was soon apparent that patients became dependent and could not manage without them.

Amphetamines were synthesised in the 1920s to combat fatigue. Again abuse was soon rife when they came to be used as 'pick-me-ups' and 'pep pills'.

Safer sedatives came with the early 1950s. The most popular of these are widely used, over-prescribed, and their side-effects little understood by those consuming them.

The abuse of highly dangerous, illegal drugs has been widespread since the 1960s. It has, however, been present in some form for centuries. Today the trade in illegal drugs is the single greatest threat to societies all over the world.

Controlled drugs

Drug pushers even lurk around school playgrounds in many Western cities. Drugs are dispensed at parties, some specially organised for the purpose.

Even for first-time users of illegal or controlled drugs there are tremendous dangers. A first-time user of heroin often experiences vomiting and nausea. Hallucinogenic drugs like LSD can produce 'bad trips' and frightening experiences. Worse still, accidental overdoses can lead to unconsciousness and sometimes death. The exact effect of a drug is dependent, to some extent, upon the personality of the user. Hence the effects of first-time use are unpredictable.

Those who introduce young people to drugs at all-night parties usually make them sound innocuous by giving them various slang names. Most illegal drugs are adulterated and diluted by the time they reach the 'consumer'. The pushers, and the syndicates behind them, make more profit if the product goes further. Police have found that drugs are diluted with anything from scouring powder to rat poison. Hence hospitalisation can result, not only from the drug itself, but from the additives.

Controlled drugs are commonly mixed. Mixing depressant drugs is especially dangerous and can prove fatal. Other complex interactions can also occur.

'Tolerance' develops with the continued use of a drug. Tolerance is where the body adapts to the repeated presence of a drug and in this way reduces its effectiveness. This means that the user will have to take larger quantities for the same effect and thus be placed in greater danger of a fatal overdose.

Police have found that drugs are diluted with anything from scouring powder to rat poison

Because drugs alter co-ordination and vision, accidents frequently occur to people under their influence. Crossing the road or operating machinery can prove fatal even to the first-time drug user.

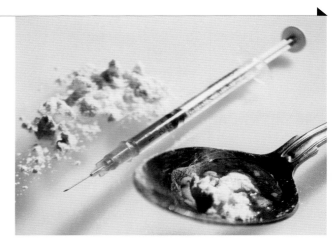

If drugs are abused over a period of time and in sufficient quantities, dependence on the drug will develop. The addict's life becomes dominated by the drug. Even before this stage has been reached the price paid in terms of both body and mind is horrendous. Eventually every area of life becomes entwined with the drug until only one thing counts: getting more.

'Physical dependence' is produced by prolonged use of some drugs. The body becomes so used to the drug that the user has to continue taking it to avoid physical discomfort or actual pain, part of the 'withdrawal effect'.

The *method* of administering the drug may also cause problems. 'Mainlining' directly into the bloodstream can destroy the structure of the veins and cause difficulties with blood circulation. If the user misses the vein, infec-tions, sores and septi-caemia can result. Non-sterile need-les pose a high risk of infection, abscesses, gangrene

and AIDS. AIDS can be passed on when contaminated blood directly enters the bloodstream. Hence intravenous drug users are at tremendous risk if needles used by

an infected person are re-used without sterilisation.

Consequences of drug abuse

✳ Disease and the consequences of self-neglect.

✳ Breakup of friendships and the near impossibility of establishing any kind of social relationship except with groups of fellow users with similar habits.

✳ The breakup of families.

✳ The impossibility of acquiring or holding down a job because of the effect of drugs on co-ordination, balance and the ability to think and retain.

✳ Crime. As the drug takes over the addict all restraints upon behaviour are abandoned to the urgent need to get money for the next fix. Theft, burglaries and muggings are commonly related to drug abuse. So over-powering is the domination of a drug, that some young people even sell themselves to finance their habit.

Whether it's a pusher or a friend who offers the drug, no matter how attractive they make it sound, the only response – if you want to stand any chance of a life worth living – is to say an emphatic No.

Chapter Eight

How to weigh what you want to

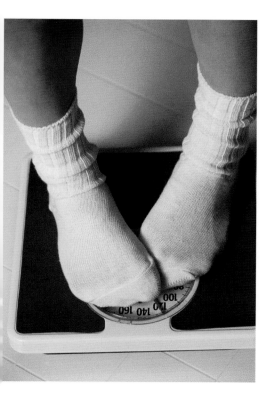

Obesity and its consequences

Obesity or overweight is the condition where excessive fat is stored in the body tissues. It is by far the most common form of malnutrition in the rich industrialised countries, but it is becoming a worldwide problem. The World Health Organisation describes it as an epidemic. It is a serious problem because it predisposes to a vast range of diseases.

Obesity is one of the major medical problems in the developed countries today, and it is also a problem wherever the sedentary, high sugar, high-fat Western lifestyle is followed.

Not only does excess weight reduce the efficiency of those affected and prevent them from enjoying many normal activities, but it is associated with a much higher incidence of many diseases and an appreciably higher death rate. Some of these diseases, for example hernias and varicose veins, are

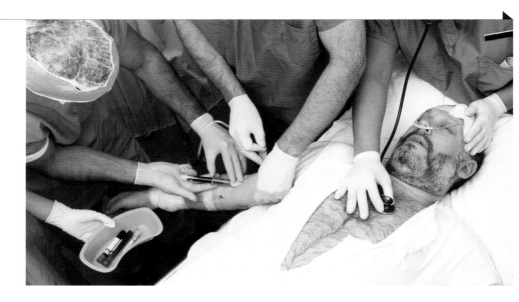

simply due to the extra volume of fat itself. Others, like osteoarthritis, are due to the excess wear and tear that extra weight puts on the spine, hips and knees. Others, like gallstones and diabetes, coronary heart disease and stroke, are due to the changes obesity produces in the body chemistry.

Life-threatening illnesses are not only commoner, but are more often fatal in the overweight. Even cancer, particularly some of the commonest types – breast, colon and prostate – are associated with excess weight.

Weigh right

Clearly being the right weight is a very important part of being healthy, as well as of looking good. If you put health first and weight second, you will find that the weight eventually normalises, but it

> **If you put health first and weight second, you will find that the weight eventually normalises**

just doesn't seem to work the other way round. In the long run, adequate exercise and a positive, cheerful outlook are as important as diet for good health and lasting weight control. Achieving the right weight should be part of an ongoing life plan and not just an isolated scheme for a few weeks. 'I must lose weight for the holidays' is not the motivation for lasting success!

If you want to maximise your health, it is absolutely essential to be in control of what you eat. You cannot allow the taste, sight or recollection of a food to dictate what you eat. Many weight control programmes fail because they don't retrain your thinking about food. Clearly if you make an enormous effort of self-discipline and deny yourself cream cakes and chocolate you may lose weight, but continue to think longingly of them, and you are unlikely to resist the urge to eat them when you have succeeded in reducing your weight. Sadly, if that's the case, as so many can testify, your weight won't stay down.

Being the right weight involves the whole person, not just the eating habits. Spiritual factors are important too, especially coming to terms with oneself and one's place in creation. In the twenty-first century the Bible has many valuable insights about health, food and weight. It tells the story of a loving God who prepared a perfect and beautiful world for his children. Everything was made according to his plan. He designed their bodies and planned their work and recreation, environment and food, and companionship, which he himself would share. The closer we can get to the original principles, including the original plant food diet and physically active life, and the communion with the Creator, the better our health will be, and that applies to our weight as well.

What is your right weight?

The first thing in weight control is to come to terms with one's body type, and then to concentrate on getting healthy because optimum health will ultimately lead to the right weight. This applies to both underweight and overweight people.

The human body is a masterpiece of design, the crowning work of God's creation, and like any machine, it works best when the instruction manual is followed. Many people are unhappy with their bodies, not appreciating the wonder of the overall design and the 'variations' that are 'normal'. Some are designed to be below average weight, some above, *but definitely none is intended to be obese.* Some people *do* put on weight more easily than others. Their metabolism is very economical, and they burn less energy and have extra left over to store. Others have a different metabolism, that tends to burn at a higher rate, and they just never seem to get fat, no matter what they eat. Actual endocrine disturbances, for example thyroid deficiency, that cause weight gain are rather rare. For most people with a weight problem, the solution is not medication so much as dedication! Following the rules of health (the divine plan) will enable each person to reach their full physical potential

Exercise

One of the most important parts of any health plan is **exercise**.

Weight is not a problem for the Masai tribesmen of East Africa, who spend all day on the run with their cattle, or with the

Hunza in Northern Pakistan who walk up and down mountains all day. We are designed to be active, not to be sitting, and we are at our best when we get vigorous activity.

One reason why some people don't lose weight even on the most frugal diets, is that exercise is necessary to stimulate the body to burn up the calories and to activate the appetite control centre in the brain. *Regular* exercise is vital for weight control, not a sport once a week or a walk on Sundays, but regular *daily* exercise. Few exercises can beat walking for safety and convenience.

Several miles a day would be good, with a gradual increase in speed and duration.

No time for exercise?

Take the long-term view. The investment of time for daily exercise from now on may add several extra years of healthy life. And incidently, it's the exercise you *enjoy* that does you the most good, so find something you really like doing.

Diet and weight

For good health and weight control you need to eat the **right amount** of the **right kind** of food at the **right time** in the **right frame of mind**.

The **amount** of food needed to satisfy the appetite depends very much on the kind of food. The more natural the food, the more fibre it is likely to contain, and the more fibre, the more filling it is. The fibre makes it bulky, and the bulk fills the stomach and makes the owner feel satisfied. The more fibre the more chewy it usually is as well, and quite a lot of the satisfaction depends on the amount of time the food spends in the mouth. Soft smooth foods like ice cream or chocolate mousse go down very quickly, and aren't very satisfying. It's the same with white bread. Its chewy fibre has been removed, and it doesn't satisfy the way wholewheat bread does.

Eating very quickly leads to overeating too, whereas eating slowly, savouring each mouth-ful and chewing it well increases the level of satisfac-tion. White bread, as well as being less filling, has more calories – two good reasons to choose wholewheat bread.

Here is another example: about ten raw apples have the same number of calories as one piece of apple pie with ice cream. Raw apples are much more filling, so who could possibly want to chew their way through more than five? But a person could easily have a double helping of pie and ice cream!

You stay the same weight when the energy in the food you eat equals the energy you use up. Clearly, if the energy output is low and the food intake is high, there's going to be a surplus to be stored away as fat. This is the case with the typical high-fat Western diet, in which 40-45% of the calories come from fat, and as much as 80-90% of the food may be refined. Most slimming diets try to solve the problem by reducing the food intake to below the supposed energy output so that the stored fat is mobilised and used up. Unfortunately, these low calorie diets are unsatisfying and demand more will-power than most people have. If the food intake is really low, the body goes into starvation mode, endangering health, and making weight loss very difficult.

What **kind** of food? **Wholefoods** win hands down every time. They are more bulky, so you feel fuller and more satisfied. They have their full complement of vitamins and minerals, and they don't contain excess calories. Refined foods have less bulk, are filling, and have more calories. Excess calorie intake is almost inevitable when these foods form a large part of the diet. In addition, they are deficient in the vitamins, minerals and phytochemicals that the body needs to metabolise all those calories and to fight disease. Their absence creates even more dissatisfaction and sometimes cravings and addictions as well.

Fat provides more than twice as many calories as carbohydrate and protein, so it makes sense to eat less of it, but in itself fat is not bad. In the right amount, as found in natural unrefined plant foods, it is good. Some is necessary to enable us to absorb the fat-soluble vitamins – and it adds flavour and interest to the diet. A varied diet of unrefined plant foods is not a fat-free diet, and need not even be a very low-fat diet. There is plenty of healthy natural fat in nuts, seeds, olives and avocados. It's not these (in moderate amounts) that cause the problems, it's the *added* fats. A very overweight person would be wise to be careful not to use too much of even natural high-fat foods, but few should cut them out completely without expert advice. The food industry has had great success with the sale of low-fat food, but it has actually been found that people get fatter when they use these foods. This is because fat gives a feeling of satisfaction, limiting the intake; what happens is that we eat larger amounts of the low-fat foods, the *total* number of calories is higher, so the weight goes up. Low-fat sweet things are *extra* high in sugar. Low-fat spreads may not be much help either, especially if you eat them in double

Regular exercise is vital for weight control, not a sport once a week or a walk on Sundays, but regular daily exercise

the quantity of the old full-fat spreads.

Two dangerous dietary myths need to be exploded: • One is that high-protein diets are the way to lose weight. While it is true that the metabolism of protein uses extra energy and that high-protein diets can result in rapid weight loss, it's at a price. High-protein intake puts stress on the liver, kidneys and heart. • The other is that starchy foods like bread and potatoes are fattening. Unrefined starchy foods are filling and prevent overeating so the opposite is true, though of course bread becomes fattening when thickly spread with butter and jam, as do potatoes when they are made into chips.

What about animal products? Even apart from the question of the association of animal foods with degenerative disease, they are not the best for a health-promoting diet, especially a weight-reducing one. They tend to be concentrated foods, high in calories, fat and protein. They contain no fibre, and often contain large amounts of fat. If they are used, it should be in small amounts and preferably the low-fat varieties. A varied whole plant food diet based on unrefined starches, with plenty of fruit and vegetables, and also some pulses, nuts and seeds is the most effective for weight loss.

What about drinks? They can be your worst enemies in the battle for weight control. Fizzy soft drinks are mainly sugared water. Alcoholic drinks are even worse, because alcohol itself is not a food, but a

rich source of empty calories. Even natural fruit juices are high in calories. The best drink for weight control is definitely water. Tea and coffee don't contain calories, unless sugar, milk or cream are added, but caffeine is a drug with withdrawal effects, a feeling of letdown that can be confused with hunger, and makes appetite control more difficult.

Should we count calories? Absolutely not! If we choose a varied, unrefined, mainly plant food diet, there is no need for this tedious exercise. The principle is to eat enough healthy food to feel satisfied, and to exercise enough to raise our metabolism enough to burn it up.

The time for food. A regular programme is one of the secrets of appetite and weight control. A large, filling breakfast will set you up for the day and eliminate the need for between-meal snacks (which are usually high fat or high sugar). Make a decision not to eat between meals, and save yourself the trouble of having to make a decision every time you are tempted.

Food eaten in the morning tends to be burned up during the course of the day's activities. Two groups of young male volun-

teers were given one identical meal a day for two weeks, with the one difference that group A ate their meal for breakfast and group B ate their meal for supper. Group A lost weight, group B gained. The groups were then reversed, with  the same result. Why? Because food eaten at night tends to be stored as fat, food eaten in the morning gets used up. Moral: eat a big breakfast, a moderate lunch and a small evening meal. The old adage 'breakfast like a king, lunch like a prince, and sup like a pauper' is especially valid for those who are battling with their weight. Those who are seriously overweight would be wise to miss the evening meal altogether.

Mental attitudes

The frame of mind in which we eat is important too. It's very easy to eat for emotional reasons. Lonely and sad people who feel rejected often eat for comfort, and unfortunately, comfort foods are usually high in sugar and fat. Self-respect and self-acceptance are healthy emotions at mealtimes, along with acceptance of the laws of life and a thankful heart. It's vital to cultivate interests in subjects other than food, and to take an active interest in other people and their problems as well as one's own. Improving one's health, or correcting one's weight both need to be long-term projects.

Usually it has taken years to gain the excess weight, and the best way is to reduce it slowly, sometimes over several years. Most diets aim at a loss of two pounds a week, but a steady half pound a week loss will add up to nearly two stones in two years. The diet and lifestyle changes that are made gradually will be more easy to maintain, unlike the usual slimming diet with its promised quick results but short-lived success. The healthy lifestyle needs to be *lifelong*.

What motivation is needed for a lasting change of lifestyle and eating habits? Gratitude to the God who created the human race in his image, designing our bodies for maximum enjoyment of life, our food for maximum health and enjoyment of eating, and our spirit for communion with him, is the best motivation one can have.

Practical suggestions for
starting a weight reduction programme

Those who are very overweight and are unwell, very easily tired or short of breath, or are on regular medication, should, of course, consult their medical advisors in case there are any specific restrictions for them. They should also take advice before starting exercise programmes or fasting. For them it's even more important to start exercise changes gradually, but some will find it helpful to start their new eating programme with a therapeutic diet, even beginning with a one- or two-day fast.

If you start with a **fast**, keep to a normal daily programme with fruit or vegetable juices or herbal teas at your normal mealtimes. Drink plenty of extra water between mealtimes. Do light exercise only, and have as interesting a programme as possible to keep your mind off food. Many people who have tried it say that fasting is

actually easier than eating less. Abstaining from food, and drinking lots of fluids has a cleansing effect that produces a feeling of well-being, a relish for healthy food once the fast is over, and a distinct confidence in your ability to control your appetite!

The best way to start the day is to get up early and have a large drink of water or herb tea, at least half an hour before breakfast. This stimulates the kidneys to get rid of the night's waste products, and gets the metabolism off to a good start. You could open the window and breathe some fresh air or do a few exercises while the kettle boils. Have a good, filling breakfast. It's the most important

> **You don't need to exclude olive oil – small amounts will make your salads and savoury dishes even more delicious**

meal of the day, and you should enjoy it! Some time during the day fit in some extra exercise, and do it as briskly as you can. Walking is always a safe exercise for anyone who is actually able to walk. Have your other main meal at midday if possible, and have a small light evening meal several hours before bedtime.

Either at the start of your diet plan, or after your short one- or two-day fast, have a **fruit diet** for three days. Eat all the fruit you want, of any kind, provided no sugar is added, and drink lots of water between meals. Fruit juices contain quite a lot of nutrition and are best at mealtimes.

Follow this with a three-day **fruit and vegetable** regime. Start with a selection of fruit for breakfast, have a selection of vegetables for lunch, starting with a salad and include filling things like jacket potatoes if you want to, but don't add any butter or other high-fat dressings. For supper have another fruit meal.

After two or three days on the fruit and vegetable regime, you can start to add some wholewheat bread or other cereal food to the fruit meals. Choose a kind of bread that is tasty enough to be eaten without the usual high-fat spreads.

The next stage is to get onto a normal **whole plant food diet** and it's worth keeping this up for a month – or, better still, indefinitely. Add some high-protein plant foods to each meal: beans or lentils, or dishes or spreads containing nuts and seeds. It's best to avoid all the refined foods. This includes many of the ready-prepared vegetarian foods, too. But you don't need to exclude *olive* oil – small limited amounts will make your salads and savoury dishes even more delicious.

Regular whole food diet suggestions

Variety is an important key to good health, because it ensures an adequate supply of all the essential nutrients, which in turn protects against food cravings and other problems. In general it's a good plan to eat fruit and vegetables at separate meals. Some find them much easier to digest this way, others find that it's easier not to over-eat if there is less variety at any one meal. On the other hand, it is important to have a

wide variety of food from day to day.

Breakfast – many people find it's nice to start the day with a fruit and grain meal – like fresh fruit, cereal and toast. Start with a couple of pieces of fruit. Choose cereals made from wholewheat or other grains, and with no added sugar. You don't have to eat them with milk, you can use fresh or cooked fruit, nut or soya milk (which tastes a lot more creamy than skimmed milk). Raw grains are hard to digest, except oats, which are quite digestible if soaked overnight. Hot breakfast cereals can be made from a variety of flaked whole grains. Sweeten them with raisins or chopped dates rather than sugar. Develop a taste for spreads that contain their full spec-

trum of nutrition – whole nut butters, tahini, avocado (which is an excellent substitute for cream cheese), mashed banana. Delicious 'jams' can be very easily made from dried fruits, cooked and mashed or blended. Then you won't need butter, with its cholesterol and saturated fat, or margarine which is just as high in fat as butter, or even 'low fat' spreads which are still 50% fat at least.

Savoury breakfasts are good too, as long as they keep to the principle of avoiding refined and deficient foods.

Lunch should *ideally* be the other main meal. Start with a big salad and the more weight to be lost, the bigger and chewier the salad should be. Base the meal on unrefined starch: potato, brown rice or pasta, maize or whatever. Add cooked vegetables and a smaller helping of the high protein food. Chicken and fish are preferable to red meat, but vegetarian foods, especially beans and lentils, are best. Beware of adding fat or high-fat sauces.

The evening meal – it is best to have the smallest meal in the evening if it's possible. Bread and spread is a good evening menu, with a vegetable soup or salad, or better still, with fruit.

What if you can't choose the menu? If you don't have any say about what happens in the kitchen you can still make choices that will improve your diet and health. First, don't add sugar and avoid all sugar-rich foods. Get your own supplies of other foods, such as fruit or nuts to take their place if possible.

Be very careful about fats. Cultivate a taste for less. Remember fats come on bread as butter and margarine, are plentiful in fried food, but are also present in large amounts in many gravies, sauces and made-up dishes such as stews and casseroles. Pastry is, by weight, at least one third fat, and cakes, biscuits and ice creams are often as rich in fats as they are in sugar. Be careful about cheese – standard hard cheeses like Cheddar are over 50% fat.

Eat bigger helpings of the vegetables and salads and smaller helpings of the high-fat foods, avoiding the richest altogether. This will save you many empty calories. And do work hard on the exercise programme too.

How strict do I have to be?

This is something you need to decide for yourself, according to how much weight you need to lose, how well your regime is going, how good your general health is, what your social circumstances are and so on.

Occasional deviations from your healthy eating plan may be unavoidable, and should not cause any pangs of guilt, but frequent indulgence in junk food makes it more difficult to develop a taste for the good things. As time passes, if you manage to avoid the dangerous fattening foods, you will find that you develop a taste for the healthy food. As you start to feel better on the new regime, you are even more motivated to continue it. Some people do find that it is best to be total abstainers from rich cakes and puddings, because if they do start, it may set off a craving that is difficult to control. Others can take them or leave them and are able to enjoy the occasional junk food meal on social occasions. The problem is when one feels the need to eat junk food to reward oneself for abstaining from it! That is likely to lead to the slippery slope of failure.

Chapter Nine

Keeping fit

'Well,' you may say, 'fit for what?'

Clearly what is fit for father may not be fit for grandfather – or grandmother, for that matter. But there is an approach to maintaining fitness without the element of risk.

Primarily we should define personal fitness in the following terms:

✳ that we are able to carry out the tasks that have to be done;

✳ that we are able to become involved in activities that, within reason, we like to do – in the first instance without stress or strain, and in the second in an acceptable and controllable amount.

The human body is basically a machine, which, by definition, means that it is 'a device for doing work'.

The simplest of all machines is the lever and we use them constantly. Consider the garden spade. Here we have the weight at one end (the soil), the handle at the other end held in the hand is the fulcrum, and

somewhere in between we grasp the shaft and apply a force to lift the weight up. It will have been noticed that if this 'lifting' hand is brought closer and closer to the handle the weight appears to become heavier and heavier, so requiring more and more effort to raise it. The result of this creates the need for more effort and strain.

The human body is a system of levers. For instance, the long bones in the arm and the forearm, thigh and leg are rigid lines and each moves at a joint which is the fulcrum. Weight is moved on these bones – the body weight in particular on the lower limbs – on the upper limbs a large variety of weighty objects from saucepans to suit-cases, from furniture to younger members of the family, and the effort (force) needed to move these weights is produced by the contraction of muscles.

For the most part the arrangement is such that the muscles are attached and therefore apply a force between the weight on the limbs and the joints, and furthermore much closer to the joints than to the weight. This compares with using a garden spade with hands close together – consequently a great deal of effort is needed and one

will be aware of the stress involved. Nevertheless, it is an impressive thought that the human machine functions on average for a little more than three score years and ten, whereas those devices that we normally think of as machines rarely match this longevity.

Machines must be maintained; they must be cared for – they must be serviced. Clearly there is a need for freely-moving joints, for muscles which produce sufficient force to move the weights that they act upon, and furthermore there is a need for an adequate supply of energy. Unlike mus-cle tissue, joint surfaces have a very limited blood supply and, for the most part, gain nourishment – energy – by absorbing fluid. This simply means that a cartilage takes up fluid in the same way that a bath sponge takes up water when squeezed and released. When movement occurs, some parts of the cartilagenous joint surface are compressed and other parts decompressed. Movement in the opposite direction reverses this effect and so consequently it is during the movement of a joint that the cartilage gains its nutritive requirements. Further to this need, surrounding the joints are capsu-lar ligaments and unless they are regularly stretched they will shrink, thus reducing the range of movement possible and so in turn lead to a reduction of cartilagenous nutri-tion. Unless a full range of movements is regularly carried out, normal complete move-ments will become less. Enquire of the older members of the family as to whether or not

The human body is basically a machine, which, by definition, means that it is 'a device for doing work'

they can stretch their arms in a straight line above the head – or perhaps produce a straight back!

Muscles, on the other hand, receive their nutritive supply through the blood capillaries within them; and in this context it is useful to consider the question of an effective circulation. Circulation is dependent on three resources:

* the heart itself,
* the respiratory pump,
* skeletal muscular activity.

Although the heart does pump blood around the body, by itself it is not maximally efficient. Separating the thorax from the abdomen is a thin sheet of muscle

in the shape of a dome, which is called the diaphragm. When it contracts the dome descends and the thorax (chest) is enlarged and the abdomen is compressed. As a result of this, the air pressure in the lungs is reduced, and as atmospheric pressure is greater, air moves into the lungs – and so we breathe in. But at the same time the pressure on the blood in the abdomen is increased and consequently this causes the blood to flow into the thorax via the large

vein to the heart. Therefore, it will be seen that effective breathing is not only essential for good ventilation of the lungs, but is also essential for circulatory return to the heart. Within the muscles of the body are soft-walled veins, therefore when muscles contract, these veins are compressed and the blood within squeezed out and moved towards the heart.

Consequently, effective breathing and muscular activity increases venous return to

the heart. When the pressure in the large veins is increased, a reflex mechanism is activated which causes the rate and force of the heart activity to increase and so pump the blood onward via the arteries to the lungs and the body as a whole. Muscular strength is dependent upon the work that muscles are required to do, and as the heart is a muscle, general muscular activity will give the heart more work to do. Under controlled circumstances exercises can improve the mechanism of the body as a whole. It becomes clear that in order to maintain this

mechanism, the following are needed:
* Freely-moving joints,
* Sufficient muscular strength to move the levers,
* An effective circulation in order to supply the energy needed.

Whereas this requirement applies to all structures, certain joints and muscles are particularly vulnerable to wear. As the years go by, joints which tend to be affected are the shoulder, hip, and spine, and this is because in everyday activities we do not move them through the full range of normal movement. It is therefore useful to do the following exercises at regular intervals.

Mobility exercises

Stand relaxed and hold the wrist behind the back. Gently pull the shoulder down and across and tip the head away.

Neck and shoulders

Neck and upper back

Kneel on all fours with your back straight. Keep your abdominal muscles tight. Lift up through your spine to round your back then gently release.

Shoulders and Chest

Stand up straight and place your hands behind your head. Gently pull your elbows back and push your chest forward.

Start with your hands by your sides. Slowly raise to shoulder height and then gently lower back to starting point.

Shoulders and Chest

Spinal stretch

Kneel on all fours. Align your hips over your knees. Slide your hands forward but do not allow your hips to move. Allow your chest to drop towards the floor.

Spinal stretch

Lie down, face up with knees bent and feet flat on the floor. One at a time, gently bring your knees to your chest and hold.

6

7

Bear your weight on one leg. Align knee of other leg with the midline of foot and rotate gently from the hip.

Hip rotation

Hip strength

8

Lie on your side, supporting head on hand. Bend body slightly at the hip. Keep body weight forward. Raise and lower the leg.

So the first requirement for physical fitness is to maintain full range of movement in the joints of the body. In the achievement of this there will, of course, be muscular activity and therefore a certain degree of muscular strength will also be maintained.

Starting your exercise programme

Do I need to exercise? Yes. Whatever your lifestyle, current physical health, age or gender, you can benefit from regular exercise.

You are never too young, too old, or too unfit to get started.

Set yourself a goal. If you're serious about improving your overall physical health, you should be working towards doing at least thirty minutes of exercise at least three times a week. (Better still if you can manage the same amount of exercise every day of the week.)

Take it steady. If you're planning to turn over a new leaf and start an exercise programme where previously your lifestyle was

What exercise can do for you*

It increases the efficiency of your lungs, conditioning them to process more air with less effort.

It increases the efficiency of your heart in several ways. It grows stronger and pumps more blood with each stroke, reducing the number of strokes necessary.

It increases the number and size of your blood vessels as well as your total blood volume, thus saturating the tissue throughout the body with energy-producing oxygen.

It increases your body's maximal oxygen consumption by increasing the efficiency of the means of supply and delivery. In doing so, it improves the overall condition of your body, especially its most important parts – the lungs, the heart, the blood vessels and the body tissue – giving you protection against many forms of illness and disease.

It improves the tone of your muscles and blood vessels, changing them from weak and flabby tissue to strong and firm tissue, often reducing blood pressure in the process.

It slows down your ageing process and physical deterioration as it restores your zest for life and youthful activity.

It may change your whole outlook on life. You learn to relax, develop a better self-image, and tolerate the stress of daily living. You will sleep better and get more work done with less fatigue.

*From *The New Aerobics* by Kenneth Cooper, MD, Bantam Books.

largely inactive, recognise that you should start as you mean to go on – at your own pace. (If your own pace requires you to stop for a cake every ten minutes you should review your strategy!)

Your heart needs a workout too

It is a good idea to get involved in some sort of general exercise or sport which provides both cardiovascular and muscular workout, for example, brisk walking, swimming, cycling, tennis, badminton, basketball and similar pursuits. Consequently, each individual should make an appropriate selection in terms of age, interest and availability.

General advice

Nevertheless, in any activity the same ground rules should be followed and these are:

＊ Start with the minimum effort,

＊ progress in a gradual manner.

For example, take walking. In accordance with your present ability, you could start with a hundred yards, the following day walk twice the distance and so on, and in case it is thought that this goes on ad infinitum, an average daily stint of about half an hour should be considered reasonable.

＊ Never overstress or overfatigue the body. Sufficient work should be done to experience an increase in heart and respiratory rate, but this rate should return to normal within a few minutes after the effort ceases. But there again it is not recommended that the pulse should be checked at frequent intervals, and anyway it is difficult to check the respiratory rate for oneself.

＊ It is essential to *enjoy* what you have decided to do. It should not be done just because 'it is good for you'.

Graduated, regular physical activity will build up muscle strength, improve circulatory efficiency and consequently increase the ability to withstand and tolerate the normal everyday stresses that we all have to put up with.

Warm-ups and cool-downs

It is good to recognise the importance of warming up before commencing a period of physical exertion. Likewise it is good exercise practice to decrease the effort required

towards the end of your workout.

'The idea behind warming up is to prepare the muscles for physical activity', says
Ben Kibbler, MD, director of the Lexington
Clinic Sports Medicine Center, Kentucky.
'You want to improve flexibility, strength,
extensibility of the tendons and blood flow
to the muscles. A muscle in a resting state
has a certain length. Warming up improves
the ability to move the muscle through its
entire range of motion without injury. While
warmth applied to outside of the body
warms the skin and parts of the muscles
close to the skin's surface, it doesn't effec-

tively warm the muscles, particularly the
deep seated muscles and tendons.'
– *fitnessonline.com*

Safe stretches

The following stretches can be done as part of a warm-up regime or after activity as a cool
down. Stretching can also be used as a workout in its own right for thirty minutes, three
times a week. For maximum benefit stretches should be held for twenty to thirty seconds at
the point of comfortable tension. Always be sure to stretch both sides of the body. Remember
too, it is advisable to consult a physician prior to starting any exercise programme. Always
drink water before, during and after exercise to remain hydrated.

Breathing

**This breathing exercise can be done either standing or lying down.
Inhale and fill the lungs, allow the chest and stomach to expand.
Exhale and allow the chest and stomach to fall. Concentrate on
pulling your navel towards your spine while exhaling.**

Posture and neutral spine

Before begining any exercise programme it is important to find the most stable position for your spine.

Rock your pelvis forward, then back, and then find the mid-point which should encourage a natural curve in your lower back. Hold this position. This is the neutral position for your spine, the central position for good posture.

②

forward   back   neutral

Spinal stretch

Kneel on all fours. Align hips over your knees. Slide your hands forward but do not allow your hips to move. Allow your chest to drop towards the floor.

③

Stand relaxed and hold the wrist behind the back. Gently pull the shoulder down and across and tip the head away.

④

Neck and shoulders

Triceps stretch

Lift the elbow above the head and drop the forearm behind the head. Slide the forearm down the middle of the back. Support the elbow with the opposite hand and apply gentle pressure.

5

Back and shoulders

Stand with knees slightly bent. Leaning forward grasp the back of the thighs. Pull away from the legs leading with the upper back. Keep the head in a neutral position.

7

Lay on your front with elbows tucked into the side of your body. Gently lift the upper body pressing the chest up and forward. Keep your elbows on the floor.

6

Trunk stretch

Lay on your back with your spine in the neutral position. Gently bring one knee towards the chest and hold. Bring your other knee to the chest and hold.

8

Spine stretch

Groin stretch

9 Support your body on all fours and slowly extend one leg to the side. Press the groin towards the floor while leaning back slightly.

Kneel down, take one foot forward as far as comfort allows. Gently lean forwards pressing the groin forwards and towards the floor. Align the front knee directly over the ankle or shoelace. **10**

Hip flexor stretch

Calf stretch

Stand relaxed and step one foot behind as far as comfort will allow. Lean forward, keeping ankle and knee of the back leg in a straight line with the hips and shoulder. Check the front knee is over the shoe laces. Rest hands on knee. **11**

Lying quadricep stretch

12 Lying on your side, support the body by resting the head on the hand or upper arm. Angle the bottom leg forward and bend slightly to aid balance. Bend the top leg and take the foot behind, holding the ankle with your hand. Press hips forward. Keep knees parallel with floor.

Abdominal muscles

Start by lying face down with your spine in the neutral position. Lift the hips off the floor, keep your abdominal muscles firm and hold the position for as long as is possible. Do not allow the lower back to sag. To increase intensity, lift the knees off the floor.

(13)

Exercise myths

'Exercise is impractical for reducing weight since exercise expends so few calories.' No. A woman needs to eat only ninety-six calories more a day from the time of her marriage until her third child five years later to have gained fifty pounds. An added twenty-five minutes of brisk walking daily would have prevented it.

The Basic Metabolic Rate (BMR) increases and with some people is still up six days after the exercise and therefore calories are expended because of previous exercising.

'Exercise increases the appetite so better not exercise.' No. Small amounts of exercise do not increase the appetite. Only large amounts of exercise will do this. In one animal experiment, those that exercised one hour a day ate a smaller amount of food than those that exercised less than an hour or not at all.

(14) Lying down face up, bend the knees and gradually curl the upper body no more than 30-40 degrees. Keep the lower back on the floor. Focus on contracting the abdominal muscles.

Abdominal muscles

Chapter Ten

We are what we eat

Countless thousands of research papers have established the firm connection between lifestyle and quality and length of life. The concept of whole person health involves the interrelationship of all aspects of lifestyle – diet, exercise, substance use, stress levels and mental status. Optimum health is not just the avoidance of all the major killer diseases.

Your body needs premium fuel

It would be difficult to overestimate the importance of diet in this. Choosing good food is a major part of choosing good health. Good food is one of the most important factors in the lifestyle that leads to health and longevity. For our food to have its optimum effect it needs to be part of a consistent lifestyle that includes vigorous exercise, the avoidance of poisons, and a peaceful frame of mind. The

high-fat, high-sugar diet of the Western countries, and their heavy dependence on animal produce is taking its toll. This, with the sedentary lifestyle and the use of poisons like alcohol and tobacco is why, although life expectancy is longer that ever, EU statistics show

that Europeans can expect to end their lives with ten or more years of chronic ill health. Degenerative diseases account for most of this suffering.

The degenerative diseases were known as the diseases of Western civilisation. In the past only the rich in most parts of Africa, India and Latin America needed to fear them, but now the increasing popularity of the Western lifestyle is adding its burden of degenerative disease there too. They are difficult and expensive to

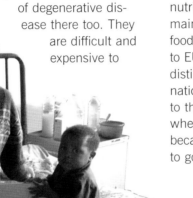

treat. Modern scientific medicine depends on advanced technology and skilled specialists. Even the most prosperous societies find it difficult to meet the demands of advancing medicine in the battle with degenerative disease. How can societies with poorly-developed economies begin to cope with such a burden?

Prevention is simpler than cure

Fortunately, prevention is a great deal simpler and cheaper than cure, and knowing the causes of the problems enables us to learn how to prevent and often even reverse them, and this is the real solution to the dilemma.

Poor nutrition is responsible for much of the world's misery and there is poor nutrition in every society. In the West the main problem is *overnutrition*, too much food of the wrong sort. In 1999, according to EU statistics, the UK achieved the dubious distinction of being the most overweight nation in Europe! This is in sharp contrast to the situation in many poor countries where undernutrition is a major problem, because they just don't have enough food to go round.

The obesity that results from overnutrition is not classed as a disease itself, but it is a very serious health problem, because it contributes to so many other diseases. Almost all the degenerative diseases are commoner, occur earlier, are more difficult to treat and are more often fatal in the seriously overweight. That includes heart disease, stroke, cancer, diabetes, gall bladder problems, arthritis, varicose veins, eczema and almost any problem you care to name. Weight reduction is very desirable and it's a serious business, a multimillion pound industry, in fact.

Many overweight people spend most of their lives on diets of one kind or another, with very little real or lasting benefit, however.

The ideal diet

Just as cars perform best when the maker's instructions are followed, so our bodies perform best when we obey the laws of health – our Maker's instructions, in fact. The story of the creation of the world, found in the beginning of the book of Genesis, gives some excellent guidelines. There we learn that our earliest ancestors lived in a rural environment, had outdoor physical work and a plant food diet. This is still the ideal situation for optimum health, and is worth keeping in mind, even if we live in a city and have a sedentary job. The principle is to do the best you can. Whenever you can, seek the most natural surroundings available – parks, gardens, tree-lined streets, for brisk walks, or relaxing moments. Choose to eat the freshest and most natural plant

foods that you can find – even growing some in window boxes or on balconies. And maintain the spiritual life with regular worship, praise and prayer.

A quick guide to nutrition

We need food for energy. It's the fuel our bodies burn to provide the energy for all our activities, and all our body's complex biochemical processes. Food energy is measured in calories. High-calorie food is high-energy food. This is just what you need if you are about to expend a lot of energy in strenuous manual work or sport, but it's not what you need if you spend most of your work and leisure sitting down in a warm and comfortable environment.

calorie – with a small c – is the term used for measuring food energy. It is the amount of heat energy needed to raise the temperature of 1kg of water by one degree centigrade. Scientists call them kcalories or calories.

Food fuel comes in three different forms: **protein, carbohydrate and fat**. For optimum health we need them in the right proportions for our own particular needs, depending on our age, occupation, state of health, and even the climate we live in.

• **Protein** is the body-building food, used for growth repair and maintenance of body tissues, and in the manufacture of all the hormones and enzymes that direct the

Three protein myths

One

'Human beings need lots of protein, the more the better' – so said Professor Karl Voigt, the great pioneer biochemist, who decided that the best way to discover the body's protein requirement was to observe how much protein healthy manual workers chose to eat. This led him to recommend 140gms of protein a day for adult males. Only a few years later, Professor Chittenden did a scientific study in which he measured the amount of protein actually used in the body, and he discovered that only 42gms a day were needed. His student volunteers tried the low-protein diet with great success, and he himself followed it for the rest of his life. Since that time many other physiologists have confirmed that low-protein diets are adequate, and over the years the recommended daily allowance has gradually dropped. WHO now recommends that 50gms a day is adequate for all adults including pregnant and nursing mothers. It's now recognized that not only is lower protein adequate, it's better as it is associated with lower incidence of degenerative disease.

Two

'Vegetarians lack protein' – not true. There is plenty of protein in plant foods. The starchy grains and vegetables that form the basis of healthy plant food diets are high enough in protein to supply most of what's needed. Pulses, nuts and seeds, and even fruit and vegetables supply the rest. In fact it would really need some careful thought to devise a plant food diet that was both interesting enough to eat and inadequate in protein. There really isn't any danger, if you choose a wide variety of foods from day to day to ensure a good supply of the different amino acids.

Three

'Plant protein is inferior' – this is the old myth about first and second class proteins. Animal proteins were considered to be first class or complete proteins, because the balance of amino acids in them was the most similar to the total balance in our own tissues. Plant proteins are more variable, some have more of one amino acid and less of another, than human tissues do, so they were designated as second class or incomplete proteins – and therefore less adequate. The fact is that our cells are able to pick and choose from the pool of amino acids in the bloodstream that results from the digestion of the different types of protein, and as long as we eat a variety of plant proteins, we are not going to have any problems on a plant food diet.

body's complex chemical processes. Plant foods are good sources of protein. The most concentrated sources are the pulses – the peas, beans and lentils: nuts and seeds are high in protein and fat, and grains average about 10% protein by weight. Even fruit and vegetables contain some protein because it forms part of the structure of all plant cell walls.

Protein-rich foods of animal origin are meat, fish, poultry, eggs and dairy products.

Our bodies are wonderfully designed machines, and if treated well they work very efficiently and economically. Much of the protein that is used for maintenance and repair is recycled, so we don't need a large intake and it's difficult to go short of protein unless we are actually short of food. Contrary to what nutritionists thought in the past, completely plant food diets contain plenty of protein, and meat eaters run the risk of getting too much.

Proteins are complex molecules made up of long chains of amino acids, each protein having its own individual, characteristic structure. The amino acids are made of carbon, hydrogen, oxygen and nitrogen. During digestion, the proteins are broken down to their component amino acids, which are then transported in the bloodstream, to wherever they are needed for growth, repair, maintenance or manufacture. Any surplus to requirements is prepared for disposal – the nitrogen part is removed by the liver, and the kidneys send it out in the urine. This gives extra work for the liver, kidneys and also the heart. The remaining part of the amino acid is used either as fuel or converted to fat and stored for later use. When burnt as fuel in the body, one gram of protein produces four calories of energy.

Recent research has shown that animal protein as well as saturated animal fat contributes to high blood cholesterol levels. Plant proteins come without the baggage of cholesterol, saturated fat and other disease-related substances. Plant proteins come with fibre and other health-promoting substances. Plant protein is *superior*.

• **Carbohydrate** – the name means that it is made from carbon and water – no nitrogen here to stress the liver and kidneys – in fact, the ideal fuel. There are two main types, **starches** and **sugars**. They are all constructed from simple sugar units of six carbon atoms with hydrogen and oxygen.

• **Sugar** is a premium fuel and is the body's first choice for instant energy. It burns very easily and cleanly, producing energy (four calories a gram), carbon dioxide and water. The best-known simple sugar molecule is glucose – widely advertised as a source of instant energy, and the form in which sugar is transported in the blood. Sucrose is the most widely used sugar. It is formed from two simple

sugar molecules joined together. It's very easily broken down in the digestive tract, and absorbed almost as quickly as glucose.

• **Starches** are long chains of simple sugar molecules linked together, each type of starch with its own characteristic pattern. These complex carbohydrate molecules take longer to break down in the digestive tract, and are absorbed much more slowly. Important sources of starches are all the

Sugar decreases the ability of the white blood cells to fight infection

grains, and the starchy vegetables like potatoes and yams.

Simple sugars have the advantage of being very rapidly absorbed for emergency energy supplies, but if large amounts are eaten, they have the disadvantage that their rapid absorption can raise the blood sugar level too quickly. This can precipitate a reflex lowering of the blood sugar, causing it to fall too fast, with symptoms of weakness, shakiness or irritability and hunger. The slow absorption of the sugar molecules from the breakdown of the starches gives a much more long lasting feeling of satisfaction after the meal, and maintains a much more stable blood sugar level. The ideal is to base the meals on the complex carbohydrates, add plenty of fruit or vegetables, and limit the use of refined sugar.

Simple sugars have more disadvantages. They are very harmful to the teeth, especially children's teeth, and especially if kept in frequent or prolonged contact with the teeth. Sweets and biscuits between meals, and the frequent use of sugary soft drinks can cause major problems. Another harmful effect is that sugar decreases the ability of the white blood cells to fight infection. Then there's obesity. In the West most sugar is eaten in the refined form. It has lost all its vitamins, minerals and fibre. The sugar eater needs those missing nutrients, but interprets the dissatisfaction for a need for more sugar –

more empty calories, worse nutrition – and where do the extra calories go? They are stored as fat or, worse still, used to provide energy for restless irritable behaviour.
• **Fats** are concentrated fuel sources, producing nine and a half calories of energy a gram – more than twice as much as carbohydrate or protein. They are complex molecules constructed from carbon, hydrogen and oxygen After digestion they enter the bloodstream to be distributed for use as fuel.

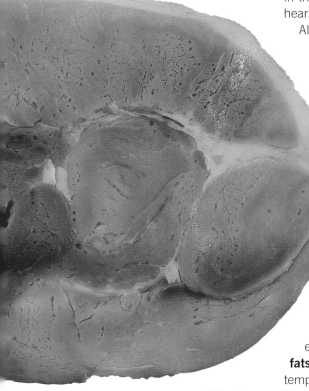

If fuel is not needed, they go to the fat storage cells. Fats are essential for good health, and as there are traces of fats and oils in almost all foods, there is no danger of going short.

The different kinds of fats are classified according to the structure of their molecules. Almost everybody has heard of saturated and unsaturated fats, if only from margarine cartons. This distinction has become very important to the food industry. This is because the **saturated fats** are associated with raised levels of blood cholesterol, which in turn is linked to increased risk of heart attack and stroke. This has led to the development of a whole industry producing 'low fat spreads' and other reduced fat foods in the hope that they will help to prevent heart disease.

Although it may sound complex, you don't need to be a food scientist to choose the right food for your heart. All edible fats are mixtures of the different kinds of fat, but usually one predominates and gives that fat its particular properties. The more saturated the fat, the higher its melting point, which means that saturated fats are solid at room temperatures and unsaturated fats are liquid at room temperature. Animals produce mainly saturated fats in their bodies – examples are butter, lard, and the fat of bacon and red meat – all of them solid at normal room temperature. Plants, with two notable exceptions, produce mainly **unsaturated fats** – the plant oils that are liquid at room temperature, and even in the fridge. The two exceptions are palm oil and coconut oil which are both mainly saturated.

As heart disease is associated with saturated fat, and saturated fat is mainly of animal origin, it is clear that vegetable fat is a

better choice. However, **vegetable oils** are usually highly refined and processed. Typical sources are soybeans, corn and sunflower seeds. To make one table-spoonful of corn oil takes many more corn cobs than any normal person would eat at a sitting, but most people could very easily con-sume several spoonfuls of corn oil if it was in the form of margarine or mayonnaise, or hidden in biscuits or pastry. As well as making it easy to over-consume, the refining process has removed many vital nutrients. It has left us with a concentrated but deficient food. Not only is it defi-cient, but it is damaged. The high temperatures to which it is exposed in the re-fining process alter the molecular structure in a way that contributes to tissue damage and ageing, and cancer. This damage is increased when the oil is cooked at high temperatures, as in frying. The reheating of oils in deep fryers com-pounds the problem. Limit the use of veg-etable oils if you are fit and healthy. Avoid them if you are overweight or have health problems.

Olive oil is completely different. For a start, it is not refined. The cold pressed virgin olive oil is a completely natural product, comprising about 16% of the olive. What has been discarded is mainly fibre. It is stable at higher temperatures than the other oils and does not undergo the unhealthy molecular changes when heated. In addition its use as the main dietary fat is associ-ated with low levels of heart disease. *Olive oil seems to be the safest form of added fat* (that is fat that is added to food, rather than being a natural part of it).

Fat adds interest and texture to food, and also helps to give a feeling of satisfaction. The best way to eat fat is as it occurs nat-urally in the different types of whole plant food. Some of these, like nuts and seeds, have a high fat content. Avocados, like olives, are loaded with fat, but it is a healthy type, and few, if any, need to cut these delicious plant foods out of their diet, unless they have specific problems with digesting them.

Progress in medicine and nutritional science is not in a straight line. New ideas tend to be accepted either overenthusiastically or not at all. This has been the case with fats. Some doctors and nutritionists went to the extreme of condemning all fat. The food industry responded with lots of low-fat foods. In many low-fat cakes and biscuits the fat is replaced by sugar. Because the low-fat versions are not so satisfying, more is eaten, and the net result of the low-fat foods is that people are gaining even more weight.

What is one to do? The secret is to avoid processed foods and eat simple natural unrefined foods. It is almost impossible to overeat unprocessed plant foods with all their fibre intact, and with their own naturally occurring fat, rather than added fat. Such food has the added benefit of improving health and helping to prevent disease. Go for the simple natural unrefined plant foods, and enjoy your food without worrying about the complicated chemistry of dietary fat.

Olive oil seems to be the safest form of added fat

Fibre is the indigestible residue of plant foods. All plant foods in their natural state contain fibre, because it is an important part of plant structure. Unrefined cereal grains are a good source. Most of their fibre is in the outer layer of bran which is removed in the refining process. Fruits and vegetables, pulses, nuts and seeds all contain fibre. Animal produce does not contain any dietary fibre at all. White flour and rice have lost much of their fibre. Sugar and vegetable oils have lost it all.

Fibre has two very important functions – **filler** and **mover**. As **filler** it gives bulk to the food, and gives a feeling of fullness, which is lacking when refined food is eaten. This feeling of fulness helps us to know when to stop eating, and lack of fibre is one of the main reasons for overweight. This is why natural high-fibre food is an essential part of any successful weight-watching programme and why it plays an important part in the prevention of many diseases.

As **mover**, the fibre bulk enables the whole digestive tract to work more easily. The bulky material also retains fluid, and this helps the colon to pass it quickly through, preventing constipation and all the problems that it causes, from piles to bowel cancer.

There is an added bonus with the soluble fibre of oat bran and fruit and vegetables – it also acts as a cholesterol trap, moving it right out of the system with the rest of the waste.

helping to prevent heart attacks, strokes and blood clots. It also helps to relieve headaches and many muscular aches and pains. A good rule of thumb is to drink enough to keep the urine pale and clear. In practical terms this will work out at six to eight glasses of water a day. A good way to start the day is take a large drink of water on rising, say a pint (a generous half litre), and then take mid-morning, mid-afternoon and mid-evening drinks. It is better not to drink very much with meals, as the fluids dilute the digestive juices, and slow down the digestive process.

Water

Fruit and vegetables in their fresh and natural state have a high water content. This is by design, and its function is to give a sense of fullness and satisfaction after eating them, and also to help maintain our water input. Another of the problems with refined foods is that, as well as lacking fibre, they also lack water. This makes them even more concentrated, and less filling.

Water intake is very important. Recommendations vary from one to two litres a day, more in hot weather, or when exercising strenuously. Good hydration has many bonuses. It boosts the immune system, so helping to resist infections. It thins the blood, lowering the blood pressure and

Other nutrients - vitamins, minerals

Vitamins are complex organic substances present in tiny quantities in food and essential for normal body function and maintenance.

They come in two varieties, *fat soluble* (A, D, E and K) and *water soluble* (B and C). The fat soluble ones come with fats and oils in food. They are absorbed along with dietary fat, which is another reason to avoid unnaturally low-fat diets. They are stored in the liver and fat tissues, and this fact makes

Water thins the blood, lowering the blood pressure and helping to prevent heart attacks, strokes and blood clots

it possible to get too much if you take too many vitamin supplements.

Fat soluble vitamins

Vitamin A works like a hormone, and has roles in vision, skin, lungs, bones, reproduction and more. Deficiency causes blindness, sickness and death, and is a major problem in many parts of the world. Animal food sources are milk, eggs and liver. In plant foods it comes in the form of *beta carotene* which is changed to vitamin A in the body. It is a bright orange colour, and it comes in bright orange, yellow and green vegetables and fruits, such as carrots, greens and apricots. *Beta carotene* is also a powerful antioxidant (see below).

Vitamin D occurs in fish oils and eggs and is added to margarine but it is also synthesised in the skin when it is exposed to sunlight. Ten minutes of gentle sunlight a day just to the face is enough to maintain the supply of vitamin D. It also acts like a hormone and is needed for bones, digestive and urinary systems. Deficiency causes rickets in children and bone degeneration in adults. It is toxic in excess.

Vitamin E works to preserve cell membranes, especially in the lungs and blood cells. It is also a powerful antioxidant. It is found in many plant foods, particularly oils, and also in fruits and vegetables. Animal sources of small amounts are meat, fish and eggs. Deficiency and toxicity are both rare.

Vitamin K is one of the twenty-eight or more factors involved in blood clotting. It is found in greens and beans, and in milk and eggs. About half our supply of this vitamin

Antioxidants and free radicals

As the body's cells use oxygen to produce energy, some highly unstable molecules known as *free radicals* are produced. These are atoms or molecules with missing electrons. They rush around grabbing electrons from other molecules to stabilise themselves, in the process creating new free radicals. An electron-grabbing chain reaction starts that damages tissues and contributes to ageing and degenerative disease.

The 'police' who put a stop to this are the *antioxidants*, among which are vitamins E, C and beta carotene. They seek out the free radicals and inactivate them – becoming inactivated themselves in the process. For this reason a regular supply of antioxidants is needed, and the best way of ensuring this is (of course) to eat a natural unrefined plant food diet.

is manufactured in our bodies by bacteria in our digestive tracts. Deficiency, which is rare, causes a problem with bleeding. Excess, usually due to unwise supplementation, is also rare, and is toxic.

Water soluble vitamins

Vitamin B complex. Vitamin B is not a single substance, but a group of over a dozen, which act together to facilitate the work of every cell, in every system, including the nervous system. Some are involved in generating energy, some in the manufacture of proteins and new cells. They are essential for the metabolism of carbohydrates, fat and protein, and deficiency leads to serious diseases. They are abundantly supplied in natural unprocessed foods, both plant and animal. The outer layers of grains are a rich

source, and serious deficiency diseases occurred when the refining of wheat and other grains became common practice. Some of the lost B complex vitamins are now added to white flour to avoid this problem. Milder deficiencies contribute to irritability and nervous tension. Other plant sources are beans and green vegetables. Nutritional yeast and yeast extract are particularly rich sources.

Vitamin B12 is rather special and mysterious. It occurs in animal produce. It is not made by plants, nor can our bodies synthesise it. This has led to the belief that animal products are essential. However, many total vegetarians survive very well for many years without either animal foods or B12 supplements. Where do they get it from? Bacteria produce it, and bacteria are working away in all sorts of unexpected places. We only need very minute amounts and most strict vegetarians probably get enough through bacterial 'contamination' of foods and drinking water. However, problems occur, even in meat eaters, when vitamin B12 can't be absorbed. The onset of these problems, which include pernicious anaemia and degeneration of the spinal cord, is very gradual as B12 is stored in the body, and most people have about a four-year reserve. As these illnesses are very serious, it's rec-

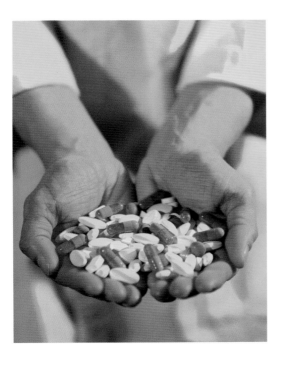

Food minerals are soluble in water and are easily lost if foods are cooked in water and the water is thrown away. To avoid this they should be cooked in as little water as possible and the water should also be used. Steaming is a good method, especially if the water is saved and used for gravy or soup, or simply drunk. Stews and soups conserve all the minerals, as do methods of baking and roasting whole vegetables (and fruits).

Water soluble vitamins are also lost if cooking water is discarded, but they are also destroyed by heat, especially overcooking. Quick cooking, starting with the water already boiling, or the oven already hot, minimises the vitamin loss due to heat. Slow cooking, starting from cold and gradually warming up gives enzymes plenty of time to destroy them.

Raw fruit and vegetables obviously contain the most vitamins and minerals, and it is a good plan to eat something raw at every meal. It is not necessary to eat all the fruit and vegetables raw, however, as some nutrients are more available when the food is cooked.

Cooking to conserve vitamins and minerals

ommended that people changing to totally vegetarian diets, especially in later life, have occasional B12 blood tests, just to make sure that they are absorbing the very tiny amounts that occur in their exclusively plant food diets.

Vitamin C has been known longer than any other vitamin. Hundreds of years ago sailors on long voyages suffered from scurvy, due to lack of vitamin C, until it was discovered that adding citrus fruit or cabbage (both good sources of vitamin C) cured them. It is another antioxidant. It maintains connective tissue, speeds up the healing of wounds, protects against infection and promotes iron absorption, among many other functions. Its antioxidant properties help to slow down the aging process and the development of all the degenerative diseases. It is found in all fresh fruit and vegetables, but it

is destroyed by heat, and once the produce has been picked, the content gradually diminishes.

Major minerals are calcium, phosphorus, potassium, sodium, chlorine and iron. Though plant foods contain all the minerals we need, and in the right combinations, large amounts of them can be lost in cooking. See above.

Calcium is used for building bones and teeth, and also has roles in nerve transmission, muscle contraction, blood clotting and other important functions. Its most well known source is dairy produce, but what is less well known is that the calcium in dairy produce is not in the most easily absorbed form. Calcium is also widely distributed in plant foods like green vegetables, grains, nuts and seeds, mostly in an easily absorbed form. Deficiency in children causes rickets, and bone degeneration in adults.

Phosphorus is also important in bones and teeth, and in cell membranes and genetic material. It has vital functions in maintaining acid-base balance and in energy production. It is highest in animal produce, but is present in many plants, and deficiency is unlikely on almost any diet.

Magnesium is necessary for the operation of hundreds of enzymes. Good sources are beans, potatoes, spinach and sunflower seeds. Deficiency has been linked to heart disease, chronic fatigue and many other illnesses.

Sodium. No known human diet lacks this element which has many important functions in the maintaining the body fluids and, therefore, the function of every organ and tissue. Excess is a common result of eating too much salt. Savoury snacks and many processed foods are very high in salt. Animal produce is also high in sodium. High sodium

intake is associated with high blood pressure, heart attack, stroke and some cancers. To eat a whole plant food diet with lots of fruit is a good way to reduce salt intake to the small amount that we actually need.

Potassium is very important inside the cells. It has many metabolic functions, including control of the action of the heart. Fresh fruits and vegetables are the best sources. Deficiency is possible in some illnesses and with the use of some diuretic medicines. Supplements can cause excess which is dangerous too.

Iron is best known for its part in the structure of haemoglobin, the oxygen-carrying pigment in the red blood cells. Iron deficiency anaemia is a worldwide problem. Diseases that cause blood loss are a major factor. Another one is inadequate iron in the diet, which often simply means inadequate *food*. Most people think that red meat is the most important source of iron, but though plant sources may contain less iron it is usually in a more easily absorbed form. The richest plant sources are the dark coloured ones – dark green vegetables, beetroot, prunes, raisins, and the dark outer layers of grains.

Trace Minerals: iodine, zinc, selenium, fluoride, chromium, copper and other minerals (including boron, nickel, manganese silicon and molybdenum) are needed in very tiny amounts. Iodine is well known for its relation to the thyroid gland. Zinc and selenium have multiple functions that involve the immune system and antioxidant

Empty calories
(junk food)

These are the calories, or food energy units, that come from refined sugar, fats and starches. They include white sugar, vegetable oil, white flour, and all foods made from them. Confectionery is mainly sugar, soft drinks are sugared water. Cakes, biscuits and puddings are usually high in all three. Crisps and other savoury snacks are very high in fat, and also in salt. These foods provide very little more than fuel because they have lost their vital nutrients and fibre. Having lost all or most of their minerals and vitamins, they don't contribute to health maintenance. Because they are so concentrated, they are not filling, and the temptation to overeat is hard to resist. They make a very major contribution to obesity and health problems of every kind.

Healthy and active people can usually cope with small amounts of junk food on an occasional basis, especially if they exercise vigorously to burn the calories up. If the junk food is a large part of the diet, there is a price to pay in present or future ill health, or both.

activities, making them important factors in preventing cancer and other degenerative diseases. Most of these trace minerals are widely available in unrefined plant foods. Heavy use of refined foods makes deficiencies possible, with important effects in all the body systems. All the trace minerals are toxic in excess. Overuse of supplements is dangerous, underlining the fact that the safest way to get your minerals is from your food.

Phytochemicals

These are being named 'the vitamins of the next century'. They are non-nutrient plant chemicals, compounds that give plants their special characteristics including taste, smell,

colour, and healing properties. In the last few years many phytochemicals have been discovered to have anti-cancer properties, and some examples of these are the brassica family – cabbage, broccoli, brussels sprouts, etc; the carrot family, which includes celery, parsnip, parsley and coriander; and the onion and garlic family. They occur in fruits and grains as well, and every plant food that has been studied so far contains valuable health promoting phytochemicals.

E-numbers and other additives

E-numbers refer to food additives permitted in the EU. Their use is a controversial subject. Some scientists reassure us that the additives are perfectly safe at the levels used, others quote research that shows the opposite. The best plan is to avoid artificial additives as far as possible. This can be done by choosing a simple, natural diet using large amounts of fresh fruit and vegetables, some of them raw, and using simple natural home-made dishes rather than prepacked ones. If this is our regular diet, we can be sure that our livers will be in the best possible condition to deal with whatever artificial additives and pollutants we may accidentally, or occasionally choose to eat.

Going organic, is it worth it?

This also used to be controversial, with conflicting evidence, but the balance of evidence now is in favour of methods of agriculture that use organic fertilisers and

The best plan is to avoid artificial additives as far as possible

avoid chemical pesticides. This is especially true with the introduction of genetically engineered food, one purpose of which seems to be to enable more pesticides to be used.

When we don't know the results of these types of interference with nature, it seems sensible to eat the simplest and most natural diet that is available. The ideal would be to grow our own food, and eat it when it's at its freshest and best. Failing that, we should eat a wide variety of the freshest and most natural food available, and that we can afford, remembering that the whole balance is what is important. Do the best you can, praise God for the food on your plate, ask for his blessing as you eat it, and eat with a thankful heart.

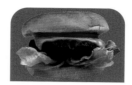

Chapter Eleven

You don't need meat

There has been a revolution in thinking about this subject in the last few years.

The received opinion used to be that human beings needed to eat meat in order to preserve life, health and strength. This view was strengthened by the theory of evolution with its ideas of 'nature red in tooth and claw', and the idea that man had fairly recently (in evolutionary terms) evolved from his carnivorous ancestors. Pictures of primitive cavemen gnawing on bones reinforced the idea. Some have even gone so far as to say that we have too recently evolved from our carnivorous past to be able to cope fully with complex carbohydrates. This they say explains the prevalence of wheat sensitivities. They completely overlook the fact that our carnivorous 'cousins' (cats and dogs are the most familiar examples) have completely different teeth, jaws and digestive systems in order to cope with meat, not to mention the many other major differences between

Meat eating is definitely not worth the increase risks of cardiovascular disease, cancer and other degenerative diseases.

human beings and their nearest so-called 'animal relatives'.

Nor did they know about the more recently discovered fact that archaeologists studying cave dwellings have found evidence that the cave dwellers' diet included many plant foods as well as animal flesh, suggesting that these 'primitive' people had a mixed diet, and were hunter gatherers, rather than just hunters.

The vegetarian: a new image

It's only a few decades since doctors and scientists questioned the adequacy of the vegetarian diet. The popular image of the vegetarian was of a pale thin person, as opposed to the strong healthy meat eater typified by the stout, hale and hearty

farmer. The facts that the farmer's ruddy complexion owed much more to fresh air and exercise than to his diet, and that many farmers died in the prime of their lives from cardiovascular disease were not appreciated. Today the

vegetarian, who is usually enthusiastic for the other aspects of a healthy lifestyle as well, is appreciated as slim and healthy. Human beings are much more similar in anatomy and physiology to monkeys and apes than we are to carnivorous or even to herbivorous animals. Most of these animals are vegetarians most of the time, only eating meat when plant food, their preferred diet, is out of season. Mainly plant food eaters, they are able to cope with meat if necessary. Human beings are similar in that they can cope with meat. Even completely herbivorous animals can adapt, at least in the laboratory, to eating meat, and may even grow bigger, fatter and stronger – but unfortunately they are likely to collapse in their prime with fatal heart attacks!

Who lives longest?

There are few human groups that survive on an entirely animal food diet. The Eskimos are one example, living in a very cold climate on a very high fat and protein fish diet. They are not noted for longevity, and when sugar was added to their diet the effect was disastrous: tooth decay, diabetes, cardiovascular disease and more, in epidemic proportions. The Masai in East Africa are another example, living very active outdoor lives herding cattle, and living on milk and blood. In both cases survival of the fittest no doubt has played an important part. Three groups are particularly known for their longevity, the Hunza in northern Pakistan, the Vilcabamba in Equador and the Georgians in the Caucasus. Although their ages have been exaggerated at times, these groups did in the past have a much higher than average number of healthy and active elderly members. These groups eat very largely plant food diets; *they also all live in rather remote mountainous areas that necessitate a lot of vigorous physical activity.*

For those living the comfortable Western lifestyle, meat eating is definitely not worth the increased risks of cardiovascular disease, cancer and other degenerative diseases. They are at least 30% more likely to have a heart attack, and 40% more likely to develop cancer than vegetarians. Increased risks of many other degenerative diseases have also been noted, including gall stones, kidney stones, diverticulitis, arthritis and osteoporosis.

At risk

Meat eaters are also much more at risk from food poisoning, especially salmonella. Food-borne infections are almost invariably associated with animal produce, not only meat and poultry, but also dairy products and eggs. Mayonnaise, custard and creamed chicken are in fact almost perfect culture mediums, and we should treat them with care, especially in warm climates. Much of the information given about cooking and preparing meat is concerned with how to avoid infections such as salmonella, some strains of which are potentially very serious, and can be fatal. Preparation areas for meat and poultry need to be disinfected after use. Eggs are notorious for their ability to spread salmonella, to the extent that pasteurised egg mix is used in commercial cooking and we are advised not to use raw eggs. Soft cheeses have been a source of listeria food poisoning, with its possible disastrous effects on the unborn, often enough for public health authorities to warn pregnant mothers not to touch them. Plant foods present no such problems.

Then there is the question of cholesterol. Meat, poultry, fish, dairy produce and eggs all contain cholesterol, which is associated with increased risk of cardiovascular disease. Saturated fat pushes the level of cholesterol even higher, and animal foods tend to be high in saturated fats. And don't be deceived about the low fat varieties. They are not good, only less bad.

Meat and bowel cancer

Another negative thing about animal produce is that it contains none of that healthy fibre that prevents constipation, reduces cholesterol levels and helps to prevent many diseases including bowel cancer. Plant fibre also gives a sense of satisfaction that prevents overeating and makes weight control easier. This is why, contrary to what used to be thought, vegetarians can lose weight more easily that meat eaters – if they choose whole foods.

Animal products produce more free radicals, the 'wild' oxygen atoms that race around and damage cell membranes, contributing to ageing, heart disease and cancer. Plant foods contain the trouble-shooting antioxidants that inactivate them.

The humanitarian argument

In the UK alone, over 800 million animals are slaughtered for food each year. This, of course, includes birds as well as large farm animals. They are all sentient creatures, capable of feeling pain and pleasure, fear and contentment. Some of them are more intelligent than many of our domestic pets. They were created for our pleasure and service, not for us to exploit and torture, keeping them in unnatural surroundings, feeding them unnatural food, denying them the satisfaction of their most basic instincts. Keeping poultry in battery cages will be illegal in Europe by 2005, but there are many other inhumane practices where animals are considered merely as meat machines, bred to exploit the characteristics that are the most financially rewarding, with little thought for the animal's comfort or health. *Many people are vegetarians because they want to have no part in this industry*. Nor is the dairy industry exempt, and vegans,

Meat eaters are at least 30% more likely to have a heart attack and 40% more likely to develop cancer than vegetarians.

(those who have chosen a diet consisting entirely of whole plant foods) have often chosen this way of eating out of respect for the animals and the desire to live in harmony with nature and the environment.

Environmental issues

Environmental and economic issues are compelling in this connection, too. *To produce meat as a staple food is an economic disaster*. It takes *ten* times as much land to produce a pound of red meat as a pound of grain. Fifty per cent of the world cereal production is used as animal

feed. It's not too difficult to calculate that the world could quite easily produce food for several times its present vast population if only plant foods were used. Animal hus-

bandry uses more land, more water, more chemicals as pesticides and herbicides, causes more pollution to water supplies and soil. It is said that in the USA raising animals uses over half the water and a third of the raw materials, including fossil fuels. Animal husbandry is the single greatest polluter of water there and is responsible for 85% of soil erosion. Meat production is actually damaging our environment beyond repair. The methane produced by cattle contributes to the greenhouse effect, and the ammonia from animal waste joins with that from fertilisers to produce acid rain that damages trees and buildings. Overfishing has depleted the seas and intensive grazing erodes the land. *Choosing a plant food diet is one of the most important contributions one can make to preserving the environment.*

Vegetarianism in vogue

Meat eating is becoming less popular in many parts of the world, particularly in the UK, where it has been estimated that 8% of the population are already vegetarians, and another 10% are nearly vegetarians. The only reasonable answer to the question, 'Why eat meat?' must be 'because I like it'. Here is where many make a mistake. They sacrifice their health because they don't realise that plant foods have wonderful flavours of their own, and that tastebuds are flexible. It takes a few weeks, or at most a few months to re-educate our tastebuds. For example, soyamilk may not taste right the first time it's tried. It tastes nothing like cows' milk. However, most people who stick to soyamilk, and don't keep reminding themselves of the taste of cows' milk, will eventually come to prefer it, especially if it is freeing them from some of the many unpleasant symptoms of cows' milk sensitivity. The solution is to decide what is best for your health, eat accordingly and be patient with your tastebuds. Concentrate on enjoying new and interesting tastes and never look back as you eat for health and not for taste alone.

The mind and the spirit

Physical health is not the only reason for choosing a plant food diet. The mind and spirit benefit as well. The Bible teaches that the Creator chose a plant food diet for his first children Adam and Eve. Their work was to care for their garden home, and the animals were to be their companions, not their diet. Joy and peace are the rewards for choosing to eat according to the Creator's original plan.

The Nacne report in 1983 revealed that people in the UK were overconsuming fat, sugar and red meat and would benefit from reducing these and consuming more starches, fruit and vegetables. This was confirmed by the World Health Organisation in 1990. Since then we have learned about the phytochemicals in plant foods – substances with specific disease-preventing properties which are found in *all* the plant foods and *none* of the animal foods. Vegetarian diets contain less total fat, less saturated fat, less salt, more fibre and many more phytochemicals. Vegetarian diets win whichever way you look at them!

Eating for health

Choose whole food and solve your nutrition problems!

For optimum health, very nearly all our food should contain its full quota of nutrients. This means it should be whole and unrefined. This will ensure that you get enough fibre as well as all the vitamins, minerals and phytochemicals that you need.

Why fibre? Fibre keeps the bowels functioning regularly, prevents constipation and related problems, such as diverticulitis, and even bowel cancer. Fibre helps *remove* cholesterol from the body. Perhaps most important of all, it is bulky, filling the stomach and giving a sense of satisfaction that prevents overeating and excess weight gain.

Which foods for fibre? All the whole plant foods contain some fibre, but the starchy grains are the main source: wheat, rice, barley, rye and so on. Beans and lentils, fruit and vegetables, nuts and seeds are other sources.

How much fibre is needed? Make the starchy filler foods like grains and potatoes the basis of the diet. Then eat as much as you need to feel satisfied while still leaving room for plenty of fruit or vegetables, and some of the concentrated higher protein beans, lentils, nuts or seeds. This will ensure that you get all the fibre you need. You really can't go short of fibre on a whole plant food diet.

Warning! It's possible to overdo the fibre if you add bran to your food. Get the bran in its *natural* state as it comes as part of the whole grain, for example in whole wheat bread, brown rice, oat porridge.

Why plant foods for vitamins, minerals and phytochemicals? Of course animal products contain vitamins

and minerals, too, but *no* vitamin C and *no* phytochemicals. These are particularly important for building a strong immune system and helping to ward off diseases, from simple coughs and colds to heart disease and cancer.

Choosing a whole plant food diet means that you will automatically be eating less fat. The average person in the UK gets about 40% of their total calorie intake from fat. *(Weight for weight, fat contains more than twice the calories of protein or carbohydrate.)* If you eat whole plant foods, there is no problem with excess fat. You get the fat in its natural state, in the right amount, and with all the other nutrients in the right amount too. If you add a few nuts and seeds, or avocados and olives to your grains, fruits and vegetable foods, you will

Change challenge

In some places, for example the UK, it is not difficult to change to a vegetarian diet. Supermarkets offer an abundant variety of vegetables, fresh, frozen, tinned or preserved in other ways. Wholewheat bread and breakfast cereals are easy to find, as is wholewheat flour, and a variety of beans, lentils, nuts and even seeds. The frozen food cabinets hold a range of meat substitutes. What the supermarkets don't supply can be found in the health food shop.

Would-be vegetarians who live in countries where the food industry is less developed may feel that vegetarianism is just too difficult an option. But actually, many people living in countries with developed market economies envy those living in tropical countries who have access to outdoor market stalls where there is an abundant variety of fresh fruit and vegetables and also beans, lentils, nuts and seeds, all in their natural state, free from the preservatives and additives of the advanced food industries.

through any refining process and is rich in monounsaturated fatty acids which are associated with healthy hearts and low blood pressure. Then there are all the other vegetable oils which are usually highly refined. For example it takes about twelve corncobs to get a tablespoonful of corn oil. All the fibre, protein and carbohydrate has been lost in the refining process along with almost all the other nutrients, making it a very concentrated food which is easy to overeat.

Choosing whole plant foods means you will also automatically be eating less sugar. White sugar is a pure energy source, containing *no nutrients whatsoever except calories*. The average person in the UK gets 20% of their calories from sugar. It takes about a yard of sugarcane to make a teaspoonful of sugar – it's very easy to overeat sugar, impossible to overeat sugarcane! Sugar is associated with all sorts of problems from tooth decay to diabetes, but the real problem is the fact that it supplies empty calories – it is deficient in all the valuable nutrients that are lost in the refining process.

get the *healthy* fat you need without having to worry about the *un*healthy kind.

A note about oil: There are two kinds of vegetable oil. There is olive oil which is about 16% of the olive and doesn't go

Warning: Don't get the dangers of refined food out of proportion. It is when they form a large part of the diet that they are so harmful. Small amounts occasionally are unlikely to be harmful to healthy active people. *Animal produce is a different problem.* Now that there is so much disease in animals it would be wise gradually to give up the use of animal flesh altogether, and to be very careful about the other animal products as well.

What about plant protein? It is completely adequate, provided you eat more than one kind of plant. Choosing whole plant food will solve the protein problem. Plant foods enable you to avoid the excess protein in meat, fish and poultry, and the stress it puts on heart, liver and kidneys.

Making the transition

Unless there are urgent health reasons, make changes in your diet *gradually* – for some it can be done in a few weeks, others need several months, or even one or two years. *The first step* is to choose more whole foods, making a *gradual* change, for example from white to wholewheat bread. Then start choosing bigger servings of vegetables and other whole plant foods, and choose smaller servings of the animal foods, gradually replacing them with a wide variety of plant foods. Learn to make some vegetarian savouries and have one or two completely plant food days

each week. Meat replacements like TVP and Quorn are not necessary for health, but can be very useful for replacing meat, especially in the transition stage if you are changing from a high animal food intake to a mainly plant food diet. *Be very careful about making major changes in diet if you live in a place where a wide variety of plant foods is not available.* Take local advice about dairy

produce and eggs. It's important that there is a good variety of different kinds of plant foods to take their place if they have been an important part of the diet.

Something Better

Living healthily *does* take more thought and care, especially in the beginning while you are getting used to it. It is possible to develop a healthy vegetarian diet anywhere where there is a variety of fruits, vegetables and pulses (beans and lentils) and a supply of unrefined cereal products such as wholewheat bread, or the local cereals. *Special vegetarian products are not necessary*. Most local diets are fairly easy to adapt as they are based around starchy foods. Use a little seasoning to help get used to the meat-free taste.

Another difficulty can be when the rest of the household don't want to change to a meat-free diet. Experiment with vegetarian dishes and try them on the family *occasionally*. It's good to approach the subject of improving one's diet calmly and unhurriedly or the stress caused could undo the benefit of the healthier food! 'Something Better' is the watchword of all true food reform, and reform is progressive – *you don't learn it all at once or make all the changes at the same time.* You do the best you can as you gradually move towards what you decide is better for yourself and your family.

Chapter Twelve

Back Pain

Back pain - the facts

Back pain has always been very common and over the last few years we have learned a great deal about it. There has been a revolution in thinking about back care, and we now approach it in a different way.

Most people can and do deal with back pain on their own most of the time. The information in this chapter is based on the latest research and government recommendations on the treatment of back pain. It will aim to give you advice on how to deal with back pain, how to avoid disability, and how to recover quickly.

Here are some facts:

✳ Most back pain settles quickly enough to continue with the normal activities of life.

✳ It affects 80% of the population at some point in their lives.

✳ Approximately half of the people who get backache will have it again within a couple

of years, but this doesn't mean it is serious.
* Most people return to normal activities
between attacks with few if any symptoms.
* During an attack the pain can be very
severe and some activities may need to be
reduced for a time.
* Rest for more than two days usually does
not help and may do more harm than good.
* It is better if you can keep moving.
* Your back is designed to move; the sooner you return to normal activity the sooner
your back will feel better.
* The people who cope best with back
pain are those who stay active and continue
with their lives despite the pain.

The anatomy of the spine

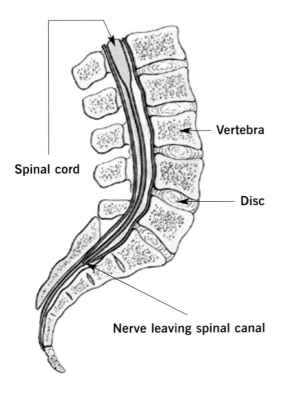

Vertebra

Spinal cord

Disc

Nerve leaving spinal canal

The spine is one of the strongest parts of
your body and is made up of thirty-three
solid bony blocks (vertebrae) joined by discs
to give it strength and flexibility. Tough
bands of tissue called ligaments act like
tight elastic bands holding the spine together and reinforcing the blocks and discs. The
whole structure is surrounded by both small
and large muscles, which move, stabilise
and protect the spine. Running down the
centre of this structure is the spinal cord,
the trunk of the nervous system. At intervals
between each block of bone and disc a
branch, called a nerve root, runs off this
central trunk and out into the body. The
nerve roots pass through the openings
between the vertebrae. Thus, a failure of
muscular support or injury may result in
pressure or 'pinching' upon a nerve, causing
pain.

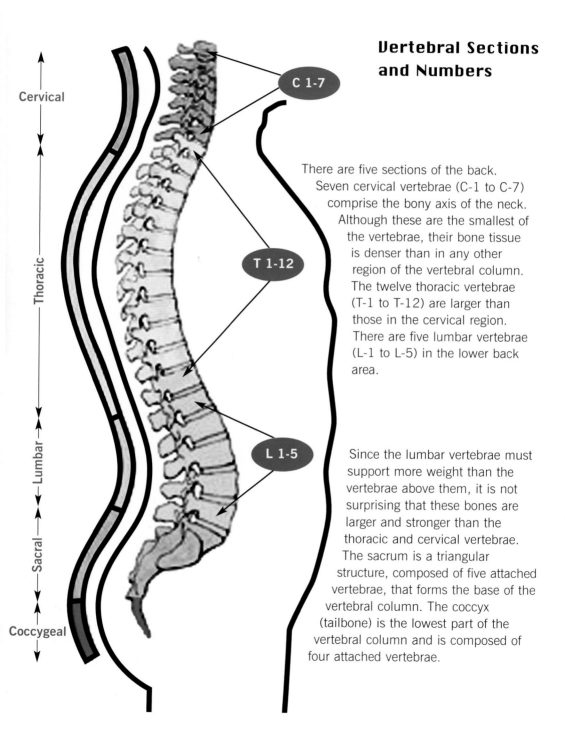

Vertebral Sections and Numbers

C 1-7

Cervical

Thoracic

T 1-12

Lumbar

Sacral

L 1-5

Coccygeal

There are five sections of the back. Seven cervical vertebrae (C-1 to C-7) comprise the bony axis of the neck. Although these are the smallest of the vertebrae, their bone tissue is denser than in any other region of the vertebral column. The twelve thoracic vertebrae (T-1 to T-12) are larger than those in the cervical region. There are five lumbar vertebrae (L-1 to L-5) in the lower back area.

Since the lumbar vertebrae must support more weight than the vertebrae above them, it is not surprising that these bones are larger and stronger than the thoracic and cervical vertebrae. The sacrum is a triangular structure, composed of five attached vertebrae, that forms the base of the vertebral column. The coccyx (tailbone) is the lowest part of the vertebral column and is composed of four attached vertebrae.

Causes of pain

It is surprisingly difficult to damage your spine. Research has shown that most people with back pain or backache do not have any damage in their spine. Very few people with backaches have a 'slipped disc' or a trapped nerve.

Low back pain is one of mankind's most common ailments. However, back pain or ache is usually not due to any serious disease. If there is a serious cause for your backache, it is usually easy for your doctor or physical therapist to diagnose. The not-so-serious causes account for 80% of the population's suffering at some point in their lives.

X-ray findings often show 'wear and tear'. However, this is the normal ageing process and most people over 30 will show these signs on X-ray. Normal wear and tear does not lead to arthritis; it is as normal as having grey hair.

In most people a detailed diagnosis pinpointing the exact source of the trouble is impossible. However, most back pain comes from the muscles, ligament and joints in your back. If they are not moving as they should, they will cause pain. The best way to consider backache is by thinking of your back as 'out of condition'. The need is to get your back working properly again. If you are physically fit you will generally get less back pain and recover faster than those who are unfit.

As stated earlier, many people experience neck and back discomfort at some time in their lives. Problems can occur suddenly after an accident or injury, or as the result of a slow, gradual process due to lack of exercise or poor posture. Incorrect posture throws the head forward and puts a tremendous amount of stress on the muscles in the back of the neck and upper shoulders. Muscles in this position maintain a constant state of contraction, resulting in injury and subsequent discomfort. Poor sleeping habits, poor work habits, and tension can all contribute to this problem. While tension is not often the primary cause it can certainly worsen pain and make you more prone to injury.

Some other specific conditions that can lead to muscle deterioration and pain may include a sedentary lifestyle, obesity, and general lack of muscular tone. A healthy, pain-free lower back also depends on the condition of your upper back. Because the upper and lower back share the same muscles, the strength and flexibility of the shoulders and upper back muscles are important for keeping the neck balanced. Pain is also generated when muscles go into spasm. While such a spasm may occur as a protective reflex, it intensifies discomfort by reducing circulation and setting up an inflammatory response. Stress of any kind, physical or emotional, may cause spasms in under-exercised muscles. Lastly, pressure or 'pinching' of the nerves in the spine can cause severe pain that can radiate (travel) down the back and leg.

Serious symptoms

While dull aches can be annoying and even ignored, severe pain or pain accompanied by other symptoms may indicate a serious underlying disease that requires medical attention. If you have any of the following symptoms associated with pain in your neck or back, you are urged to seek medical assistance:

- **Fever** – May indicate an infection.
- **Frequent, painful or bloody urination** – May indicate a kidney problem.
- **Leg pain travelling down to or below the knee** – May indicate a possible disc problem.
- **Numbness, tingling, weakness or loss of bladder or bowel control** – May indicate a nerve or disc problem.
- **Persistent pain that hasn't improved in six weeks and cannot be relieved** – May indicate a serious back disorder or injury.

Seeking help

If you have any of the symptoms listed above or have other concerns about your neck or back, you are encouraged to consult a medical provider or your physical therapist. Evaluation of your problem may include a discussion and review of your medical history, a physical examination and diagnostic tests.

Treatment/self-care

Self-care and treatment can be responsibly done under the consultation of a medical provider. The following are some safe and effective methods, but remember, if your back still hurts after a week of self-treatment, seek medical advice from your physical therapist or doctor.

✳ Rest or exercise?

The old fashioned treatment of back pain was weeks of bed rest. This has long been shown to be bad for your back. If you lie

down for a long time your –
bones get weaker,
muscles get weaker,
you get stiff,
your ligaments get slack,
you get out of physical condition,
you feel depressed,
the pain feels worse,
it's harder to get going again.

It is no longer recommended that you use prolonged bed rest to treat backache.

Bed rest is bad for your back

However, you must give your back time to recover, this involves doing less for a while. Listen to your back and follow good posture, lifting and twisting advice.

There are many treatments which can help back pain. They may not completely stop the

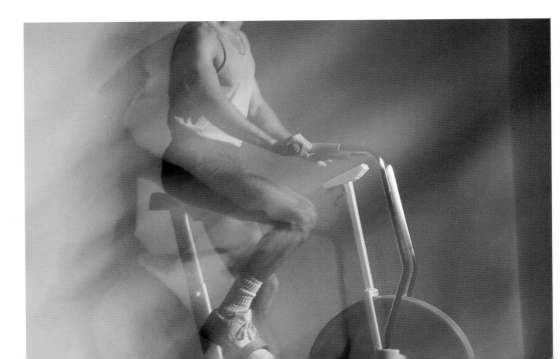

pain but they should control the pain enough for you to get active.

＊ **Medication** If you are taking any other medication you should consult your pharmacist or doctor

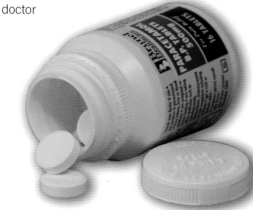

before taking more. Paracetamol or soluble aspirin are the simplest and safest painkillers. Follow the instructions on the package and never exceed the recommended dose. Anti-inflammatory tablets like ibuprofen can also prove very useful.

You should take painkillers for a couple of days to a couple of weeks, but *do not take aspirin or ibuprofen if you have indigestion or an ulcer.*

Remember painkillers do not cure your back problem; they are a means of helping you stay active while your back is healing.

＊ **Acupuncture** can be of help as a pain reliever. However, it is still unproven as a method of curing the cause of the back pain so should be used with the same precautions as painkillers.

＊ **Application of heat or ice** Apply heat and/or ice in a way that makes you most comfortable. To relieve initial pain, you may want to apply ice packs wrapped in towels for 10 minutes every two hours for the first one or two days. Then you may apply heat or ice. Always make sure you have a cloth of some type between your skin and the ice, to prevent freezing the skin and frostbite. *It is not recommended that you lie on an ice pack.* Since back sprains and strains don't usually cause much swelling, some people find moist heat, such as a hot shower, wet towels, or hot water bottle, to be more effective than ice. Limit heat to 15-20 minutes every few hours. Too much heat can make you feel drained and tired, rather than relaxed.

＊ **Rest** Try to lie comfortably in a well-supported bed. The best position for your back is on your side with the knees bent. A pillow between the knees may also help increase comfort. Another good resting position is on your back with a pillow underneath your knees. Lying on your stomach or flat on your back with your legs straight out are not recommended positions. Remember, do not rest for long periods.

Spinal manipulation

Sometimes joints become locked or get stuck together. In such cases a low velocity, high frequency, painless manipulation can often free the joint with a dramatic relief of pain and return to function. This should always be performed by a trained physical therapist. Back pain from this cause, however, is relatively uncommon and often happens suddenly with the sufferer unable to move in any direction. Manipulation can help in other cases of low back pain. A physical therapist will advise you on posture, ergonomics, appropriate exercise and healthy lifestyle. You must ensure that any physical therapist is appropriately qualified before seeking treatment.

Physiotherapists will have the letters

The short answer to back pain: Get your back moving and working properly. Get into condition and physically fit.

MCSP SRP after their name. This ensures they have undergone at least three years of training and are fully qualified. Manipulating physiotherapists may have in addition the letters MMACP. This shows that they have undertaken a high-level postgraduate training exam in manipulation.

Exercise

You can exercises even when your back is sore. It is important to use your muscles and get your joints moving. Walking, exercise bikes, and swimming all help you make a start without putting too much stress on your back. They make your heart and lungs work and are a start to increased physical fitness.

Build up exercise gradually over a few weeks and then exercise regularly and keep it up. Remember, fitness takes time.

Different exercises suit different people. You may need to experiment to find out what suits your back the best. Try walking instead or going by bus or car, remember that when you are training your muscles they can ache. This does not mean you are damaging them. Exercises are not easy. Painkillers and other treatments can help to control the pain and let you get started. Exercise can often hurt at first but the longer it is put off, the harder and more painful the recovery from your back pain will be. If you experience any significant pain, stop

immediately and seek medical attention. Gradually increase the amount, intensity and frequency of exercise as tolerated. Do not perform any exercise with pain that is increasing or not improving.

Exercise caution
You must be aware that certain exercises can put an excessive strain on your back and should be avoided especially if your back is 'weak'. Avoid bending over to stretch the hamstrings, any kind of leg lift, and flexion or rotation exercises.

✳ **Massage** helps increase the blood flow to your muscles, improves muscle tone and helps your muscles to relax. Make sure your masseur knows you have a back problem before starting treatment.

✳ **Stress and Tension Management**
Techniques such as progressive muscular relaxation, exhalation breathing and meditation can help create a more relaxed body that is receptive to healing. Soothing music

played on a stereo or radio and resting your body and mind may also be beneficial.

✳ **Recreational Activities** Some activities can be helpful in toning and stretching muscles while reducing the possibility of further injury. Swimming, walking, and water walking are recommended. Conversely, some activities can cause problems if done before symptoms are gone and strength, flexibility and conditioning are restored. Avoid tennis, golf, bowling, racquetball, diving, high-impact aerobics, and other activities that combine sudden bending and twisting.

How to avoid back pain

Most back pains are avoidable and the measures recommended here will help to prevent a recurrence as well as a first onset. The first step is becoming physically fit. One of the best methods is to walk at a moderately brisk pace for 20 minutes at least three times a week. You should be slightly breathless after this walk. This raises the heart rate and works the lungs, getting the muscles, joints and ligaments moving again. Swimming and cycling are also good forms of exercise. Swimming exercises the body while the water buoyancy takes the body weight, reducing any stress or strain on the joints of the body.

Prevention of problems with proper posture

Correct posture in sitting, standing and lying will ensure that no strain is being put on the back. Slouching, lolling, dropping and bent and twisted postures all put undue stress on the back. Repeating these positions during a lifetime will predispose you to having longer and more frequent episodes of back pain.

A healthy neck supports your head, keeping it aligned with the rest of the spine in a proper, balanced posture. The neck has a slight natural curve, which sits on top of the two curves in the middle and lower back. Correct posture maintains all three curves and prevents undue stress and strain by distributing body weight. Actually, when your back is balanced, it is self-supporting and requires little help from your back muscles.

Correct posture is important no matter what position you assume – standing, sitting, lying down, exercising or moving in any way. In correct, fully erect posture, a line dropped from the ear will go through the tip of the shoulder, the middle of the hip, the back of the knee cap and the front of the anklebone. And, with correct posture, your

internal organs have room to function normally and blood circulates freely for best total fitness.

Good posture is not simply a matter of 'standing tall'. It refers to correct use of the body at all times. To prevent problems, avoiding strain must become a way of life, practised while lying, sitting, standing, walking, working, and exercising. By learning to live with good posture under all circumstances, you will gradually develop proper carriage and stronger muscles, which are needed to protect and support your back.

✳ In a sitting position:

When sitting in any position, the three back curves need to be maintained. If you cannot sit without slouching forward or backward, you need to support yourself with hands and arms or lean against a wall or chair back.

Ensure that you are positioned well back in your chair and that your legs touch the floor comfortably.

Sitting properly

Your back's 'best friend' is a straight, hard chair. If you can't get the chair you prefer, learn to sit properly on whatever chair you have.

Recommended

Caution

Relieve strain by sitting well forward; flatten the back by tightening abdominal muscles; and cross knees.

 A

TV slump leads to 'dowager's hump'; strains the neck and shoulders.

 A

Use of a footrest relieves swayback; have knees higher than hips.

 B

If the chair is too high, swayback is increased.

B

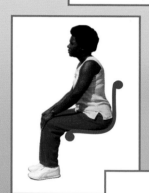

The correct way to sit while driving is close to the pedals. Always use a seat belt.

C

The driver's seat too far from the pedals emphasizes the curve in the lower back.

 C

Keep the neck and back in as straight a line as possible with the spine. Bend forward from the hips.

 D

Forward thrusting strains the muscles of the neck and head

 D

Recommended

A Use of a footrest relieves swayback.

B Bend the knees and hips, not the waist.

C Hold heavy objects close to you.

D Never bend over without bending the knees.

Caution

A Try not to keep both feet on the ground when standing in the same position for any length of time.

B Do not lift heavy objects using your back muscles only.

C Do not hold heavy objects at arm's length.

D Bending over without bending the knees puts undue strain on the back

Lifting correctly

✳ Do **NOT** attempt to lift beyond your ability – if in doubt always seek assistance,

✳ Plan your lift, i.e. know where you are going to put the load and how you are going to get it there; do a warm-up stretch,

✳ Keep your back straight during the lift,

✳ If the load is on the ground or a low bench, make sure you crouch beside the load with one foot in front of the other,

✳ Use the whole of your hand to grip the load,

✳ Keep the load as close to your body as possible,

✳ Lift smoothly using your legs to lift you, not your back,

✳ It may help to tighten your stomach and bottom muscles before you lift to 'brace' your back,

✳ Never bend and twist at the same time with a load in your hands,

✳ Never lift when tired.

Putting your back to bed

The average person spends a third of his life in bed. The bed and, more importantly, the mattress that you buy should be considered an investment in your health. Usually the more expensive a mattress the more supportive it should be. You should check that when lying, your mattress supports you fully and your spine should be in its appropriate curves. A too-firm mattress can be just as bad as one that is too soft. Sleeping on a board will *not* help most people. However, if your bed is very soft, putting a ¾ inch plywood board under your mattress may give it some additional support. The position you lie in can make a difference to your back. If you are in any doubt consult your physical therapist.

Recommended	Caution

Lying on your side with your knees bent effectively flattens your back. A pillow may be used to support your neck, especially if your shoulders are broad.

Lying flat on your back makes swayback worse.

Sleeping on your back is restful and correct when your knees are properly supported.

The use of high pillows strains your neck, arms, and shoulders.

Raise the foot of your mattress to discourage sleeping on your abdomen.

Sleeping face down exaggerates swayback, strains the neck and the shoulders.

Ideas for daily living

Packs and Sore Backs

If you're in the habit of slinging a backpack full of books over one shoulder, your back could be in for trouble. Among students, this is a common cause of pain in the back and shoulders. Instead, carry your backpack properly over both shoulders.

Bicycling and Your Back

Adjust bicycle handlebars and seat to support correct posture. Upright handlebars, rather than racing types, may be better for avoiding injury.

Footwear

Wear flat-soled shoes that are designed for comfort and support. High heel shoes increase the forward curve of the lower back. Do not stand in one place too long; shift your weight and change positions. As you walk or stand, remember the three natural curves of the back and maintain correct posture.

Neck Tips

Do not lean over your work, hobbies, projects, etc. Angle work so that you can look straight ahead, or sit closer to your work area. Do neck exercises throughout the day. For advice on proper neck exercises see the following pages. Also try taking frequent 'mini-breaks' to relieve tension and avoid overhead reaching. Use a ladder or step stool instead.

Sex

Avoid stress on your back during sexual intercourse. Try positions which seem most comfortable such as having your partner on top, or lying on your side.

Pregnancy

During pregnancy, special precautions should be taken since ligaments soften. Also, the added weight of pregnancy can cause further strain. Consult with your doctor or physical therapist about any problems you may be having.

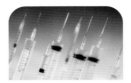

Chapter Thirteen

Reducing Cancer Risk

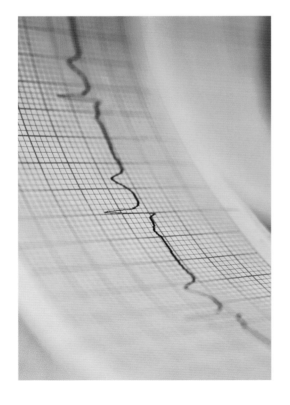

A *Europe Against Cancer leaflet,* produced as part of a cancer reduction programme, asks the question *'Is cancer on your agenda?'* Many people fear the onset of any form of cancer, but relatively few take the necessary steps to reduce the possibility. From an early age cancer needs to be on our personal agenda. After heart disease it is the next most important cause of death worldwide.

Cancer is started when the cell DNA is damaged following exposure to a cancer-causing agent (carcinogen). The cell multiplies at an uncontrolled rate thus resulting in the abnormal cells forming a tumour. The tumourous growth may affect adjoining tissues and spread to other parts of the body, leading to secondary tumours.

In spite of its fearsome reputation as a killer, the good news is that it can be avoided in some of its forms and markedly reduced in incidence in others. One of the world's leading cancer researchers,

Professor Sir Richard Doll says:

>'On a worldwide scale the differences in incidence that have been observed encourage the belief that all the common types of cancer are largely avoidable, in the sense that it should be possible to reduce the risk of developing each type by at least a half and often by 80% or more.'

Ernst Wynder, former president of the American Health Foundation, states:

>'It is our current estimate that some 50% of all female cancers in the Western world and about one third of all male cancers are related to nutritional factors.'

While it is true that not all cancers are caused by diet, our diet either exacerbates the problems or protects us against them.

It has been estimated that about one third of all cancers are directly related to diet and alcohol; one third to tobacco use; and the remaining one third due to all other factors. This latter third would include occupational hazards, pollution, industrial products, infections, some medicines and medical procedures, and other as yet unknown causes. The top three causes of cancer death in men are lung cancer, colon cancer, and cancer of the prostate. In women the three leading causes of cancer deaths are breast cancer, colon cancer, and cancers of the ovaries and uterus.

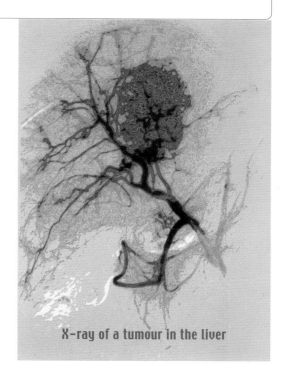

X-ray of a tumour in the liver

The regional cancer context

A higher-than-average incidence of some forms of cancer is to be found on the continent of Africa. These include:

Cancer of the liver

✶ This is the commonest cancer in males, with the highest rate in the world occurring in Shangaan-Tsonga men living in Mozambique.

✶ Usually associated with liver infections, high alcohol intake (and following *cirrhosis* of the liver), or spread from cancers anywhere else in the body.

✶ Characterised by pain in the upper right abdomen, *jaundice* and a fluid distension of the abdomen *(ascites)*.

While it is true that not all cancers are caused by diet, our diet either exacerbates the problems or protects us against them.

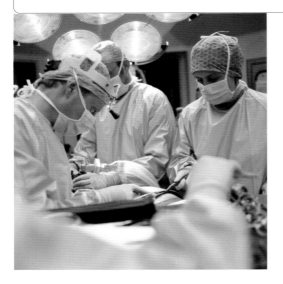

Treatment
✳ Difficult to treat even if detected early.
✳ Diagnosis confirmed by ultrasound scanning and liver biopsy.
✳ Removal of the tumour may be possible, otherwise the progress of the condition may be slowed by anti-cancer drugs.
✳ Abstaining from alcohol (while the damage has already been done, to continue drinking will only hasten death).
✳ In some circumstances a liver transplant might be considered.

Cancer of the oesophagus (gullet)
✳ Particularly common in Xhosa men in South Africa (second only to north-east Iran).
✳ Difficulty in swallowing at first, and eventually reaching a painful state when it may be too late to treat successfully.
✳ Mainly related to drinking very hot fluids, smoking and alcohol.

Treatment
✳ Barium swallow and X-ray to confirm diagnosis, with a tissue biopsy if necessary.
✳ Radiotherapy and chemotherapy.

✳ Avoidance of hot fluids, smoking and alcohol.

Cancer of the cervix (neck of the womb)
✳ Commonest cancer in black women.
✳ May be caused by erosion of the tissue cells, infections, a polyp (growth), a tear (following childbirth), or a wart resulting from a virus (*human papillomaviris* HPV) of which there are a number of high-risk strains. HPV 16 and HPV 18 have been present in around 90% of squamous-type cancers of the cervix, and also in 50-70% of pre-cancerous conditions.
✳ Having early sex and many sexual partners increases the risk of cervical cancer.
✳ Cigarette smoking may be a contributory factor.
✳ The more pregnancies, the greater the risk.
✳ Use of oral contraceptive pills may increase the risk slightly.
✳ There may be a genetic factor not yet identified.
✳ If untreated the cancer will spread to other pelvic organs.

Treatment
✳ Changes in the tissue of the cervix may be detected by smear tests (*PAP smear*) which may be followed by colposcopy (use of instrument called a colposcope for investigating cervix and womb), and biopsy if a cancer is suspected.
✳ Electrocoagulation, diathermy, radiotherapy and/or chemotherapy depending on extent of the condition.
✳ Surgical removal of the cervix and other affected organs.
✳ Early detection and treatment offers the best survival rate.

General cancer sites

The top three cancers listed earlier as causing male and female deaths are to be found everywhere but with varying degrees of incidence. The latest available annual WHO figures show:

* Deaths worldwide from all malignant neoplasms (new growths) amount to 1,174,112 for men, and 968,351 for women.
* Colon cancer kills 62,039 men, and 70,080 women.
* Breast cancer kills 134,081 women, and 5 men.
* 33,716 ovarian cancer, and 10,477 cancer of the uterus deaths.
* 95,505 men died of prostate cancer.
* Cancers of the trachea, bronchus and lung killed 365,549 men and 132,104 women.

Not every country reports, so these figures are only as accurate as the reporting. Therefore they are likely to be under-reported. Consider also the number of people who have either been treated or who are currently undergoing treatment and you will gain a more complete picture of how cancer can cause such massive problems worldwide.

Now seems like a good time to put 'cancer on our agenda'. If we do, we can be encouraged by knowing that our risk of any of these conditions can be markedly reduced, and that early detection increases our recovery chances. Risk can be reduced further by avoiding, where possible, exposure to things known to cause cancer.

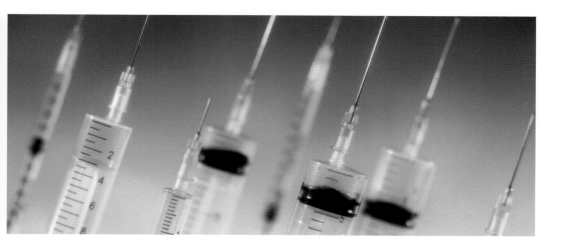

BREAST CANCER

Breast lumps are very common. Most turn out to be benign, but symptomatic cancer of the breast usually presents as a lump.

Although not a modern disease, breast cancer is increasingly being diagnosed, particularly in British women. About one in twelve women in Britain are affected at some time in their life, one of the highest rates in the world. Half of those with the disease will not die from the cancer, but 15,000 do die every year in Britain, and 25,000 women are newly diagnosed. Breast cancer is by far the most common type of cancer in women, accounting for 20% of all new cases, and it is the leading cause of female cancer death in the United Kingdom. A few cases occur in early age, and the majority are in older women. But for women aged 35-54 years, breast cancer is the commonest single cause of all deaths.

The earlier a breast cancer is diagnosed the better are the survival rates.

Causes

Scientists make a distinction between causes that are 'initiators' and causes that are 'promoters'. Initiators are factors which at present we cannot control, such as a defect in the cellular DNA system. But other factors also come into play. Factors which are known to increase the risk of breast cancer include increasing age, carrying a first pregnancy after the age of 30, having had no pregnancies at all, early commencement of periods and late menopause, a strong family history, radiation and obesity. But most women can do very little to protect themselves against these factors. High fats in the diet, prolonged use of hormone medications, smoking, alcohol and stress are still under evaluation.

Treatment

Four types of treatment – surgery, radiotherapy, hormone treatment and chemotherapy – are used in the management of breast cancer. Over the last thirty years or so it has become increasingly clear that the extensive operations devised early this century, often with mutilating results, make no difference at all to the overall survival. The main effect is to prevent disease recurring at the site of the breast. Such recurrence, although unsightly and troublesome, does not of itself become fatal: it is the spread of the cancer cells to distant and important sites such as the liver and the brain which cause death. So radical mastectomy is not commonly carried out now. But most breast cancer patients will have some form of surgery. This ranges from localised excision of the lump within the breast, to some form of mastectomy. Many women have a combination of treatments and may

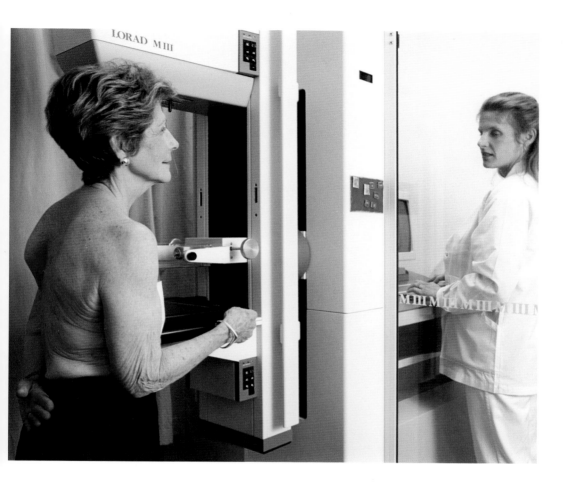

receive combinations of surgery with radio-therapy or chemotherapy as the primary treatment. The antioestrogen drug tamoxifen has been shown to be useful in post-menopausal women, but the situation in pre-menopausal women is less clear. If a tumour is excised locally then most patients also need to have a course of radiotherapy to the breast. This usually takes the form of an outpatient visit to a radiotherapy centre several times a week for up to three weeks. So the treatment team will not only include a surgeon but will usually also comprise a specialised cancer physician, a radiologist, a radiotherapist and specialised nurses.

A proportion of women still need a form of mastectomy because of the size or partic-ular type of tumour, and for these patients techniques of plastic surgery may make the loss of a breast so much easier to bear. Reconstruction can be done in many different ways with tissue expanders and implants or transferred skin and muscle flaps. The cosmetic result can often be very good but usually more than one operation is required to reconstruct the body's shape.

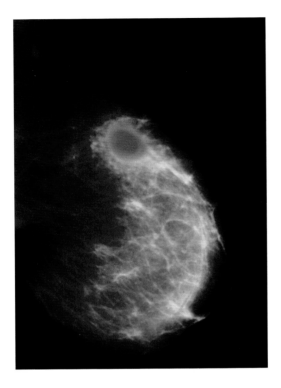

The earlier a breast cancer is diagnosed the better are the survival rates. ⊙

The commonest time for a women to notice that something is wrong with her breast is while bathing. Examination of the breast with the flat of the hand and soap can reveal little lumps or dimples which are different from the usual shape of the breast. Examination should be done after the menstrual period for pre-menopausal women. *A typical breast cancer doubles in size approximately every 100 days, so in one year a typical breast cancer will increase in size by a factor of 8 if untreated.*

Screening programme

Britain, in common with many other countries, has devised a national breast screening programme. These are based on single-view diagnostic breast radiographs or mammograms. It makes sense to try to diagnose cancers when they are still so small that they cannot be felt with the fingers. The procedure has improved survival in the over-50 age group by 25%. Breast screening units are either at local centres or in mobile units. The mammogram films are repeated every three years.

The decrease in mortality from breast cancer of 25% applies to the population offered screening, and there is a decrease of 40% in those who actually attend the examination.

Chapter Fourteen

Planned Families are Happier Families

Bringing a new individual into the world is an immensely important under-taking, demanding the full commitment of both the partners responsible. Contrary to current custom and practice, it should not be entered into lightly. In today's uncertain world, it's wise for families to be planned.

The responsibility of planning

We all need to seek divine wisdom in such major life decisions as education and work, choosing a life partner, when to get married and where to live, whether to have children or not. The decision to start a family is one of the most important decisions a couple will ever make, and having children is one of the greatest privileges they can ever enjoy. Our Creator intended that the whole experience should be one of the deepest joys we can know. Ideally, the decision to have a child should be made very carefully, after work, marriage and home have all been established. In an ideal world all pregnancies would be carefully planned and pre-

> **The decision to start a family is one of the most important decisions a couple will ever make, and having children is one of the greatest privileges they can ever enjoy.**
>
> (!)

pared for and all births awaited with joy. Unfortunately, as we all know only too well, in this far-from-ideal world there are many accidents and mistakes in this area and many babies are denied the welcome that should be their birthright; some just not wanted at all; others unwisely brought into the world at an inappropriate time in their parents' lives.

At the one extreme there are mothers in their early teens pregnant by fathers of the same age, children having children with all the problems that brings for every member of their families, not least the baby itself. At the other extreme is the successful career woman, using contraception responsibly and effectively over the years, and finding that she has left it too late to conceive without the help of high-tech medical intervention, with all its stresses and uncertainties.

When individuals are valued and respected, childbearing, motherhood and fatherhood are highly esteemed. Children and youth grow up to value and respect themselves and their bodies,

honouring them as gifts from their Creator. Encouraged to grow up with healthy bodies and disciplined lives, they will be prepared for the future time when, with their partner, they choose to have children. They need to plan their *lives* as well, as far as is possible, so that their children can have the support and security that they need.

One of God's greatest gifts

There is much more to sexual activity than the momentary pleasure that comes from the gratification of a physical need, as many would have us believe. Sexuality is in fact one of the Creator's greatest gifts, designed to give great pleasure. It is also designed to help to bond indissolubly those couples who already know and love each other well enough to be willing to be faithful to each other for the rest of their lives. This is the sort of partnership that our Creator planned for each home. In such a home, each additional child, carefully planned and lovingly awaited, would be welcomed as a gift from God, by parents who would consider it their highest duty and joy to care for that child with wisdom and love.

But, clearly, things are very

often far from ideal. Babies are not planned, often make housing and financial problems worse, and seriously interrupt career plans. The good news is that, even if you have started at the wrong place, things can still turn out well, especially if you accept your limitations, and seek for wisdom from above as you struggle to get back on the right track.

half the marriages end in divorce. Single parent households with their economic hardship and other traumas, and blended families with their own unique stresses and strains, have become almost as common as traditional families.

Each family, whatever its history and composition needs love, understanding and respect. Each breakup involves immense personal suffering, for some or all of the individuals concerned, and often economic hardship too. In society as a whole, family breakdown is associated

Trust and faithfulness

In fact today's world is much more confusing in these areas than was our parents' and grandparents'. This is because the old social customs have broken down, the old rules have been abandoned, and there are no satisfactory new ones to take their place.

Western civilisation developed in societies where the rules of social behaviour were based on Bible principles. The ten commandments, with their emphasis on trust, honesty and faithfulness in marriage and respect for parents, were the basis of family life. Homes tended to be stable, and the two parent family was the norm, except where broken by death. Of course there were exceptions and unhappy homes, but in general family units were stable, with the result that society itself was stable. Today, the rich countries in the West have abandoned their Bible heritage, and society's basic building block, the home, is disintegrating. Almost

Choosing to start a family

In the past choosing to start a family was not a problem for most people. Because very little was known about human physiology few people had access to contraception, and what there was, was not reliable. For many people that meant that sexual abstinence before marriage was the norm and they expected to start their families soon after marriage. In other societies this pattern was reversed. The marriage took place once the pregnancy was established. In either case it was very different from the situation in the Western world today, where safe and reliable contraception gives the option of limiting the number of children in a family, and also of timing their arrival. It is only in this century that really reliable methods have become widely available.

with increases in many other problems: homelessness, mental illness, drug and alcohol abuse, crime and suicide. However, no situation is hopeless. Our Creator looks with loving concern on every person, and has resources of strength and wisdom for all who sincerely seek his help. As far as a healthy family life is concerned, we have to start where we are now, not where we wish we had started, or someone else thinks we should have started. We always have some choices, and by God's grace we can ask for His wisdom in making the right ones.

The advent of the contraceptive pill in the 1950s rapidly brought about a major social revolution. Sexual intercourse could now, with any luck, be completely separated from the risk of pregnancy. The sexual revolution with its resultant breakdown of the home and family began at once.

On the other hand, the advent of reliable contraception has been of tremendous bene-

fit to a great many couples, enabling them to choose when to have children, and to limit their families to the number that they can take good care of.

Only those with rich material and family resources can afford to have large families in today's world. Most couples nowadays will want to use some method of family planning at some time in their life, to postpone the first child until they feel ready for that responsibility, to space their children, or to prevent further pregnancies once they feel their family is complete.

Methods of contraception

Here is a brief survey of the methods available. Their effectiveness is expressed as the percentage of women who use that method for one year and avoid pregnancy. This means that if only one of every hundred women using that method for one year becomes pregnant, that method is 99% effective.

✳ The Pill

The contraceptive pill is perhaps the most widely known method, for most people the easiest, and definitely the most reliable. The hormones in these pills have the effect when they are taken regularly as prescribed, of preventing ovulation, and making other minor changes in the reproductive tract that prevent conception from taking place. There are two types, the **combined pill** and the **progesterone only pill.** The combined pill is more reliable, there's less danger of failure if one is missed, the monthly cycles become very regular, and are usually pain free. Side effects with a few exceptions are unusual or mild and tolerable. The progesterone only pill is a lower dose (it's sometimes called the minipill) and this means that side effects are less likely, but failure is more likely if one is missed, and the cycles are liable to be much less regular.

The contraceptive pill has been monitored and studied much more than any other

medication in the history of pharmacology. It has been in use for over forty years so a vast amount of data has been collected. The original pills were much stronger than those used now. In the early days there were some fatalities. Such tragedies are very rare indeed now that we understand that the pill, while being safe for most, is dangerous for a very few easily identified women. This is one of the reasons why in most countries the pill is not available without some form of medical supervision.

The research has rightly concentrated mainly on the most dangerous side effects, and suggests that for most women the risks of pill taking are considerably less than the risks of pregnancy.

However, taking the contraceptive pill is not natural, and it does alter other biochemical processes. Blood levels of Zinc, Vitamin C, Vitamin B6 (pyridoxine), and B12 are altered, and these changes may have subtle effects on the immune and nervous systems that are not yet fully understood. There is always some sort of price to be paid for interfering with nature, and the jury is still out on exactly what that price is for the average woman who takes the pill for many years with no apparent problems. The failures that do occur are most often due to such human errors as forgetting to take it, but can also be due to conditions or medications that prevent its being absorbed.

✳ Intrauterine devices

Even in ancient times it was known that if a foreign body could be inserted into the uterus it would prevent pregnancy. In its modern form the **intrauterine contraceptive device** is a tiny plastic and copper object, which is inserted through the cervix by a specially trained doctor or nurse. It then remains in place for as long as it is wanted. It works by causing a mild irritation that prevents fertilized eggs from implanting in the lining of the uterus. They need to be replaced after five years, but they can be removed at any time. Periods may be heavier and more painful and there is an increased risk of infection, but it is about 98% effective. Failure can be due to the device slipping out unnoticed, but pregnancy does sometimes occur with the device in place. Babies have even been born with the device in their hands! There are new models that contain long-acting, slow-release progesterone, which make it an even more effective contraceptive, with the added advantage of very light menstrual blood loss. Both types also have the advantage of not needing much medical supervision.

✳ Injections and implants

Slow release progesterone **injections and implants** are used to suppress ovulation and prevent the sperm from entering the uterus. The injections must be repeated at regular intervals, usually twelve weeks. They cannot be removed, so any side effects, like weight gain or nausea have to be endured. Periods may become irregular, or stop altogether, and it may take up to a year for menstrual cycles and fertility to return to normal. Implants work in the same way, but last much longer, up to five years, and they can be removed, sometimes with difficulty, however. Both methods are over 99% effective.

✳ Barrier methods

Barrier methods of contraception, as their name implies, involve the placing of some sort of material barrier between the sperm and the egg. The most commonly used is the **condom** – this is the sheath, usually made of very soft and delicate rubber,

which is rolled over the erect penis before the act of penetration takes place. To some the idea of interrupting the sexual act to put it on is quite intolerable, but with the coming of the AIDS virus, and the 'safer sex' campaign, the condom has become much more popular. It has several important advantages: it doesn't need any medical supervision, and is on sale in a wide variety of places. It helps to protect against sexually transmitted diseases as well as pregnancy, and it is usually pretty easy to tell after use whether it has worked or not (that it hasn't slipped off or split or otherwise spilt its contents). The disadvantages are obvious – it *can* slip off or split. When used carefully, the success rate can be as high as 98%.

The **cap,** another barrier method, is less popular. Starting its use involves a visit to a doctor or clinic to have it fitted. There are several different kinds. The most popular is the diaphragm, which is a soft thin circular rubber diaphragm attached to a soft springy coiled wire ring. First, its inner surface is coated with spermicidal cream in case any very robust sperm should venture round the edge, then it is folded in half and slipped into the vagina where it springs into shape and forms a barrier between the cervix and the penis during intercourse. Unfortunately there is no way of telling whether it actually does stay in place. Eight or so hours after use it needs to be removed, washed, dried and put away until next time. Its success rate averages less than 95%.

✷ Chemical methods

There is a variety of **chemical methods** – vaginal creams, foams and tablets, none of which is recommended for use on its own but which makes a useful backup for barrier

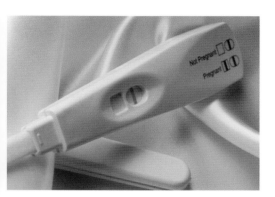

methods, or even the intrauterine device at the most fertile period. They don't appear to have any harmful effects, though an individual may find some of them cause local irritation.

✳ Emergency contraception

Accidents are far from being rare events when barrier methods are used. And of course there may be the accident of losing the device, or forgetting to use it altogether, and it would be truly unrealistic to suppose that all sexual activity is carefully planned with contraception in mind. Far too often it's the act of intercourse itself that's the accident. In all these emergencies, **the morning after pill** comes to the rescue. If taken within 72 hours of the 'accident', it can be expected to prevent pregnancy. It is not 100% effective, and should be looked upon as an *emergency* method – certainly not something to be used every couple of months. Another effective emergency method is the insertion of an intrauterine device within five days of the 'accident'.

✳ 'Natural' methods

Many people feel unhappy about using 'unnatural' methods like the pill, the intrauterine device or barrier methods. This is the official view of the Roman Catholic church, among others. They recommend

natural family planning, which is also called the rhythm method. This involves discovering when the woman's fertile period is and avoiding having intercourse at that time. This method has received adverse publicity. Few family planning agencies have the time and personnel necessary to teach it. Carelessly used, it is notoriously ineffective. However, most women who are willing to take the time and effort can easily determine when their fertile period occurs and, if their cycles are regular, can use this knowledge to plan their families.

At the time of ovulation the body temperature rises slightly and remains up until the period begins, when it returns to normal. This is quite easy to measure with a special fine-gauge clinical thermometer – the best time is each morning on first waking.

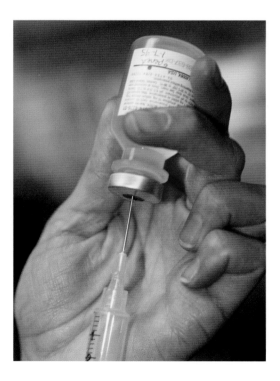

Ovulation time can also be recognised by noting the type of mucus produced by the cervix at ovulation time. Thin slippery mucus, rather like eggwhite is produced to enable the sperm to swim easily through the cervix. Most women are aware of this change in mucus and it's a very reliable indication of ovulation and indicates the time to have intercourse if you want a baby, and to avoid if you don't. However, it's a bit more complex than that. The sperm can normally survive for five days, so you are in danger if unprotected intercourse takes place five or less days before ovulation. The

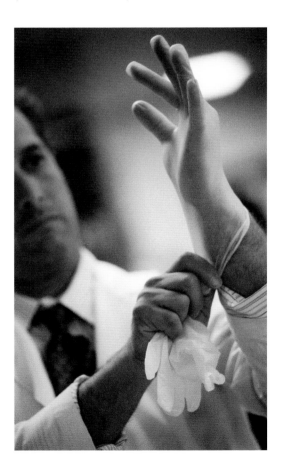

God gives help for the future and abundant forgiveness for the past. ⚠

eggs survive for two days. This means that the potentially dangerous time lasts for a whole week. For some, for instance those who have frequent separations and only limited time together, this is very limiting, but for others, who have the good fortune to be able to live more regular lives, it works well. Those who are well organised, enjoy regular routines, and like to live their lives according to natural rhythms and without outside interference or supervision may find this is the method for them. But even they may have problems, as the menstrual cycle can be upset by such things as minor illnesses, travel, or even stress.

Another 'natural' method is the **withdrawal** method. This is not recommended because it is unreliable, and really is not natural. The penis is withdrawn before ejaculation takes place, so the sperm, one hopes, does not enter the vagina, but some of the sperm may well leak out, or the self discipline this demands may not be quite accurate enough, and it can be frustrating for both partners. However, some do manage to use this method to good effect. It doesn't cost anything, nor is there medical involvement, except of course when it fails, and antenatal care is needed!

✳ Sterilisation

Sterilisation is a very final method, not to be used without long and careful consideration, because, although it very occasionally fails, it is very difficult to reverse. Requests for

reversal are increasing now that so many marriages break up and so many people remarry and want to start a new family with their new partner.

Male sterilisation is the easiest operation. It involves a tiny incision in the skin of the scrotum, and the cutting and tying off of the duct that takes the sperm from the testicle. It's a minor operation, takes minutes to do, and seldom needs hospital admission or follow up, except for a semen analysis three months later to check that it has worked.

Female sterilisation is more complex, as it involves opening the abdominal cavity to cut and seal off the fallopian tubes which take the eggs from the ovaries to the uterus. Even so it's a fairly minor procedure. In many ways it's preferable for the woman to be sterilised, especially in a world of unstable marriages. Women are usually less likely to want to start new families.

※ **Abortion?**

Sometimes **abortion** is viewed as another method of contraception. It is very commonly practised in societies where reliable contraception is difficult to obtain. For some it is a last resort in a desperate situation, a lesser of two evils. For others it is an alternative when other methods fail. In the past, in many societies, abortion was forbidden by law. Although the operation is very safe and free from complications when performed by experienced operators in well equipped clinics, it is dangerous when done by untrained people or with unsterile instruments, and many lives have been lost in this way. Even in the most ideal clinical situations, abortion is not a natural or happy experience. There is an often unrecognised price of guilt and mental anguish.

Much time and energy has been expended by Christians and others, discussing the question of abortion. Is it acceptable in *any* circumstances? (For example in cases of rape, or if the foetus is deformed.) Is it *murder?* Have human beings the right to interfere with nature in this way? Certainly people, whatever their religious persuasion, would agree that it is not right for us to bring life carelessly into being and then to destroy it purely for our own convenience. This sort of behaviour, when widely practised, does not lead to lasting happiness or a successful society. On the other hand, is it right for us to judge one another, or for one person to deny another the freedom to choose to use a service which is legally available?

'Conduct not condoms'

The right path for an individual to take is to determine, by God's grace, to do what is right, whatever the circumstances they find themselves in. He gives help for the future and abundant forgiveness for the past. His plan is that sexual relationships should add to our joy. One man and one woman in a faithful loving lifelong relationship makes for the greatest happiness and the superlatives of sex. Sociologists have found, to the surprise of many, that religion does make a difference – they have found that those who regularly take part in religious worship most enjoy their sex lives. Changing partners, even temporarily, brings the possibility of many problems, including sexually-transmitted disease. Using condoms may limit the spread of infection, but doesn't heal the hurts that accompany irregular relationships. 'Conduct not condoms' is a much better plan for preventing disease and unhappiness.

Chapter Fifteen

Pregnancy and Childbirth

Preparing for pregnancy

How soon should one start preparing for pregnancy? The sooner the better. Even before a baby girl is born her body is being prepared for possible future pregnancy. Her egg cells are already formed at the time of her birth, although they will only start to mature at puberty, and normally only one at a time. Before her birth the foundations are being laid for her future health, and this continues throughout her childhood. So marvellous are the body's self-healing powers, that even if poor foundations are laid early on, right choices later can help to reverse the harm.

Is it ever too late to make such choices? No, whatever your stage of life or pregnancy, it is always worth improving your lifestyle.

> **Our Creator designed that human beings should live together as couples, one woman and one man, and if they so choose, to have children together.** ⊙

Rules for healthy pregnancy

The rules of health for pregnancy are the same basic rules that apply to everyone else: • healthy eating; • daily vigorous exercise; • avoidance of poisons; and • a cheerful frame of mind. These will all stand a woman in very good stead when she plans to start a pregnancy, and they are important for fathers, too. Good health is one of the best gifts parents can pass on to their children.

Another valuable heritage is a healthy attitude to pregnancy and child bearing. At a time when the UK leads Europe in the number of teenage pregnancies, clearly many people need some help in this area. Bringing a new baby into the world should not be a matter of chance, but of decision. It's one of the most important decisions a couple can ever make, and it needs to be made thoughtfully, seriously and responsibly. For the sake of the child such decisions should be made together by two people who love each other enough to be committed to each other and their child for the rest of their lives. Our Creator designed that human beings should live together as couples, one woman and one man, and if they so choose, to have children together. This is the pattern that provides the best environment for the child to grow up in. This is not to say that all such families are a success, or that all other types of families are failures, but that this is the ideal.

✳ Diet

Starting with food, it's common sense and a widely observed fact that healthy mothers are likely to have healthy children, and that mothers who have a poor diet in pregnancy have less healthy children. It would be difficult to overestimate the influence of the mother's diet on the unborn baby's development and its future life. Countless scientific studies, ranging from animal feeding experiments to observations of human mothers and babies, show the profound relationship of the mother's diet in pregnancy to the baby's health at birth. And not only at birth,

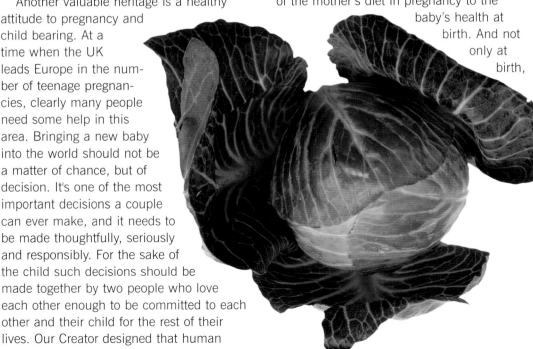

but in childhood and even adult life. Child health records from the thirties and forties have been followed up and have revealed that the underweight babies (of malnourished mothers) had grown up to be the unhealthy adults who succumbed to heart attacks and strokes some fifty or sixty years later.

Mothers should go for optimum rather than adequate nutrition. This means nutrition-dense food; food that is completely nutritious and has not had any of its precious vitamins, minerals and phytochemicals refined away, a diet based on simple, natural, whole, plant foods. This food will help to ensure the best health for both mother and baby.

It will also help with weight control, which is important because excess weight is associated with many more problems in pregnancy. It is uncomfortable and tiring too: good reasons for preparing for pregnancy early, and getting any weight problems sorted out before conception. Keeping the weight down has many advantages to the mother. It's more comfortable and avoids strain on muscles, joints and ligaments, and also the heart. It helps to prevent serious complications like high blood pressure and pre-eclampsia (a life threatening condition for both mother and baby), and also gestational diabetes (a temporary type of diabetes which develops in pregnancy and disappears after delivery, but predisposes to diabetes in later life). It helps to prevent heartburn and other forms of indigestion which are due to the fact that there simply isn't enough room for the baby, the digestive organs, the stored fat and a full stomach. It also discourages the development of varicose veins and piles.

✳ Exercise

Exercise in pregnancy can be vigorous, but should not be stressful, violent or excessive. It's wise to avoid heavy lifting and carrying, especially if you are not used to it. This is not because of risk to the baby, so much as to protect the mother from muscle or ligament strain, which is more likely in pregnancy, as the tissues, especially those in the pelvis, loosen up. The best plan is for the exercise to be enjoyable and regular, every day if possible. Walking is excellent and very safe. Swimming is good, along

with other sports that the mother is used to and enjoys.

Almost all mothers feel the need of more rest during pregnancy, and they should not expect that everything will be exactly the same as usual. The amount of energy to spare in pregnancy diminishes as the mother gets older. She will be much more energetic at 20 than she will be at 35.

What about work? Twenty-first-century culture in many parts of the world demands that mothers remain in paid employment outside their homes for most of at least their first pregnancies. For many this is no great problem, and with an understanding partner and a few more early nights all goes well, but for others the whole thing becomes extremely tiring and the months of pregnancy, which should be a peaceful happy time, become a wearying burden.

Shift work, especially if it involves night duties, should be outlawed in pregnancy! So should commuting long distances and twelve-hour

days away from home. This is a time when a regular schedule is important, especially where sleep is concerned. Many vitally important metabolic functions involving hormones work according to daily rhythms, including rhythms of light and darkness. During pregnancy these cycles are even more important and this is why shift workers have more problems in pregnancy as well as poorer health in general. Regular hours and adequate rest are also important for those who are trying to conceive, especially those who need medical assistance.

Circumstances are seldom ideal for pregnant mothers, and they have to do the best they can, taking whatever chance they can to put their feet up, even if it's only for a few minutes. Pregnant mothers who have the chance to lie down for an afternoon rest are fortunate. Those who already have several small children may have little hope of a proper daytime rest, but at least if they can sit or lie down for a short time, they will get some benefit, even if their children are sitting or climbing on them! In the evening the children need to go to bed early, so their mothers get a short break before getting an early night themselves.

✳ Poisons

Drugs. The avoidance of poisons is particularly important when pregnancy is planned. There are several types of poisons that need to be avoided. The first is unnecessary medication. The thalidomide disaster of the early sixties alerted doctors to the possible dangers of other medications in pregnancy. Thalidomide was a tranquilliser that was used for morning sickness in early pregnancy until it was discovered that it interfered with the development of the babies' limbs. Some thousands of babies were born with absence or severe deformity of some or all of their limbs. No other drug has been found to have quite such a specific and devastating effect, but many widely-used medications have the possibility of damaging the unborn child, especially if they are taken at the very sensitive time during the early weeks of pregnancy when the organs are being formed. For this reason everyone – doctors, midwives, pharmacists and lay people – are very cautious about the use of any medication at all in pregnancy unless it is absolutely necessary, and known to be safe.

If you have a chronic health problem that needs medication, talk to your doctor or other health care provider, about whether there are any natural therapies you could use instead. Do this when first starting to plan for pregnancy. Many problems will respond to diet, exercise and other types of natural therapy and remove or reduce the need for medication. Learn simple remedies for headaches, indigestion, backache and other minor problems, or better still, learn how to avoid them altogether. Even herbal remedies are not all safe in pregnancy. Take qualified advice before you use them. Some medicines do have an excellent record. Many antibiotics are considered to be very safe for use in pregnancy, so you need not fear if they are needed.

Smoking. There are many other harmful substances that people use voluntarily. Tobacco is a poison that damages the unborn child. Smokers have smaller babies and an increased rate of miscarriage, premature labour and stillbirth.

Alcohol. Less well known is the harmful effect of alcohol on the unborn child. The foetal alcohol syndrome, which involves a number of abnormalities including mental handicap, is well known and is caused by heavy drinking. The exact threshold for lesser degrees of alcoholic damage is less clear, but currently is thought to be below four drinks a week. Alcohol is a cell poison with a special affinity for the brain and nervous system, so the safest policy for pregnancy is not to use it at all. This goes for fathers, too, at least until after conception because even a few alcoholic drinks a week can lower the sperm count to infertile levels.

Caffeine. What about caffeine? This is usually thought of as a very mild poison, and one that is extremely widely used with no apparent problems, but in some research it, too, is associated with a higher rate of miscarriage.

Sperm Production in male testis

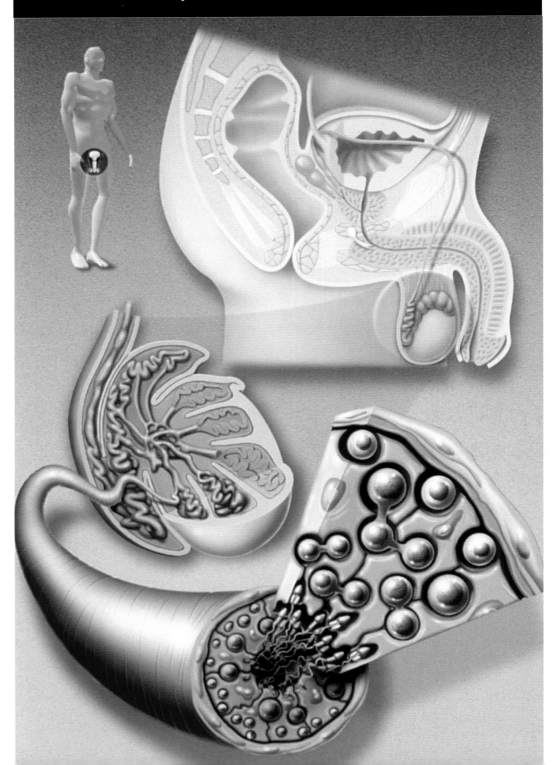

Female Reproduction, ovulation to foetus

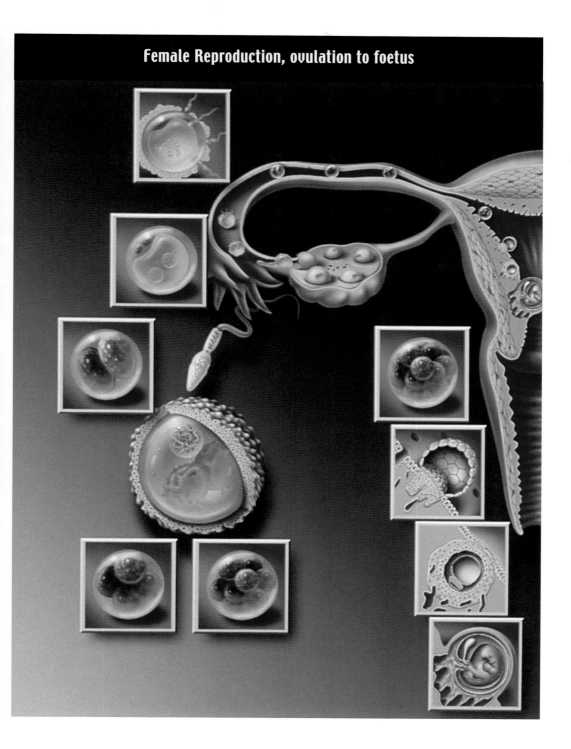

> **As you learn about the wonders of the human reproductive process, marvel at the fact that as you pray you actually converse with the one who designed it.**

Mental and spiritual preparation

What about the mental state in pregnancy? How can one be mentally and spiritually prepared? Obviously it's more pleasant for the mother if the pregnancy has been planned, and the baby is awaited with happy anticipation. But does it matter to the baby? Does the mother's mental state make a difference to the baby's mental state?

Peaceful, calm mothers tend to have peaceful, calm babies, and nervous, anxious mothers tend to have nervous, irritable babies. But how can an anxious mother change her temperament? Nothing will give such peace of mind as trust in divine power.

The Bible has many secrets of lasting mental health and happiness that elude psychologists. If you have not yet given much time or thought to spiritual matters, pregnancy is a very good time to begin, while you are actually experiencing in your own body the creation of a new human being. As you learn about the wonders of the human reproductive process, marvel at the fact that as you pray you actually converse with the one who designed it.

Pregnancy should be a time of joy and rejoicing. Even if things have not gone according to plan, and there are problems and difficulties, make the most of every moment when you can relax, look up, think of cheerful and beautiful things, and thank God for them.

Help with infertility

Although some couples manage to conceive every time they try, others may need a year, or even longer, and some will never manage without medical help. It is estimated in the UK that one in six or seven couples has difficulty in conceiving. This problem has increased in recent years, partly because society has changed, and more women are delaying pregnancy on account of their careers. Fertility decreases with advancing years, and many women of over 35, and most women over 40, will need some medical help before they can conceive. On the other hand, advances in obstetric technology have made pregnancy in older women much safer and, with help, many can have children who would not have been able to do so a generation ago.

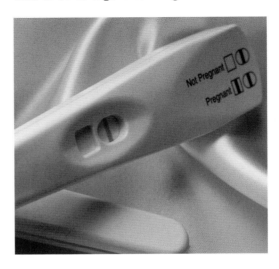

What about preconceptual check-ups?

These are especially important if either partner has a history of genital infection, inflammation or other problem with the reproductive system. Irregular periods, pelvic pain or abnormal vaginal discharge are some of the problems about which a woman should seek advice.

If there is no reason to suspect past or current genital health problems, at what stage should one seek advice about infertility? After a year of unsuccessful trying is a good general rule, but couples can take some very simple steps themselves, long before a year has passed, by asking themselves some simple questions.

Conditions for conception

* On a physiological level, are the testicles cool enough to give the sperm a chance? They need a lower temperature than the rest of the body, which is the reason for their position. Tight hot clothing and too many hot baths can reduce their efficiency. Instead go for cool, loose underwear (boxer shorts rather than briefs), cooler showers and active exercise.

* Is ovulation happening, and is intercourse at the right time? The chapter on family planning explains how to recognise the fertile period. Is intercourse happening so often that the sperm production can't keep up? Most experts advise abstinence for a few days before the fertile period to be sure.

* Does the semen actually reach the cervix? Even such a simple thing as the position during intercourse can make a difference for many couples. If the woman lies on her back the semen will be deposited in the best possible position, and if she remains on her back for a few hours, better still.

Having checked all these things and patiently tried for a year or more, it's time to seek expert advice, either from a fertility expert, or from your GP, who will usually start with some investigations before sending you on to a fertility clinic.

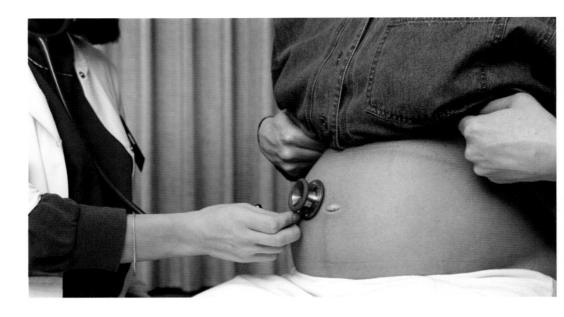

What form does medical help take?

Infertility investigations include a detailed medical history of both partners in case of any relevant problems in the past, an examination of them both, and a number of tests. The semen analysis looks at the number, form and activeness of the sperm. A blood test will indicate whether the woman is ovulating, and whether her hormone levels are normal. Another blood test will tell whether she is anaemic or not. She will have an ultrasound scan to check that her internal reproductive organs are normal and some tests to ensure that she is free from any sort of genital infection. If there is any doubt, a laparoscopic (keyhole surgery) examination can be done, and there are other more specific tests if they are needed.

When the cause is found, the treatment can begin, but in many cases there is no obvious cause, or there may be several minor causes, none of which on its own would be enough to cause infertility. But even when the cause is unclear, there are possible treatments, and the fertility specialist will be able to explain and advise about the different assisted fertility options.

Normal pregnancy

❋ **First signs.** When conception has taken place, the first sign will normally be the missed period, though some women, especially if this is not their first pregnancy, will have the feeling that they are pregnant even before this. Soon there will be an increased frequency in the need to pass urine, as the enlarging womb presses on the bladder. As all the extra hormones start to work the breasts will start to develop, and they will probably feel different before any change can be seen. Other signs caused by the changing hormone levels are feeling more tired, being more emotional and feeling nauseated, especially in the mornings.

✳ Calculating the date. Pregnancy is usually reckoned in weeks, counting forty weeks from the first day of the last period. This means that one is 'four weeks pregnant' when the first period is missed, though conception probably took place only two weeks before. If the periods were very infrequent or irregular, or if the crucial date can't be remembered, an ultrasound scan will give the answer more accurately.

✳ Antenatal care. The important part is what the mother does herself in choosing a healthy lifestyle. Apart from this, there are three major parts to antenatal care. There are the routine visits to doctor or midwife, to confirm that all is well at the various stages. Then there are the tests and scans to detect and deal with possible abnormalities, and finally there are the preparation classes where both parents can learn how to prepare for their new baby and its birth.

Routine antenatal visits are very helpful for getting to know your medical attendants.

In most countries the midwife is the most important one. As well as organising the various special tests at the appropriate times, she will be keeping a watch on the blood pressure to make sure there is no danger of high blood pressure and its complications. She will check the urine for kidney function and for infection, both of which can cause problems before the mother is aware of them. She will monitor the baby's development by checking the size of the womb. She will also be concerned with the mother's general health and state of nutrition, which may seldom be a problem in prosperous areas, but can be a very serious one elsewhere.

✳ Antenatal tests and scans. This is another area of rapid development. The aim is to detect abnormalities as early as possible so they can be dealt with quickly. Unfortunately, at the present time, the only solution science has to offer in many of these cases is the abortion of the damaged baby. This poses tremendous ethical questions, and not all mothers want the option of aborting their baby, even if it is likely to be damaged. The damaged unborn baby's life will be ended to spare suffering for both the parents and child, but does this mean that the lives of handicapped people, for example with Down's syndrome, are so painful that they should never have been born? This clearly is not the case, as many people with Down's syndrome and their parents, will testify. And what about handicapped people who are already here? What message does it give to them? A mother may also feel under very strong social pressure to conform to this policy, feeling that it would be irresponsible to bring a handicapped child into the world.

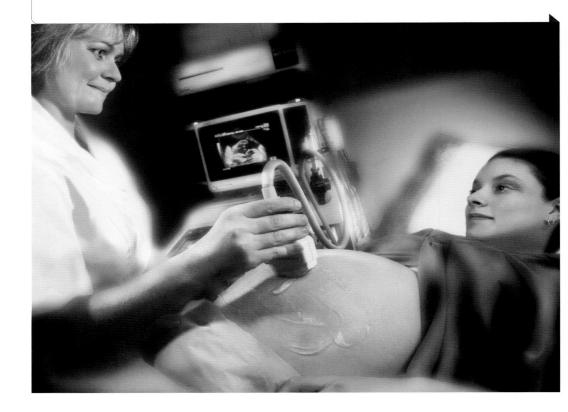

There are some severe handicaps that seem to be incompatible with any sort of meaningful life, but the parents of handicapped children have many encouraging stories to tell about how the children bring love with them, and how their often short lives are far from meaningless. So although it is desirable to prevent abnormal births, many would feel that killing the foetus is not the way to go. It is good when research stresses the actual prevention of abnormality, as well as its early detection. A successful example is spina bifida, a congenital abnormality of the spine and spinal cord, that was found to be due to a deficiency of folic acid in the mother's diet, and folic acid supplements before conception and early in pregnancy are now recommended. A varied whole plant food diet also ensures against this deficiency.

✳ **Waiting time.** Apart from the ethical questions, some tests can cause a great deal of stress, as suspicions are raised and some weeks of waiting must pass before the final diagnosis can be made. No tests are guaranteed to be absolutely accurate, either. False negatives and false positives are not unknown, and in addition, invasive tests occasionally precipitate a miscarriage, a particularly tragic outcome if the baby was normal anyway. But they can save lives. When a correctable abnormality is recognized in advance, the baby can be born in a hospital where there are facilities for dealing with the problem at or soon after birth.

✳ **Ultrasound scans.** Ultrasound scans are now routine in many parts of the world. Scans are done early on to confirm that the foetus is growing, that it is the right size for the dates, or to check on the dates if the mother is unsure about them. Later detailed scans check that the unborn child has no abnormalities. Scans are invaluable whenever there is a suspicion that anything may be going wrong. The information they provide enables the medical team to take life-saving action.

In the UK and other industrialised countries, it's very rare for babies to die at or around the time of birth, and extremely rare for mothers to die. This is one of the great success stories of modern scientific medicine. The wonderful equipment now available enables highly-trained staff to predict and avoid emergencies. They can make potentially dangerous situations safe, and save the lives of babies who otherwise would not survive. Not all societies are so privileged and in the developing world

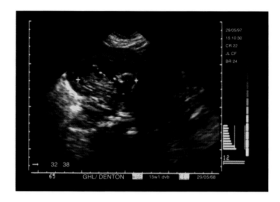

preventable birth-related problems are one of the main causes of infant mortality. There is also an appreciable maternal mortality in these countries. Many of these mothers are undernourished and unwell to start with, and to compound the problem, good medical care is often not available.

Miscarriage

Bleeding in early pregnancy is fairly common. Some women continue to have periods for the first three months, so blood loss does not always mean that a miscarriage is on the way. If there is persistent bleeding, especially if it is heavy or is accompanied by cramping pains, medical advice should be sought. Bleeding with one-sided pain in the early weeks could be due to ectopic pregnancy (pregnancy in the fallopian tube). This can develop into a very serious emergency if there is severe internal bleeding, so early medical advice is essential.

Miscarriages (andectopic pregnancies) are very disappointing outcomes, even more so now that reliable tests are able to confirm pregnancy at a early stage. The reason for many miscarriages seems to be that the embryo or foetus was damaged in some way, and so nature removes it. Normal embryos or foetuses are very firmly attached, and strenuous activity (including sexual intercourse) will not dislodge them. Miscarriages are common, especially if you include the ones in the very early weeks. Some estimate that as many as one in five pregnancies ends in this way. Usually there is no difficulty in conceiving a second time, and in most cases the pregnancy will go ahead normally. If miscarriage happens several times, investigations are needed, and will often reveal a treatable cause.

Trimesters

Although pregnancy is counted in weeks, for convenience it is also divided into three-month sections or *trimesters*.

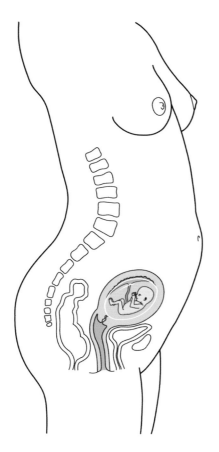

✳ **The first trimester** is the crucial time when the baby's organs are formed, and it's particularly important to avoid all poisons at this time.
⇨ At *six weeks*, the embryo is about the size of a fingernail, and already has the beginnings of eyes, ears, limbs, brain and heart.

⇨ By twelve weeks all the major organs are already formed. The baby is fully formed by *28 weeks*, and is able, with special care to survive birth at this stage.
⇨ By *34 weeks*, the baby weighs around 3kg, is about 45.5cms long, and has an excellent chance of survival if born now. This is when viral illnesses like rubella are most able to damage the developing baby. It's also when miscarriages are most likely.

Another hazard of the first trimester is sickness, which is due to the changing levels of the various hormones. A certain amount of nausea, especially in the mornings when the stomach is empty, is common and fairly normal. A mother needs medical help if she actually vomits more than a few times, or if the nausea is preventing her from getting adequate food and causing her to lose weight. This may all sound rather alarming but, in fact, the majority of pregnancies progress normally, and those who are taking good care of themselves should not expect problems, but should know when to seek help if they do occur.

✳ **The second trimester** is usually the easiest time. Most women will find the nausea has gone by the twelfth week and the danger of damage to the baby, either by illness or poisons, is much less. The baby is still quite small, so does not cause any major discomforts, and the mother can relax and enjoy these middle months.
⇨ By the *twentieth week*, the top of the uterus can be felt at the level of the umbilicus. The baby will have been moving since its limbs were first formed, but the mother doesn't become aware of them until around the twentieth week. She can

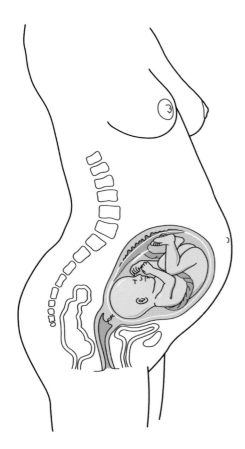

and planning for the birth. It's important to keep the antenatal appointments now, because this is when serious problems like rising blood pressure or placental insufficiency can occur. Warning signals that need urgent attention from your doctor or midwife are bleeding, unexplained pain, unaccustomed headache, sudden increase in water retention with swollen hands and feet, or a marked decrease in the movements of the baby. Usually a few tests, an ultrasound scan or a baby heart monitor reading, will very quickly reveal any danger, and show the medical staff when to take action to put it right.

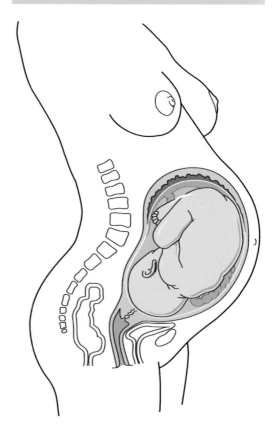

now notice the baby growing as the uterus increases in height by about one finger-breadth each week.

* **The third trimester.** The baby is taking up quite a lot of space by the third trimester. As the due date approaches, it may not be possible to do all the energetic things that one could do in the middle months. Good habits of eating, drinking and exercise will go a long way to preventing some of the problems like heartburn, piles, and varicose veins that make life uncomfortable for a lot of mothers.

⇨ This is an exciting time of preparation

Some simple remedies for common problems

> **Heartburn.** This type of indigestion is very common, especially towards the end of the pregnancy. It happens partly because the baby is taking up more space and there isn't quite enough room for both it and the food in the stomach. It's often worst at bedtime, as one lies down, with food still in the stomach. Small drinks of hot water can provide rapid relief for the burning pain, but in the longer term, give your stomach the best possible chance by observing these simple rules: eat regular meals, never eat between meals and drink very little *with* meals. These measures ensure that the stomach doesn't get overfilled, gets its work done quickly and has time to rest. If the evening meal is small, light and several hours before bedtime, the stomach can rest while you rest, and cause less trouble.

> **Piles** are very common in pregnancy in the West, and anywhere else where low-fibre food is the norm. They are a direct result of constipation, and the presence of the baby compounds the problem. To avoid piles avoid constipation by drinking plenty of water, eating plenty of fruit, vegetables and high-fibre cereal products, and getting regular exercise. Dried fruits like prunes and figs are some of the best natural laxatives.

> **Varicose veins** are part of the same refined food problem, but in addition to the other measures, it's important to avoid standing for long periods. Take every chance to sit down, if possible with your feet up. If you must stand for long, make sure you don't stand still. Step around, because flexing and extending your feet contracts the calf muscles, pumps the blood back up and relieves the congestion in the veins.

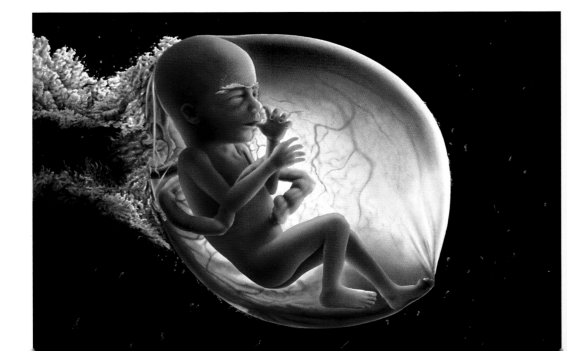

Preparing for the birth

Birth customs vary from one society to another. In Western countries it has been the custom for many years that mothers lie on their backs to give birth. Hospital births have become the norm in most places, and home births have been discouraged.

Dr Grantly Dick Reed, an English doctor, pioneered the idea of natural childbirth. His theory was that fear caused muscle spasm and this was the reason for most pain in childbirth, and could be eliminated if mothers were educated about birth and were taught to relax. Although there is truth in this, it is not true that childbirth is pain free for every well-prepared woman.

A French doctor, Fernand Leboyer, reacted to the lights and high-tech ambiance of the delivery room, urging that birth should take place in a quiet, comfortable place, with soft shaded lights. In other countries it has been the custom for mothers to walk around during labour, and to give birth in a squatting position. Europeans have looked down on this, thinking it very primitive, but another French doctor, Michel Odent, pointed out that it is much more natural to give birth with the body upright, as in squatting, standing or kneeling. This way gravity helps to bring the baby down. On her back the mother actually has to push the baby uphill through the birth canal. He found that his mothers gave birth much more easily, and did not need such interventions as forceps delivery, or even episiotomy and, having been spared those traumas, recovered much more quickly afterwards. (Some mothers whose pelvis was too small did need caesarian section.)

All these pioneers have made important contributions, and it should now be accept-able for a mother to choose the type of preparation and delivery she would like. There are different relaxation techniques to use in the early stages of labour, different medications to use for pain relief and different positions for delivery. A flexible birth plan can be made with the midwife, understanding that emergencies may arise and the plan may have to be changed for the safety of mother and baby. Changes of plan are not failures, but call for thankfulness for the help that is available.

Fathers in the labour room? In most societies throughout recorded history they have been excluded. Now they are warmly welcomed in many places, and cynics might say that as the shortage of midwives has increased, so has the welcome for fathers in the delivery room. Fathers certainly have a place beside mothers to give them comfort and encouragement, and to share what should be one of the greatest experiences of their lives.

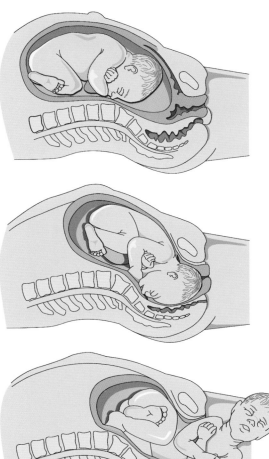

There are three stages to labour.

1) During the first, the regular contractions dilate the cervix and start the baby on its journey down the birth canal. They gradually become stronger and more frequent until the cervix is completely opened. This can take up to twelve hours, or even more if it's a first baby. It's usually much shorter for later babies. Sometimes, especially if the mother is tired, the contractions slow down. A very simple natural method can be tried to stimulate them – gentle massage of the nipples. The same reflex which causes the womb to contract, and speed up its return to normal when the baby is at the breast, can stimulate contractions in labour. If necessary, hormone medication can be used to stimulate contractions.

2) In stage two, really powerful bearing down contractions start, completely different from the previous ones, and there is an automatic urge to push. It helps if the mother is upright and gravity can assist the baby on the final part of its journey. This stage takes an average of an hour for the first baby, but may only be minutes for later babies. Eventually, the top of the baby's head appears, the moment of crowning. The midwife holds the head so it doesn't descend too rapidly and cause a tear, and this is the point at which the episiotomy may be done. The shoulders and the body quickly follow and there is the newborn baby, rather blue or grey for a moment, but quickly taking its first breath and turning bright pink, to everyone's delight. The baby can be given to its mother immediately, placed on her abdomen or put to her breast, while the midwife waits for the cord to finish pulsating, before she ties and cuts it.

3) The third stage is the passage of the

When labour begins

Labour begins with one of three signs:

❄ 'a show', which is a small amount of blood-stained mucousy discharge, as the mucus plug which has sealed the cervix throughout the pregnancy is passed;

❄ contractions at regular intervals;

❄ waters (the amniotic fluid that surrounds the baby) breaking, which can be a trickle or a gush.

placenta, which happens shortly after the birth. The midwife checks that it is complete, any episiotomy or tears are sown up, and the father can go to tell the good news to the rest of the family. The mother can relax now, in a wonderful glow of fulfilment, achievement and thankfulness.

The mother's reaction

Mothers are all different. Some have very strong maternal feelings and love their future baby passionately from the moment they know they have conceived. For others, maternal feelings develop more gradually, and for some, not until they actually hold their baby in their arms. Yet others struggle with their lack of maternal feelings for longer, especially if the birth has been difficult. Some are devastated by an early miscarriage, while others take it in their stride,

viewing it merely as a temporary interruption in their plans. Many of these emotional differences are due to reactions to the different levels of hormones in the circulation, and also to varying degrees of tiredness. Mothers should not feel abnormal or guilty if their feelings are not what they think they ought to be, and, to avoid becoming overtired, they should accept all the help they can get, from fathers, family members, friends, neighbours and professionals. However, persistent feelings of gloom and despondency, exhaustion, and failure to bond with the baby are not normal and are signs that help is needed. In the UK, midwives, health visitors and family doctors are trained to recognise and help with these problems. Effective help *is* available, so there is no need to struggle on alone and unaided, missing out on what should be one of the happiest times of one's life.

CLOTHES IN PREGNANCY

Comfort is the keyword. Nothing should be tight, but gently-supporting bras and possibly a maternity girdle in the later months help to support the extra weight, and save excessive stretching of the skin and other tissues. Shoes should be particularly comfortable, and may even need to be a bigger size. Comfortable need not mean dowdy, and it helps if you try to look your best!

THE MENSTRUAL CYCLE

The days of the cycle are reckoned from the first day of bleeding. While hormones from the pituitary gland are stimulating the ovary to produce the egg, other hormones from the ovary are acting on the lining of the womb, repairing it after the monthly blood loss and developing it over the next two weeks so that by day 21 it is thick and spongy, ready to receive a fertilised egg. If there is no fertilised egg, the lining starts to degenerate and produces the next period around day 28. When a fertilised egg embeds in the lining there is no menstrual period and pregnancy has begun.

Hormones from the pituitary gland stimulate the ovary to produce one egg each month. The egg develops in a fluid-filled sac called a follicle. At around day 14 of the menstrual cycle the egg is released. The feathery ends of the fallopian tube fold around the pinpoint sized egg, and guide it on its way to the womb. The egg can survive for about forty-eight hours. If it meets some sperm on its journey along the tube, and one of them fertilizes it, it will continue its journey and embed itself in the specially prepared wall of the womb at around day 21. The follicle will now be busy producing hormones to maintain the lining and the fertilised egg.

EGG PRODUCTION

SPERM PRODUCTION

Hormones from the pituitary gland act on the testicles to produce the hormone testosterone, and together these hormones stimulate the testicles to produce the sperm. Sperm are produced continuously, and in vast quantities. They have a long journey through many twisted tubules where they are matured and stored and have secretions added to them to form the semen. An average ejaculation of a few millilitres of semen might contain a hundred million sperm, of which only one will be needed to fertilise the egg. The father is responsible for the baby's sex, which is determined by the sperm at the time of conception.

THE EMBRYO

This term is used for the unborn child from the time when the fertilised egg starts to divide until the time at the end of the second month of pregnancy when all the organ systems have started to develop. Fetus (or foetus) is the scientific name used from then until birth.

TESTS FOR ANAEMIA

The most important blood test is for anaemia. Worldwide, this is a very major problem, responsible for much ill-health and sometimes loss of life. Even in developed countries anaemia is common. It is usually very easy to correct by the use of iron supplements.

'AN EPIDURAL'

Epidural anaesthesia is a method of pain relief by an injection of anaesthetic into the fluid-filled space around the spinal cord. It is very useful if some intervention such as forceps delivery or even caesarian section will be needed. It completely deadens pain in the lower half of the body, but it can slow down the contractions, and it does mean that the mother is less mobile while it is working. It is ideal for planned caesarian section because the mother is fully awake, can hold her baby as soon as it is born, and has none of the after-effects of a general anaesthetic.

FERTILISATION AND IMPLANTATION

Fertilisation, the union of the egg and the sperm, normally takes place in the outer third of the fallopian tube. Around day 14 of the menstrual cycle, a newly-released egg meets vast numbers of sperm which have propelled themselves up from the vagina. One of them enters the egg, their chromosomes unite and the fertilised egg starts to grow as it is gently propelled to the womb. Around day 21, it will implant itself in the specially prepared lining. It is already composed of two different types of cells, one of which will form the placenta, and the other will form the baby, and is now called an embryo. The ovary is already producing the hormones to maintain the lining and to develop the embryo. Some of these hormones can be detected in the urine, and this fact provides a reliable method of diagnosing pregnancy, and is the basis of the widely available do-it-yourself pregnancy tests.

THE PLACENTA

This is where the mother's blood is in close contact with the baby's blood. They are separated only by a very thin membrane, and this is where oxygen and nutrients from the mother's blood pass to the baby and waste products from the baby pass back. Helpful antibodies pass across the placenta, enabling the newborn baby to resist infections. Unhelpful substances like alcohol, nicotine and caffeine cross the placenta, and also many medicines, which is why such care is taken about prescribing in pregnancy. The placenta also manufactures hormones that help to maintain the pregnancy. Sometimes the placenta deteriorates towards the end of pregnancy. It is smaller and less efficient and the baby can't grow so well. The mother's blood pressure can increase in the attempt to get the placenta to do its work. Careful monitoring will be needed to ensure that the baby's life is not in danger, and its birth may need to be induced early. At the same time, anything that helps improve the mother's circulation should help to improve the placenta, so if she has not already done so, the mother should eat the healthiest food possible, and avoid every poison, particularly tobacco.

WEIGHT - AT VARIOUS STAGES

A seven-pound newborn baby has increased in weight by 2,000,000,000 times since the moment of conception nine months before. Four weeks after conception it is fingernail size, but already the beginnings of eyes, ears and limbs can be seen. By twelve weeks it is about 6.5cms long, and all its organs are in place. The womb can now just be felt behind the pubic bones. By twenty weeks the baby will be about 20cms and will weigh about 350gms. It will be moving freely, and its mother will be starting to feel the movements, a little earlier in second and later pregnancies. By 34 weeks the baby will weigh about 1.36kgs and will have an excellent chance of survival should it be born at that stage. By 37 weeks the baby is almost completely ready for birth.

EPISIOTOMY

Episiotomy is a cut made under local anaesthetic to enlarge the vaginal opening if it is not big enough and the tissues are likely to tear. Usually the tissues do stretch enough, especially if the mother is kneeling or squatting. After the birth the cut is stitched up, and it should be completely healed within a few days.

Chapter Sixteen

Keeping Children Well

Improvements in child health

Doctors in western countries seldom see seriously-ill children nowadays. The children in these countries are much healthier than they were in the past. This is very clear if we compare the mortality statistics of today with those of a hundred years ago. We are apt to put the differences down to advances in medicine, but in fact the main reasons are improved nutrition and living conditions, though of course better medical care does play an important part, too.

A hundred years ago, serious infections were frequent and often fatal. Many of those illnesses are practically unknown in the West now. Measles was very common, occasionally fatal and sometimes caused brain damage, resulting in blindness or deafness. Well into the twentieth century TB was causing serious problems in bones and lungs. Before the days of antibiotics parents could expect to spend an appreciable amount of their time looking after sick children.

Although life-threatening conditions are now quite rare in the UK, children are still often unwell and lose time from school, sport, holidays and other activities. As health standards rise, so do expectations, and the workload of family doctors seems to be as great as ever.

Thankfully, they see few seriously-ill children (and those they do see can be quickly admitted to hospital where their problems are usually diagnosed in a couple of days). There are, however, a great many worried parents, anxious for reassurance that their children are *not* developing serious diseases, or that illness will not disrupt their children's education or holidays. In many families both parents are working full time, and if there is no extended family to look after a sick child, even a minor illness needing only a few days at home can have serious financial consequences for the parent who has to take time off work. If there are several children in the family who go down with the illness in turn, or if one child has a series of illnesses, it's that much worse.

The geography of child health

This situation is in marked contrast with that of developing countries where, sadly, life-threatening diseases are much more common, and where good medical care is much less widely available. WHO immunisation programmes are making progress with measles and other problems, but malaria and gastroenteritis both take a high toll of children's lives. Statistics, of course, don't tell the whole story. They hide the fact that there are pockets of poverty in the richest countries, while in the poorer countries there are rich people whose lifestyle and health profile is similar to that of rich people in any part of the world. Nor is poverty reckoned by absolute standards. If it was, few people in the richest countries would be considered to be poor. In the UK, one is considered to be poor if the per capita income in one's family is less than half the average. To be poor in a developing country is obviously much worse.

However, whether we live in rich or poor countries, there are choices we can make that will affect our children's health. Disease never comes without quite a number of causes. For example, we look at viruses as the cause of common colds, but some children get very few colds, while others may have colds almost all the time. The child's immune system is what makes the difference, and the health choices the parents make and teach their children are an important factor in building up those immune systems.

The rules of health for children are the same as those for adults and can be easily remembered in four groups.

Nutrition The simple, natural, unrefined plant foods are the best for children as well as adults. They have their full quota of nutrients, in the proportions designed by the Creator for the human family to eat. A diet based on a variety of whole plant foods, including grains, fruits, vegetables, nuts and seeds, will provide everything that is needed for maintaining health, and will also help to heal disease. Refined foods like sugar, white flour and vegetable oil are deficient, having lost many of their valuable nutrients. They are not necessary for health, and in fact they promote disease, lowering resistance, contributing to weight problems and preparing the way for degenerative disease in later life. Their use should be strictly limited. Healthy children can cope with small amounts, but it is better for sick children to

avoid them, completely if possible.

Parents in the rich countries need to choose a better diet for their children. Many children in the West are overfed. They eat too much fat, sugar, refined food and animal produce. Good medical care ensures that serious problems seldom develop in childhood; however, the foundation is being laid for serious problems in later life. Many children in developing countries provide a stark contrast to this. They are underfed, underweight, lack energy, strength and resistance to infection. Frequently there is little medical care and this explains the tragically high childhood mortality in many parts of the world.

Avoid junk food and choose the simple, natural plant foods that maintain health and prevent future problems. Even in poor countries choices can be made about food, especially in the cities. Limited resources need to be used for simple, wholesome, nutritious food, rather than unnutritious junk food.

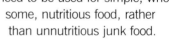

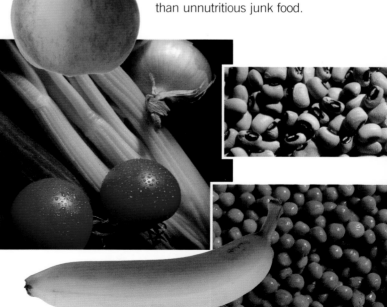

Exercise and rest Children need exercise. Well-fed children have abundant energy and this needs to be worked off by vigorous physical activity, at home, in the playground, on the way to and from school. Over the last few years children in the UK have become more and more sedentary, and many take no exercise at all. They are driven to and from school, they opt out ofsports and they spend a great deal of their leisure with TV, computers or electronic games. This is part of the reason why so many are over-weight. These children may not get enough real rest, either. Lack of physical exercise with mental overstimulation can interfere with sound, healthy sleep. Both growth and immune system mainten-ance take place during sleep and the hormones concerned are affected by light and darkness. So ensure that your children get as much rest as they

need, and early to bed and early to rise is the best plan.

Avoiding poisons Thankfully, most parents discourage their children from using harmful substances such as alcohol and tobacco, but parental example is much better than parental advice. Sociologists tell us that the average child in the UK now has their first cigarette at the age of 9 and their first alcoholic drink at the age of 12. Passive smoking is harmful for children, especially for babies. Most parents try to avoid smoking in their small children's presence, but even so, smokers' children have measurably worse health, with a higher incidence of all the ear, nose, throat and chest problems and also of the sudden death in infancy syndrome. Other poisons are seriously damaging to health too. Childhood asthma seems to have increased in proportion to the increase in car exhaust pollution, and there are many thousands of synthetic chemicals that pollute homes, schools, workplaces and the environment in general. Another source of poisoning, which should be fairly easy to avoid, is medication. All medications should be safely stored, well out of the reach of children, as should all potentially harmful substances used in the home, workshop, garage and garden.

Peace of mind Children are happier and healthier when their lives are predictable, secure and free from artificial excitement. Diet does make a difference to mind and behaviour: healthy food has a calming influence. A regular programme including physi-

> **Many children have little peace of mind because they have experienced the trauma of domestic conflicts.** ⚠

illness during the early years after the split. Emotionally, some never recover. At the beginning of the twenty-first century, the contrast between children's lives is as great as it has ever been. In the rich countries, most children are materially comfortable, but often emotionally desperate. In other parts of the world war, famine and pestilence cast their deadly blight over children's lives. There, many children are hungry, homeless orphans.

cal exercise is important too. Irregular hours, exciting television, video games and noisy rock music have the opposite effect.

Sadly, many children have little peace of mind because they have experienced the trauma of domestic conflicts and the break-up of their parents' marriages. It may take them many years to recover as far as their education is concerned, and they will frequently have an increased rate of minor

Caring for sick children

The rules of health are even more important when children are sick, but they work best when the child is used to the good health habits already. A sick child may not be very keen to be denied all the unhealthy goodies that he usually eats! The rules of health are actually also the principles of healing. Completely nutritious food at the right time and in the right amount greatly encourages recovery, as does fresh air, sunlight, plenty of rest, and the right amount of activity, and for children as well as adults, cheerfulness is one of the very best medicines.

✳ Minor illnesses

In everyday minor illnesses a child's appetite is usually a good guide, at least so far as quantity is concerned. In a child already used to a healthy nutritious diet, it may also be a guide to what to eat as well. Often our bodies need a rest from the work of digesting food in order to concentrate on the task of recovery. So don't worry about a few meals missed in the course of a minor illness. **Fluid intake** is important, and many children do need to be encouraged to drink. Water is best for both well and sick children. Sugary soft drinks are especially harmful in

> Parents who have faith in a divine power have a tremendous resource as they pray a threefold prayer – help for their child, strength for themselves and wisdom for the hospital staff.

illness. Pure fruit juices are better diluted if they are to be used in large amounts. As far as **activity and rest** are concerned the child's wishes are usually the best guide. Children will lie down and rest when they feel the need, and will bounce back to lively activity as soon as their energy is replenished. Sunlight and clean air are healing agencies too. Unless the weather is extreme, and as long as they are appropriately dressed, an unwell child can benefit from going outdoors.

Even in minor illness, the **home atmosphere** is very important. Quiet entertainment, with peaceful music, and reading, or being read to, rather than television or video, and the quiet supportive presence of

parent or carer are just as important for recovery as any treatment or medication. But just be careful that the atmosphere isn't so enjoyable that it encourages the child to be ill more often!

✳ Acute serious illness

Children with acute serious illness are usually in hospital, being cared for by experts, but parents still have a very important role. They can be a consistent, quiet, reassuring presence, comforting and encouraging their child, often simply by just being there. Communication between the parents and the medical staff and the child is very important. Parents and patient should not be afraid to share their doubts and fears with the medical staff, or to ask for explan-

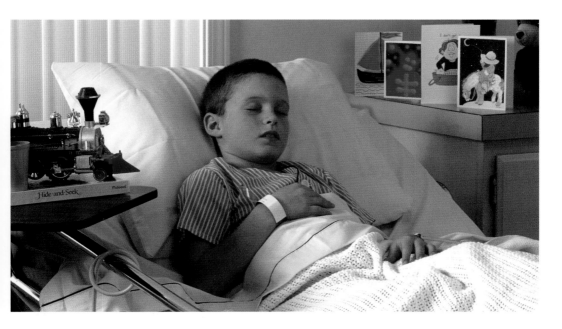

ations. Parents who have faith in a divine power have a tremendous resource as they pray a threefold prayer – help for their child, strength for themselves and wisdom for the hospital staff. Their courage will help everyone, and especially the sick child.

Few children are kept in hospital for longer than is absolutely necessary. Once the danger is over, home is the best place, the parents or other trusted relatives or friends the best carers. In the familiar surroundings of home, simple wholesome food, fresh air and sunlight and the proverbial tender loving care, will all make for a speedy restoration of health.

✳ Chronic serious illness

The same principles apply in **chronic serious illness**. The good diet that maintains health will also help to heal. Even in incurable disease it will make a difference, the aim

being to keep the child as well as possible for as long as possible, and to diminish the symptoms of the disease for as long as possible. Try to keep the food simple, appetising and varied, encourage activities according to strength and ability, and be sure that there are interesting things to look forward to. Chronic illness in the family can be very wearing for parents and carers, and maintaining optimism and cheerfulness can be very difficult. They need to take advantage of all the help they can get from family members, friends, neighbours and professional services. There are many associations for parents of children suffering from particular problems, and these can be a real support, too.

It can be a time of very real distress and hardship when a child has a long-term illness. The phrases 'For better or for worse, in sickness and in health' in the marriage vows apply equally well to parents and their children, too. To have a chronically or terminally-ill child can be one of the greatest strains a marriage can endure. This is where human resources are seldom enough and commitment to divine power makes an incalculable difference.

If you can reach out and grasp the fact that there is more to be achieved in this life than health and material prosperity, and that there is a wise, loving, Creator God who sees and shares your sorrow, take your burdens to him and accept his love and strength.

✳ **Incurable illness**

Incurable illnesses are rare in children in the developed countries, but sadly this is not the case everywhere else. Parents need to take advantage of the specialist care resources that are available. It's also important to remember that whatever the treatment prescribed, the laws of health are always relevant. A seriously-ill child will benefit more from natural nutritious food than from junk food. He will be more comfortable with regular times for food, sleep, treatments and so on. This is a time when an atmosphere of hope and cheerfulness that comes from trust in God is of the greatest value. As they draw strength from above, parents and carers can transmit their trust and hope to their child, and surround him with peace and joy rather than gloom and despondency, so making the most of whatever health and strength is left.

Meningitis

Meningitis is surely the most alarming illness in the UK. Although rare, it is very serious and can be fatal. It responds to urgent treatment with antibiotics, and if treated quickly, most recover completely. One reason why it is so worrying is because it can begin like flu or other viral illnesses. The symptoms are variable and the disease can progress very quickly. Here is what to look out for, not all of which will be present at one time:

High fever, severe persistent headache, neck stiffness, dislike of bright light, joint pains, vomiting, drowsiness or change in consciousness, dark red or purple rash that does not disappear when pressed. The rash, both in babies and older children may be the last sign to appear.

With babies, additional possible signs are refusing feeds, pale, even grey colour, rapid breathing, unresponsiveness – unusual drowsiness or difficulty in awaking, irritable high pitched whimpering cry, stiff neck, bulging fontanelle (soft spot on the top of the head).

If you suspect meningitis, get your child to medical help immediately. Call an ambulance if necessary.

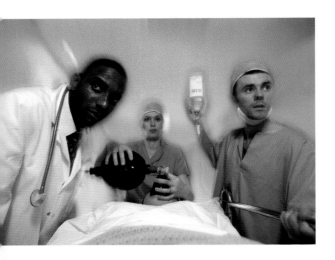

When to seek medical help urgently

Emergencies do happen even in the very healthiest of households. There are a few situations which seem to be beyond anyone's ability to prevent – rare situations that seem to come out of the blue and every parent and carer needs to know the advance signals of serious illnesses. In the following cases get medical help urgently:

> **Acute persistent pain** in any part of the body, especially the abdomen. It can develop slowly or quickly, can be steady or intermittent with spasms that cause the child to double up. Pain in the lower right abdomen is typical of appendicitis, which is a surgical emergency, but pains in other places can be dangerous as well.

> **Persistent vomiting and/or diarrhoea** – dehydration is especially likely if severe vomiting and/or diarrhoea has continued for more than 24 hours, or if the child is unable to retain water for more than half an hour, is unwell between the episodes, and the urine output is low. Babies are much more at risk than older children, especially in hot climates (or hot weather). In severe dehydration the child is ill and weak, with dry skin, sunken eyes, and little or no urine output. It is a grave medical emergency. Immediate intravenous fluid is needed and is lifesaving.

> **Change in consciousness** – unusual drowsiness, difficulty in awakening, unresponsiveness or confusion (not recognising people or knowing where he is, or not making sense when he speaks). These signs all demand urgent diagnosis and treatment.

> **High fever** – a temperature of 40°C or 104°F not responding to tepid sponging or temperature-lowering medication, especially with severe headache or other pain, rash, cough or other signs of serious illness.

> **Convulsion (fit)** – usually there is a sudden loss of consciousness, the child may become pale, or even blue, stiffen and make jerking movements. Most fits in small children are due to a sudden rise in temperature in the course of an otherwise mild viral illness. Although extremely alarming, they seldom last more than a few minutes, and have no serious after-effects, but medical examination and skilled nursing observation for the next few hours is advised for all first fits.

If a small child's temperature begins to rise rapidly, tepid sponging can help to prevent a fit, as can the appropriate dose of the medication, paracetamol or ibuprofen.

If a child starts to have a fit,

place the child in the recovery position on a safe surface – bed, sofa or floor. Do not try to open the mouth. Stay with the child until the convulsion ends or help arrives.

> **Skin rash** – The really dangerous one is the dark red or purple spots of bleeding into the skin, which can be due to meningococcal infection. This is rare, but is an extremely important and urgent sign in an ill child. Do the glass test: press a clear transparent glass against the skin. If the spots don't disappear under this pressure, seek immediate medical help, especially if there is fever, headache or change in consciousness.

> **Serious breathing difficulty** – This can be seen as a faster rate, a different sound such as wheezing or stridor (croupy breathing, often with a barking cough), or grunting in a baby, or severe coughing spasms. An important sign of **respiratory distress** is the use of the accessory muscles – those between the ribs and in the neck – you can recognise this when the lower ribs seem to stand out and the neck muscles tense with every intake of breath. A child with any sort of unexplained fast breathing, with or without these signs or strange sounds, needs medical attention as soon as possible. If the child looks greyish or even blue the situation is even more urgent.

>> **More about breathing difficulties:**

Croup is usually viral and is usually not serious. Irritation of the larynx (voice box) causes croup in babies and small children, hoarseness in older children and adults. Croup usually starts at night and is alarming for both parents and child. It often responds to comfort and reassurance in a steamy environment, and seldom lasts for more than one or two nights. The type of breathing and the general state of the child indicate when medical help is needed. Noisy breathing, especially if it is laboured, is an indication, but a child can have serious breathing difficulties without much noise, and whatever the breathing sounds or whatever he looks like, if the child is lethargic, floppy, pale or even greyish, urgent medical help is necessary.

Wheezing is due to spasm of the main breathing passages, the bronchi. This happens in the chronic disease asthma, and it can also happen in the course of a mild viral respiratory infection. Mild wheezing due to a viral infection usually lasts only a few days, and gets better by itself, and the child is no more ill that he would be with a normal cold or flu. Mild wheezing can of course become severe, and if that is the case, then medical help should be sought.

Asthma in the UK at the present time is treated almost exclusively by medication, and in an

> **Emergency oral rehydration fluid for babies and children:**
> 1 tablespoon sugar (15ml)
> 1 teaspoon salt (5ml)
> **in one litre of sterile water.**
> **Small drinks, at room temperature.**

emergency, the bronchodilator drugs can be lifesaving. The real danger with asthma is when the medications fail to work. An asthmatic child who is weak or lethargic, has difficulty speaking, whether wheezing audibly or not, and whose medication has not given the expected relief, is in grave danger, and needs immediate medical help.

In the long term, many children with asthma have been greatly helped by change in diet and lifestyle. Milk sensitivity seems to be a factor in many cases, and a trial of dairy-free eating is well worthwhile.

Some preventative measures to help stop minor problems from becoming major:

> **Recurrent abdominal pain**
> **'Tummy aches'** whether caused by viruses or dietary factors, often respond to a rest for the digestive tract in the form of a short fast – missing one or two meals and drinking lots of water instead, or in the form of fruit or other light and easily-digested food for a few meals. Both the kind of food and the timing of the meals are important for preventing recurrences. Simple, natural unrefined foods at regular intervals with no in-between snacks is the policy to follow.

Vomiting and/or diarrhoea. The vital thing is to maintain the fluid input. These are not usually serious problems in temperate climates where children normally have enough to eat, and hygiene is good. Withholding solid foods for a day or so, avoiding dairy produce, or diluting the milk for bottle-fed babies may be all that is needed. If vomiting occurs several times, small drinks of warm (body temperature) water should be offered. If the problem is mainly diarrhoea, rice water is soothing. If the diarrhoea is mild or lessening, dry toast or crispbread, apples raw or cooked, and boiled rice are all helpful foods. Always keep an eye on the urine output during episodes of vomiting or diarrhoea, especially both. Urine output is a very good indicator of the state of hydration. As the child becomes short of fluid, the body reduces the urine output to conserve it. The urine is more concentrated, and darker in colour. Pale clear urine is what to aim for – encourage more drinking until it is achieved. If the vomiting or diarrhoea occur more than two or three times, use oral rehydration fluid.

In babies and young children persistent diarrhoea and vomiting can quickly result in dehydration, especially in the tropics where virulent organisms are commoner and hygiene may be more difficult to maintain. This is the main cause of death in developing countries. Gastroenteritis is a completely curable disease if there are adequate treatment facilities. Oral dehydration fluid can work wonders and is a mainstay of treat-

Oral rehydration fluid

In an emergency you can make your own oral rehydration fluid, but it is always preferable to use the proprietary products if they are available, because they are very accurately formulated and provide a more complete supply of minerals. However, a homemade fluid can be lifesaving in a serious emergency. Always make the fluid very carefully, using accurate measurements, as there is a very real danger of actually making the child much worse if the proportion of salt is too high.

To make a simple emergency oral rehydration fluid for babies and children with vomiting and/or diarrhoea dissolve one tablespoonful (15 ml) of sugar and one teaspoonful (5 ml) of salt in one litre (1¾ pint) of sterile water. Give the child small drinks at room or body temperature until the danger of dehydration is passed – vomiting and diarrhoea lessening, and urine output good.

Better still, be sure always to have a supply of dioralyte, rehydrate or other recognised proprietary rehydration fluid available for emergency use.

Rice water. Boil one or two spoonfuls of rice in one or two pints of water, and use for drinks, sweetening a little if necessary.

ment (see box). A child too ill to take fluids by mouth needs intravenous fluid replacement, easily supplied to those who are blessed with access to good hospital care.

Constipation

Constipation can be uncomfortable, and can cause quite severe pain in children. It is a factor in appendicitis as well. There are three main causes for most cases of constipation – lack of fibre, lack of fluids, and lack of time in the toilet. For the first, gradually increase the fibre in the diet, by changing to natural, unprocessed high-fibre foods – wholewheat grain products, fruit and vegetables, and pulses. For the second, encourage water drinking at regular intervals, and for the third, it may be necessary to reorganize the family schedule, to give time for a large early morning drink of warm water, an unhurried breakfast and an unhurried visit to the toilet. For babies already on solids, extra fruit, especially dried fruit added to the meals, and extra fluids may solve the problem.

Coughs, colds and other catarrhal problems

Healthy eating makes an enormous difference with these problems, both in prevention and cure. This is because some foods encourage healing while others have the opposite effect. The fresh raw foods, with their high vitamin, mineral and phytochemical content, encourage healing. The onion and garlic family of vegetables are particularly helpful in preventing and treating ear, nose and chest problems. Sugary foods reduce the activity of the white blood cells, so reducing the immune system's ability to fight disease. Dairy produce encourages the

production of excess mucus in the respiratory tract in those who are sensitive to it, causing more congestion. Cows' milk is now recognised to be a major factor in ear, nose and throat problems, including allergic conditions such as hay fever, perennial rhinitis (year-round running nose) and asthma. Children with any of these or any other catarrhal problems do much better when they avoid sugar and dairy products, and eat simple natural plant foods.

Sensitive breast-fed babies can actually react to cows' milk in their mother's diet, producing more catarrh and getting more colds.

Soya milk looks and tastes milky, but the composition is different from cows' milk. It's a useful alternative to dairy milk for older children, and soya formula milk is available for babies who have real problems with cows' milk.

Fluid intake is important – water, herb

teas (see below), lemon and honey, *diluted* fruit juices, *not* sugary soft drinks!

Steam can help with all sorts of coughs, colds, chest problems and sinusitis, especially in centrally heated houses, where the air tends to be dry. A warm bath in a steamy bathroom may be enough for a baby. A vaporiser in the bedroom, or wet towels on radiators, can help too. For a more intense steam treatment, keep the child in the kitchen with the doors and windows shut and a kettle (safely out of reach!) boiling for ten or fifteen minutes.

Some recipes for older children

Herb tea – rosemary, sage and thyme are all soothing to the respiratory tract. To make tea, you can simply infuse by pouring boiling water over a teaspoonful of the dried herb and allowing it to stand for five minutes, then strain, cool, dilute to the child's taste and sweeten (if necessary) with honey or apple juice concentrate before serving. Another method is to boil the herbs in the water for five minutes before serving. This can be used several times a day, with the caution to avoid too much or too frequent honey.

Honey and Eucalyptus cough mixture – take a small jar of liquid honey, add a couple of drops of eucalyptus oil and mix well. A teaspoonful can be used as an occasional cough medicine, either as it is or in hot water.

Chapter Seventeen

Allergies

Who among us does not enjoy the pleasure of a walk in the country with the air heavy with the smell of new-mown hay and the bees buzzing from flower to flower collecting the precious pollen to make into golden honey? Or the sight of a long-haired cat purring contentedly in front of a blazing fire, or the gastronomic delights of a bowl of strawberries and cream?

For some people, however, these spell nothing but misery in the form of running eyes, sneezing and wheezing, and perhaps even an itchy skin rash. The common factor which accounts for each of these perverted reactions can be summed up in a single word . . . ALLERGY!

Allergy can be defined most simply as a *hypersensitivity to various substances which would normally be harmless to the average person.* It can take various forms and can involve a bewildering range of possible stimuli. When we consider all the stories about supposed allergies – some bizarre and even amusing – we realise that there may be a tendency to blame allergy for more than we should. However, modern research has

shown that allergic responses are due to very well defined mechanisms. These involve particular chemical stimuli or antigens; antibodies or chemical substances, produced by the individual to counteract the antigen, and the activities of certain cells in the body which release chemicals producing the inflammatory features of the allergic reaction. There is nothing vague or imprecise about allergy. If genuine, it is a reaction to a specific substance to which the individual has unpredictably become sensitised, and it is likely that his symptoms will appear each time he is exposed to that stimulus.

Exposure to sensitising agents can be by a variety of routes.

Inhalation of airborne allergens – such as pollens – may give rise to respiratory forms of allergy such as hay fever and asthma.

Ingestion may cause food allergies and rashes, and contact with skin can produce dermatitis. The symptoms, whether sneez-ing, wheezing, or itching, are due to inflammation at the site of entry of the allergen into the body, although once absorbed, the reaction may result in more general symptoms.

Some of the most sudden and serious allergic reactions occur when the sensitising agent is introduced directly into the circulation as with bee stings or following the injection of certain drugs to which the individual may have become sensitised by previous medication. We should remember, however, that the development of a specific allergy is very much an individual peculiarity, and that most people similarly exposed will have no problems at all.

The range of substances to which we may become allergic is enormous, and many of these

childhood. These individuals are known to produce specific antibodies known as 'reagins' in response to a variety of allergens, and this phenomenon can be demonstrated by the doctor when using skin tests, or by more specialised and expensive laboratory methods. The same tests can be carried out for food allergies but normally have no relevance to the incidence of eczema.

will be common items present in our food, or our physical environment in the home, at our work, or in our leisure activities. Whether we develop symptoms of allergy or not is largely a matter of chance, although certain individuals appear to have a particular inherited predisposition to allergic conditions such as hay fever and asthma. Such people, known as 'atopic' subjects may also have a tendency to eczema, a skin rash which may take a variety of forms and appear for the first time in infancy or later in

Common food allergens include dairy products such as eggs and cows' milk, nuts, shellfish, and strawberries, and the symptoms which follow ingestion of these may take the form of swelling of the lips or

mouth, a stomach upset, or an itchy rash of 'hives' or urticaria ('nettle rash'). Large weals appear on the skin within a short time of eating the offending item of food, and will persist for several hours unless relieved by appropriate medication. Similar allergic reactions can occur in some individuals who develop intolerance to the colouring agents and preservatives used in the processing of many foods.

Respiratory allergies, due to inhaled allergens, are most frequent in the pollen season, and the first symptoms will appear in the early summer months when the sufferers begin to be troubled by sneezing, running eyes, and perhaps by asthma. The severity of the symptoms often parallels the 'pollen count' which is recorded in many daily papers and on television weather forecasts, and is an indication of the amount of various plant pollens in the air. House-dust mites – tiny microscopic creatures in bedding and house dust – are also an allergic stimulus for many patients with respiratory allergies.

Dermatitis or eczema can result from skin contact with sensitising agents. Itching eczema will develop at the site of actual contact, and a careful history of the appearance of symptoms and the distribution of the rash may provide a strong clue as to the agent responsible. Allergy to rubber, chemicals, nickel, certain plants, animal dander, and even to wool fat (lanolin) in cold creams is not uncommon. The modern dermatology clinic provides facilities for the investigation of contact dermatitis due to the vast number of allergens in our environment, and suspicions can be scientifically confirmed by patch testing.

Dealing with allergies

As it is not practicable to regulate one's life to avoid sensitisation, it will be more helpful to consider how one can deal with allergies which actually develop.

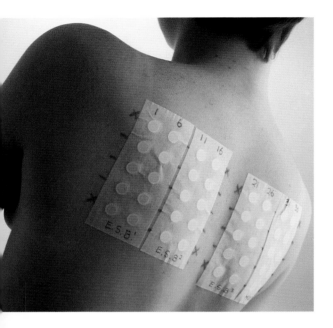

Identification of the allergen. The most useful clue to the identification of the sensitising substance may be provided by a detailed history. The individual may be able to link the onset of symptoms to a particular time, environment, or set of circumstances. The presenting features will probably indicate whether the allergen is in the air, in the diet, or in contact with the skin. Such suspicions can often be confirmed by specific tests which a doctor can carry out. Food allergies or reactions to food additives may be identified by using 'elimination diets' in which the suspected item is excluded for a period of several weeks to determine if the symptoms are alleviated. Skin allergies can similarly be confirmed by patch testing.

If the allergen can be identified with certainty it may be possible to avoid further contact with that substance. This may merely entail minor adjustments such as the avoidance of a particular cosmetic or plant, the substitution of plastic gloves for rubber ones, or the elimination of a particular item from the diet. In some situations, however, it may be necessary to make more radical changes in one's employment or lifestyle to eliminate further contact with the allergen.

Hyposensitisation. If the allergen cannot be avoided completely it may be possible to make an individual less sensitive to it by a process known as desensitisation. This is used by doctors particularly for the treatment of hay fever and can be of considerable benefit. The patient is given a series of injections of minute quantities of the antigen and over a period of several weeks he will develop a tolerance to it, and will be able to survive the effects of the pollen season with

> **A very large range of 'antihistamine' drugs is now available which can effectively relieve the distress of the allergic patient** ⚠

few or no symptoms. Such tretment of course be given under strict medical supervision. Similar hyposensitisation techniques may occasionally be used for other allergens, such as bee or wasp stings and certain life-saving drugs to which the patient may have become allergic.

Drug treatment for allergies. We have seen that the symptoms of allergy are due to inflammation, triggered off by the reaction between the antigen and the corresponding antibody or sensitised cells in the individual. This process releases chemicals such as histamine and other agents which cause inflammation in the tissues. The symptoms of allergy can thus be relieved by the use of drugs which will neutralise these substances. A very large range of 'antihistamine' drugs is now available which can effectively relieve the distress of the allergic patient. These will be helpful whether the symptoms are in the respiratory system, alimentary tract, or skin, and are an invaluable form of treatment.

Other drugs such as cromoglycate have been used similarly for the relief of allergic asthma in children and in

some food allergies. The most serious reactions – such as severe asthma, certain sting or drug reactions – may require emergency treatment with adrenalin or corticosteroid drugs to relieve the more acute symptoms which may threaten life.

Drug treatment is of greatest value in suppressing the symptoms of allergy in those situations where the allergen cannot be identified or exposure to it eliminated. An attempt to discover the cause of the allergy is the first priority, but the judicious use of antihistamine and other drugs can relieve the considerable distress which many sufferers from allergy must otherwise endure.

Modern medicine has made considerable advances in the understanding of allergic conditions, and effective treatment is available for all who require it.

We must remember, however, that allergy is responsible for only a very small proportion of our ailments, and that others will require alternative solutions.

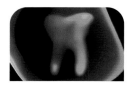

Chapter Eighteen

Teeth

Tooth decay is Britain's commonest child-hood disease – each year, Britain's children lose four million teeth, weighing four tons! By the time they are adult about 40% of people have no teeth at all!

Is our appalling dental health just a misfortune, or is it our own fault? In this chapter we shall endeavour to show that it *is* avoidable, and what steps we can take to avoid the time when our teeth are like the stars – they come out at night!

You may be thinking:

'Sorry – there's no hope for me – I've inherited weak teeth.'

True – some people's teeth are more sus-ceptible to decay than others. However, the *most* important cause of dental decay is *bad eating habits.*

'But surely we eat better now than ever before?'

Maybe we do have a greater variety of foods now, but instead of eating natural whole-foods, we have gone over to more refined products. Let's look at some of these changes:

1) Sugar Before the sixteenth century sugar was very scarce. Only the wealthy could afford it. Ancient skulls and records show that generally there was very little tooth decay up to that time.

During the sixteenth century many more sugar plantations were established around the world, and supplies in Britain gradually became more plentiful – along with tooth decay! The following table shows this trend in increasing sugar consumption:

Estimated consumption of sugar per head per year

1750	1.75kg	(4lb)
1850	11kg	(25lb)
Now	54kg	(120lb)

This means that on average each man, woman, and child consumes over 1 kg (2 lb) of sugar *each week!*

Only during world war rationing was this trend reversed – sugar consumption was halved, and whole grains replaced refined cereals to a large extent. Just look what happened to tooth decay in those few years of the Second World War:

Percentage of decayed permanent molars of seven-year-olds

1939	90%
1945	25%

Sugar, so tempting and cheap, is taken in lots of different ways during the day – in hot drinks, sprinkled on cereal, cakes, jams, marmalade, puddings, sweets, chocolates, peppermints, ice cream, jelly, biscuits, squashes, fizzy drinks, etc. It's amazing how it all adds up.

2) Refined grains Since about 1900, 100% stone-ground flour has largely been replaced by refined white flours, which are much finer, and have lost their fibre. Bread made from these flours doesn't need much

sugary foods can stagnate for some time.

3) Once decay reaches the softer sensitive dentine, it spreads rapidly unless treated by a dentist, who will remove the decay and fill the cavity.

4) If untreated, as decay spreads outwards the enamel surface will collapse, and as it spreads inwards infection reaches the pulp and travels down the roots to form an abscess. Often this causes severe pain and loss of the tooth.

If you are now smugly thinking your teeth aren't decaying like that – wait a moment – you've only heard half the story. After thirty-five years of age you are more likely to lose your teeth through *gum disease* than any other cause.

chewing, and rapidly forms a sticky mess which clings to the teeth.

3) Natural fibrous food This food, which would help to cleanse the teeth and stimulate the gums, is eaten less.

Yes, dental decay is a disease associated with our modern 'civilised' diet. Even now, as we watch the change from a natural to a refined diet taking place in many developing countries around the world, we see a corresponding deterioration in dental health.

'What happens then, when teeth decay?'

1) First of all colonies of bacteria stick to your teeth. These colonies are called 'dental plaque'.

2) When you eat sugar, or sugar-containing foods and drinks, these bacteria change the sugar into acid. Within just *one minute* the acid formed is strong enough to start dissolving your teeth.

Most decay starts in the fissures on the chewing surfaces of the back teeth, or between teeth – these are places where

'How do I know if I have gum disease?'
At first you may not be aware of it, although your dentist could tell you. Later your gums may bleed, be swollen, or discoloured. Other signs are bad breath, or an unpleasant taste. These symptoms lead to a gradual loosening of the teeth.

'What causes gum disease?'

It almost always develops in a dirty mouth.

1) Again, the first stage is formation of that sticky coating of bacteria on the teeth – dental plaque. Plaque produces substances which irritate gums, causing them to become inflamed and bleed (gingivitis).

If this plaque is not removed it usually goes on to form a hard scale, or 'calculus', which causes even more irritation and inflammation.

2) The gums shrink away from these irritants, leaving a gap, or 'pocket', between the teeth and gums. Plaque and calculus can now build up even more in this pocket, causing inflammation deeper in the gum (periodonitis).

3) The tissues supporting the teeth shrink away from the irritation more and more, until the affected teeth become loose, and are eventually lost.

'Can gum disease be treated?'

Yes, but the chance of success depends on how far the disease has progressed – the earlier your dentist sees you the better. Treatment always includes scaling and polishing your teeth, and then it is vital that you keep them thoroughly clean at home. Your dentist will advise you on the best methods of doing this, and may suggest other helpful measures.

Now we're depressed by looking at what can go wrong with our teeth and gums, let's be positive, and think about what we can do ourselves to improve matters:

1. Better eating habits As we showed earlier, we eat too much sugar and soft refined foods, so let's cut down on the amount of sugar we eat, and *avoid completely* the more sticky forms of sugar – they cling to the teeth for hours, allowing a high concentration of acid to be formed.

Avoid completely eating sweet foods between meals or just before bed, as this keeps a high concentration of sugar in the mouth for much longer. Try to eat sweet things all together at a meal, and clean your teeth immediately after. There are so many appetising natural foods – let's enjoy these instead!

2. Keeping our mouths clean The importance of removing that sticky bacterial plaque from our teeth should be obvious by now, as it is so closely involved in both dental decay and gum disease. Plaque doesn't build up *so* quickly if we are eating a more natural diet, but it is still there, and needs to be thoroughly removed.

'How often should I clean my teeth?' Ideally the teeth and gums should be brushed after every meal. If this is not possible, they should be cleaned at the very least after breakfast and last thing at night, and a cleansing food such as an apple, raw carrot, or celery should be eaten after your other meals.

'How should I brush my teeth?' The most important answer to that question is thoroughly. Sticky plaque everywhere needs to be removed. Remember, each tooth has five sides, and all of these surfaces need cleaning, so be methodical.

It's a good idea to check on how well you're brushing your teeth by chewing a 'disclosing tablet' afterwards. These are available from chemists. After chewing, swish the solution from the tablet around your mouth, and then rinse once with water. The tablet, which just contains vegetable dye, will stain red any plaque still on your teeth. The results may surprise you! If you keep brushing until all the red stain has gone from your teeth, you will know that they are now thoroughly clean. You will also have discovered that it takes several minutes to do this – a hasty 'flick and a promise' isn't enough. Make one of your daily brushing sessions longer than the others so that you have time to do a really thorough job.

'I can't brush my teeth very much – it makes my gums bleed.' This is a sign of gum disease, indicating that an area needs cleaning more thoroughly, not less. The bleeding should then gradually stop. If it doesn't, consult your dentist.

'What kind of brush should I use?' It is important to have the right tool for the job, so choose a brush which is not too large to clean round corners; not so hard that it damages your gums; and not so soft that it doesn't clean your teeth properly.

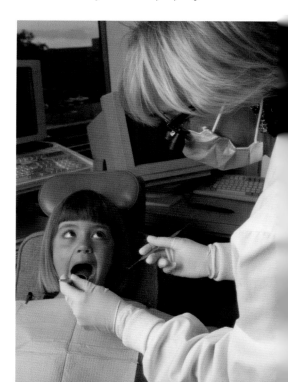

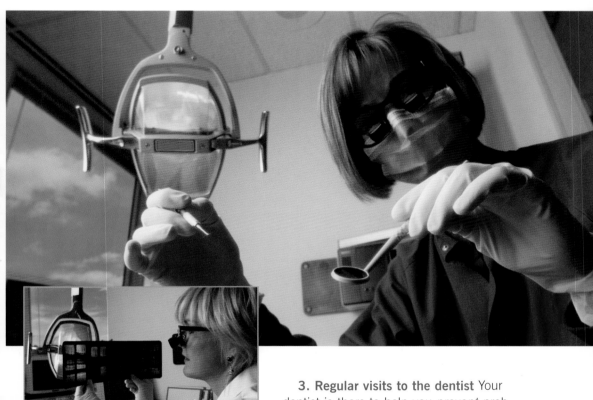

A small nylon brush of medium texture is usually best unless your dentist tells you otherwise. When the bristles *start* to flatten, it's time to buy a new brush! A single tuft 'interspace' brush is very useful for cleaning awkward nooks and crannies.

Your dentist may also advise you to use wood sticks or dental floss for cleaning between your teeth.

'Is toothpaste really necessary?'
Toothpaste does assist in cleaning and polishing your teeth. Use one containing fluoride – this will also help protect against decay.

3. Regular visits to the dentist Your dentist is there to help you *prevent* problems, not just to repair damage after it has occurred. So don't wait until you have toothache. Regular six-monthly checks enable your dentist to give you advice, spot early signs of trouble, and treat them before they become serious.

The introduction of fluoride into the water supply in most districts in Britain has led to a dramatic reduction in the number of cavities

Children's teeth

Children deserve a special mention, as this is the time of life, ideally, when the foundations of future dental health are laid. As the old proverb says – 'prevention is better than cure'. Let's follow through the story of children's teeth:

Before birth Expectant mothers should visit their dentist for advice, and their diet should be wholesome, balanced, and low in sugar – there is even evidence that the more sugar an expectant mother takes during pregnancy, the more her *children's* teeth will be prone to decay!

Baby's teeth start to form a few weeks after conception, and by the time he's born there are twenty baby teeth, as well as some permanent teeth, in the bones of his jaws.

When teeth come through The chart adjacent gives approximate timings, but growth varies from child to child, so mothers should not worry unduly if their children's teeth are early or late in appearing. Your dentist will keep a check to make sure all is well.

First visit to the dentist Usually all the baby teeth have appeared by two and a half years, so this is a good age to start taking your child along to the dentist with you. The

TIMES OF APPEARANCE OF TEETH

BABY TEETH	TIME OF APPEARANCE (IN MONTHS)
Lower central incisors	5-7
Upper central incisors	6-8
Lateral incisors	7-9
Canines	16-18
First molars	12-14
Second molars	20-24

PERMANENT TEETH	(IN YEARS)
Central incisors	6-8
Lateral incisors	7-9
Canines	9-12
First premolars	10-12
Second premolars	10-12
First molars	6-7
Second molars	11-13
Third molars (wisdom teeth)	18-21

The ages given are approximate. Many normal babies do not conform to this pattern.

Watch the sugar! Eat a balanced wholesome diet at home so that your child will not develop such a taste for sweet things, or feel the need of between-meal snacks. The eating habits adopted in childhood often remain for the rest of life!

When sweet things are eaten make sure they are the less sticky kinds, and are eaten at mealtimes, then brush the teeth afterwards. Sweets should never be used as a bribe.

Avoid giving young children bottles of sweetened fruit drinks to suck for long periods – this can cause serious damage to the teeth. Dummies or 'comforters' should never be given dipped in sugary solutions.

visits can then be short and friendly, and will accustom him to the sights and sounds of the surgery. Your dentist can advise you how to care for these new teeth, and may suggest other preventive measures.

Don't make your child go through the pain and sleepless nights of toothache before you apprehensively take him along to a strange surgery, where he may have the more frightening experience of an extraction as his introduction to dental care.

Baby teeth *do* matter – children need teeth as much as adults

> they need to chew their food properly

> learning to speak correctly is easier for children with a normal healthy mouth

> baby teeth guard the gaps meant for permanent teeth, making the need for orthodontic treatment later less likely.

Cleaning children's teeth Until children develop the ability to clean their own teeth parents should brush them really thoroughly once a day, and after every meal if possible. Brush over the gums and all surfaces of the teeth with a small toothbrush. Use a fluoride toothpaste.

Watch for the first permanent molars which appear at the back of the mouth at about the age of six. Make sure these teeth receive special care as they are important and can decay very quickly if neglected.

A fresh healthy mouth is a big asset in life. We use our mouths for some important things, like talking, eating, kissing, tasting, and smiling! Our parents may have thought that full dentures were inevitable in life, but we have seen that this is not so, and the effort put into caring for our own, and our children's teeth – precious God-given assets – is really worth while.

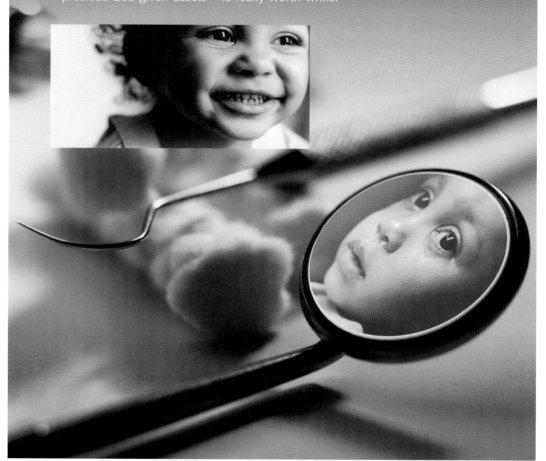

Chapter Nineteen

Whole-Person Health

There are four interrelated aspects of a person's health and being: the *physical,* the *social*, the *intellectual* and the *spiritual.* In each of these four aspects there may be disease or dysfunction. Whole-person health depends on health in all of these components of being.

Physical

Dysfunction in the *physical* component is comparatively easily recognised and diagnosed.

Much attention and mountains of cash are spent on keeping physically well, or in regaining physical wellness if – in regard to any of a thousand and one causes, real or imagined – it is believed to be lost. Nevertheless, despite the example of their fellows and the amount of advice and information available, the frantic lifestyle of many still often results in an irremediable physical dysfunction before they have regulated their lifestyle to meet physical limita-

tions. Not recognising the interrelationship between the social, intellectual and spiritual, and the physical, the demands of lifestyle and appetite have not been modified to accommodate the body's ability to cope.

However, health-consciousness has been on the increase for thirty years, as has the belief that other areas of being – especially morale, sense of optimism, self-confidence, intellectual fulfilment, stability of personality, spiritual peace – impinge upon the physical. But these other areas, where disability is less easily diagnosed, are still, to an alarming extent, left to the province of the quack.

Social

In the same way that some folk adjust to living at 'not quite 100%', or 'a few degrees under par', there are those who have never known the meaning of high-level wellness – socially. They become used to the moods from which they 'suffer'. They come to accept that not being at ease with other people is 'just me0, without digging out a cause. In the same way, their lack of self-confidence and sense of inferiority – together with whatever ways their subconscious may choose to have them compensate for these disabilities socially – are seen as character traits that they, and those whose paths cross theirs, must accept as the norm and learn to tolerate.

They can cry defeat in the face of everyday problems. They struggle and whine and flounder and bleat through their days with a sense of dull resentment at life in general – and the concepts of diagnosis and cure are far from them. They can burden their minds with problems and obstacles until they come to dominate their thought patterns and they are mentally subservient to them – and do not look for a way of escape. They have a sense of inferiority or inadequacy to the point where it interferes with the attainment of their goals – and simply do not ask questions. Negative thoughts are pushed through their brains until their sense of perspective becomes warped. Tension has so disrupted their inner harmony that they are 'living on their nerves'. That unhealthy, destructive private habit, worry, so possesses their thinking that shock-waves are carried from 'the social' to 'the physical', and soon manifest themselves in the physical person in all kinds of grisly ways. They are mastered by all manner of fears and phobias. They fume and fret at the frustrations that go with life – a travesty of *the adventure* that life really is or should be. Yet through it all it does not occur to them that there is a cure, a panacea for the human condition. Used to treating symptoms rather than causes, they do not even set out in search of the cause of their social maladies, let alone grasp the prescription for cure.

Intellectual

The same fast-paced world of mobiles, laptops, deadlines, conveyor belts and a vertical social ladder which helps produce such people, also has other, more direct side effects. They stem directly from modern industrial and commercial processes and practices and their consequences affect all four components of being, most notably *the intellectual.*

How many of the machine-minders and desk jockeys, each a cog in some vast wheel of industry or commerce, have minds dulled and spirits bored by repetitive work? How many, under a five o'clock sky, then leave work – to pursue trivial interests, their years spent in the pursuit of vacant goals?

They are oppressed by the aimlessness of life. They have been told that life has no meaning, and they almost believe it.

They reach out for sense and meaning; they have a glimmer of a belief that, despite all they have been told, life really is an adventure with a meaning, a beginning and an end. And that glimmer remains even though they may spend hours anaesthetising their brains with the second-hand adventure of the celluloid world of television and videos which enables them to enjoy, vicariously, the excitement which is conspicuously absent from their own boring lives of workaday routine.

But those boring lives, and the sense of aimlessness and meaninglessness they produce by way of side-shadow, lead to problems (diseases?) in the intellectual realm of life. The consciousness that a large proportion of the brain will never be utilised, that abilities must remain unstretched, that the frustration of life may be without significance, must beget tensions and discords for the mind. . . .

Spiritual

Then there is the *spiritual* component. Here the sense of oppression by the meaninglessness, aimlessness, lostness and rootlessness of modern life is painfully acute. But dysfunction in the spiritual area is especially difficult to diagnose because symptoms take so many forms and do not always have an obvious connection with the condition.

At base, post-modern man suffers spiritual problems because he has lost his way. And not only his way, but his address. In times past he asked the questions. Now he has become a question to himself. Today's culture – art, literature, music and political and social activity – thunders the message: 'Man is sick, and his sickness is a sickness of the spirit'.

And man is spiritually sick because he is lost.

Darwin demoted man to the status of an animal driven on by 'his collective ancestral impulses'. Marx said man was propelled by economic necessity, his stomach. Freud denied man a mind by insisting that he was motivated, not by reason, but by 'hidden unconscious instincts', his libido. By denying man a mind and reducing him to an urge-powered beast, they denied him a spiritual dimension.

Man has not taken kindly to his reduced status. A host of problems exists today because the Darwin-Marx-Freud convention-al wisdom has taken hold. Because it has taken hold the problems are not traced to source. That source is the spiritual dimen-sion of man. To heal diseases of the spirit is to heal the problems of society – and to create the harmony between the four com-ponents of being necessary for whole man health.

What 'problems of society' do we have in mind?

Anything from vandalism and crime through juvenile

> **We live in a world like an echo-chamber deafening the ear with a cacophony of many dissonant voices, all trying to shout the loudest**

delinquency and the collapse of marriages to that sense of 'not belonging', upheaval of the mind, psychiatric disorders enough to fill a dictionary and the belief that 'there's no point carrying on' which have at us on newscasts and through newspapers.

Part of the modern spiritual *malaise* is the want of *roots*. To be rooted is perhaps the most important and least recognised need of the human soul. Roots anchor, nourish, even *explain* a person. They are invisible links by which an individual is held within his spiritual and social context. If roots are violently broken or if a person is uprooted, he becomes a starved off-shoot, shallow and unstable.

The want of *aim* and direction, the fact that, walking in dark-ness, he knows not where he goes, is also part of man's spiritual, as well as his intellectual, problem.

But underlying all other causes of man's spiritual dis-ease is *lostness*.

He lives in a world like an echo-chamber deafening the ear with a cacoph-ony of many dissonant voices, all

He lives in a generation in which the moral signposts, the frontiers of behaviour have been broken down. Authority is out. Absolutes are out. Behaviourist accounts of thought and conscience – destroying homes and parental discipline – are in.

Rootlessness, aimlessness, lostness: all aspects of the cancer eating at the heart and entrails of spiritual man.

But is the cancer of 'high-grade malignancy'? Can it be cured or prevented? The diseases of the physical, the social and the intellectual components of being: can they be prevented or treated?

The physical you

Surveys list 'good physical health' at the top of the majority of people's priorities, and 'ill health' at the top of the list of their fears.

Quite right too. 'The physical you' is the most complex and exquisitely fashioned mechanism there is. No way should it be taken for granted. But it is. Even by those who list 'good health' at the top of their priorities. More often than not they take no account of the long-term effects of lifestyle upon their bodies, so intent are they on climbing the ladder of success, winning friends and influencing people – or simply keeping their heads above water. Their only concession to their number one priority is pill-guzzling when they get sick. A healthy, balanced diet is of the essence; as is a regular programme of exercise. And remember: if it doesn't make you sweat, it's not exercise. Remember too the World Health Organisation's definition of health:

'Health is a state of complete *physical, mental, social* and *spiritual* well-being; not merely the absence of disease or infirmity.'

Having got that straight, let's pass on to:

trying to shout the loudest. Enticing voices. Strident voices. Persuasive voices. Words that soothe, words that titillate, words that inflame. He stands like a person in a surrealistic fantasy: frantically turning his head, listening to this voice and that, these words and those words, confused, bewildered, spiritually dizzy. Not knowing where to turn.

The social you

Is 'the social you' in good health? Do you 'suffer' from moods? Are you at ease with other people? How is your self-image? Do you lack self-confidence? Do you live with a sense of inferiority? If so, do you try to cover up your inner feelings of inadequacy by anti-social habits such as talking too much, showing off, playing aloof, acting brusque and hard-to-handle? Do you give up in the face of everyday problems and whine? Fill your mind with negative thoughts until your sense of perspective disappears? Are you tense and difficult to live with? Do you fume and fret?

If the answer to any of these questions is 'Yes' be it known: these things ought not to be. More to the point: these things *need not be.*

Dysfunction in the component of our being spoils our enjoyment of the adventure of life. The puritan inside some of us kicks out at the concept of 'enjoyment'; but we are ignoring the evidence of a God-made creation if we have not grasped that there is a sense in which life is for the sheer enjoyment of living! Of course there are greater purposes, and grander causes; of course there is a moral and spiritual dimension which gives living a higher significance. But none of these detracts one jot from the fact that life is to be *enjoyed.* And among the main impediments to enjoyment are self-consciousness, a sense of inferiority and the other types of dysfunction in the social sphere of being.

Too many are hampered by that popular malady the *inferiority complex.* Yet without a humble but reasonable confidence in your own powers you cannot be successful and will miss out on the joys of life's adventure. The first step to a cure is to discover why you have feelings of inferiority. Basically these feelings

arise from a deep, profound self-doubt and their genesis is in the cobwebbed depths of your past: some emotional violence done to you in childhood, something you did to yourself, the unasked-for circumstances in which you were born, brought up and educated. The roots of the inferiority complex are in *feelings,* not reasons or objective fact. Find the root cause in the dim recesses of your personality then rationalise and throttle it.

The greatest antidote to the inferiority complex is faith. Norman Vincent Peale used to have sufferers repeat a Bible verse whenever feelings of inferiority set in: 'I can do everything with the help of Christ who gives me the strength I need.' (Philippians 4:13.)

The fact is that faith in God gives you faith in yourself. The reason for that is that the Bible is brimful of assurances that to God the value of one soul – for 'one soul' read your name – is beyond all creatures, beyond all sacred institutions, beyond the value of all the world. Never forget it!

How do you acquire faith?

It is a gift from God.

How do you acquire this gift from God?

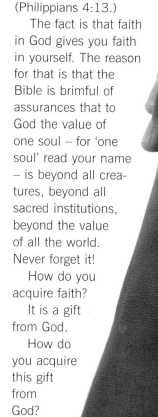

By communicating with God and allowing God to communicate with you.

How?

First through prayer. Not superficial, perfunctory, formalistic *Book of Common Prayer*-type prayer. Just you talking to God as a Friend. No set pattern of words is required; no Elizabethan prose.

Second, having prayed for help, read God's printed letter to man, the Bible. If you have never read it before, begin with the Gospel of Luke in the New Testament. Unless you have a penchant for sixteenth-century prose, read it in a modern version.

In this way, over a period of time, God will fill you with his gift of faith. That done, you will come to realise what your part is in the divine scheme of things and your self doubts will give way.

Drive your prayers deep into your doubts, fears and 'inferiorities'. When you pray you are on the hotline to the greatest power in the universe. Not to a shadowy being in a distant galaxy, but someone by your side, in your office or car or home; always nearby as a partner. If you fill your mind with affirmation of God's involvement in and concern for your life the domination of insecurity will be destroyed.

Of course, the problems which weigh us down and make us insecure are not 'all in the mind'. Life can throw some sharp missiles our way. But any fact facing us, however difficult, is not as important as our attitude *towards* the fact. Victims of the inferiority malady see all facts through discoloured attitudes. Psychiatrist Dr Karl Menninger has said: 'Attitudes are more important than facts.' The best corrective is to gain a normal view, slanted to the positive side. Begin by making a list of all the things you have going for you.

Worry is an unhealthy, destructive private vice. You were not born with it. You let it grow on you. The effects of worry carry over into all four spheres of life, especially the physical and the social. It is founded on fear and fear can only be overcome by faith. Master faith and you will automatically master fear. And again; you will only master faith if you spend time each day with God. Worry is a cancer which spreads through the mind and fills it with thoughts contrary to God's care. Cancel each day as you scrunch a page of your calendar. Live a day at a time, 'forgetting the past and looking forward to what lies ahead,' (Philippians 3:13). Expel worry. Fill your mind with thoughts of God's power, God's protection, God's goodness.

'Fret not yourself,' a wise man said (Psalm 37:1). But fretting and fuming consume a disproportionate amount of our lives. We must reduce our pace by

changing the character of our thoughts. Over-stimulation, fatigue, frustration, debilitation, even emotional illness, result from the ultrasonic pace of our lives.

Slow down and receive the peace 'which passes all understanding' (Philippians 4:7).

If you are a town-dweller, take time to enjoy the peace of the countryside; heart-expanding views from great heights. Lush fields where cattle graze. Crystal air hung with the smell of everything that grows. Untamed hillsides, heather-clad. The golden glory of autumn in misting woods. The solitude of bare fells. 'Let's get away from the

> **'I can do everything with the help of Christ who gives me the strength I need .' (Philippians 4:13.)** ⓘ

crowds for a while and rest.' (Mark 6:31.)

Relax; and receive the peace of God – into your joints, as well as into every facet of your personality.

Because attitudes are more important than facts, *choose* to be happy. By your thoughts and attitudes you distil out of the ingredients of life either happiness or unhappiness for yourself. 'The cheerful heart has a continual feast.' (Proverbs 15:15.) Do not harbour negative feelings – 'Everything always turns out for the worse. It's just my luck', 'Trust *him* to come up from the canal with a new pair of boots on. If it had been me, I would have gone head-first into the mud'; enjoy the continual feast of the happy man.

When you adopt a positive outlook on your life your social life will blossom; you will enjoy the adventure of living – become popular, well-liked, and feel an all-pervasive sense of well-being. In short, the social component of your being will be in 100%, A1, healthy condition.

The intellectual you

Don't be put off by that sub-heading. You may not class yourself as an 'intellectual', but it still applies to you. The alternative would have been 'The mental you', and you would have liked that even less. But you take the point: the part of you we are talking about is the part that thinks – *the mind.* In other words – that element in your make-up which, though often suppressed, is searching for answers to life's problems, a sense of purpose, fulfilment, and yearns for first-hand experience that makes of your life a meaningful adventure. The intellectual you cries out to be challenged, to pursue some great goal, and rebels against the boredom of life. The truth is, of course, that man's most obvious missing component is a built-in direction finder, a psychological equivalent of the automatic pilot. And *without aim there is no challenge.* Jesus saw how a vacuous, pointless existence left the spirit of man like an empty house – prey to invasion by devils of all kinds, mischief, despondency, despair, mental turmoil. He put forward a dominating, life-fulfilling purpose – salvation by grace through faith in him. He knew that rich talent lies buried beneath the soil of self-pity and injured self-importance. To him the individual was of supreme importance. He set each human life against the background of eternity, extending to an infinite perspective each individual's struggle for worth and hope. He never spoke in terms of large-sounding abstractions like 'humanity' and 'mankind'. Always of *you* and *you* and *you*. Within God's great purpose every man's life-work makes its own unique contribution. Accept his leadership and you accept adventure and reject futility.

In the hectic, noisy pattern of life these days a daily 'quiet time' can have a strong therapeutic value. For minds in turmoil this daily practice of silence can bring peace. In it do not read, do not write, do not worry. Thomas Carlyle said: 'Silence is the element in which great things fashion themselves.' After your period of silence pray that the tensions of life may be kept at bay and the inner harmony of the mind may be restored. Reject futility and begin 'great things', the supreme adventure into which Jesus Christ invites you.

The spiritual you

The spiritual you harmonises all the other aspects of your living. Unless the spiritual you is at peace, you are a walking civil war. And if you do not recognise the existence of a 'spiritual you' you are seriously under-estimating your importance and the significance of your life.

Remember, dysfunction in the spiritual being is often caused by a sense of 'uproot-edness'. You know: 'Roots, the things you come from, the things that feed you. . . .' Psychiatry is no more than a highly-developed skill in root-investigation and root-pruning. But of vaster importance: Christianity has to do with the root-system of the individual, the permanent soil from which thought, aspiration, belonging, aim, self respect, stability and feeling, spring and are sustained.

Man moves and grows and journeys – he may even pass from the scene – but he has roots among eternal things. These roots remain though all else changes. And man's spiritual being develops as they grow. Those roots are in a loving Creator God who cares and guides and empathises. They go down to the nourishing stream that flows from God through Christ who came to Earth, lived, died and on the third day rose again from the dead that we might know freedom from guilt, and the assurance of salvation.

The pilgrim spirit of mankind has its home – a background from whence man came, a goal towards which he tends. For whole-person health, the spiritual you requires an unshifting faith in the eternal God, the assurance of salvation through his Son Jesus Christ, the moral shelter of his reverent, unaccommodating code and the deep emotional resource of the comfort of a divine love which knows no limit.

When the spiritual you is rooted in God, the diseases and dysfunctions of the spirit require no healing. Your problems are off-loaded on broader shoulders than your own. Your mind is no longer filled with echoing, strident, conflicting voices. You are no longer lost, for God has found you and, in him, your life has meaning. You have peace and joy: a peace that passes understanding and a joy that no man takes from you.

For whole-person health each of the interrelated aspects of man's being – the physical, the social, the intellectual and the spiritual – needs to be in health. And basic to all is the spiritual.

Chapter Twenty

Simple Home Treatments

Many accidental injuries and some illnesses respond very well to treatment given at home. Simple treatments can be achieved by the application of cold or heat, and one of the best ways of doing this is through the medium of water. Using water, and articles to be found in most homes, many simple forms of treatment can be carried out quite effectively.

The application of heat and cold to the body changes the blood supply in that area. Heat dilates the smaller blood vessels and increases blood supply, while cold constricts the smaller blood vessels and reduces blood supply. Cold, for instance, is very satisfactory in the treatment of soft tissue injuries such as a sprained ankle.

Important. Simple home treatments are inexpensive, readily available and effective. Home treatments are for immediate first aid only and never replace the advice and prescription of your doctor. Consult him early with your problem and he will be pleased to advise on your self-help programme through hydrotherapy which is the scientific term for the use of water as a therapy.

Water in the treatment of burns

This is an emergency treatment. It is pain relieving and effective in reducing damage but must never take the place of carefully controlled medical care, which must be implemented as soon as possible.

Immerse the burnt part in cold water. Hold a burnt fingertip under a running tap. Use a basin for a burnt hand. An arm or leg needs a bucket, sink or bath.

Areas such as the forehead, cheek or abdominal wall should be drenched with cold water and the burn covered with clean wet cloths. Renew the cloths as they lose their coldness. A small trickle of water is of no use. Drenching or submersion is essential for at least ten minutes or for as long as the pain persists. This method cools the tissues deep in the skin, reduces inflammation from the burn and reduces later redness, blistering and scarring.

DO NOT USE ICED WATER. The extreme cold can be more painful and is less effective. *Even if the burn has been of half an hour or longer duration it is still worth while using cold water.*

The immediate use of whatever water is at hand might increase the risk of infection, but this is offset by other benefits and by the availability of medication in the form of antibiotics.

If at all possible keep the burnt part elevated, raised on a pillow – or, if an arm or hand, supported in a sling. Get medical help without delay.

Chemicals in the eye

Children like to play with bottles and containers. In a domestic situation this might be harmless but some bottles and containers do contain substances which can be dangerous if taken internally or splashed into the eye. Immediately wash out the chemical with a continuous and copious, but smooth, flow of water. The patient may be keeping the eye tightly shut because of pain, so you must pull the lids firmly but gently open. Hold the head so that the affected eye is at an angle and the water flows off sideways on to the floor or into a basin. It should not pour over the rest of the face or into the other eye. In this way the chemical is diluted and removed. You may have to irrigate the eyes for a full ten minutes. An adult person could immerse the face in a basin of cold water and blink the eyes rapidly. *Get medical aid as soon as possible.*

The hot foot-bath

The hot foot-bath is a simple but very effective procedure. It is valuable because of its effect on the entire circulation of the body. By dilating the blood vessels in the feet and legs, it may relieve congestion in other parts of the body – brain, lungs or abdominal organs. The blood is shifted from one part of the body to another. This is called derivation.

During cold weather it is easy to become chilled from exposure. Precaution against taking cold may be accomplished by stimulating the circulation and warming the entire body with a hot foot-bath.

This simple hydrotherapy procedure will also aid in relieving nervous tension by lessening the congestion in the brain and thus balancing the circulation. When a person is nervously fatigued the feet are usually cold, with an unequal circulation; thus a hot foot-bath can be a valuable measure for relaxation.

Articles needed:

◆ Foot-bath (a clean bucket or a plastic wash bowl may be used).
◆ Bath towel.
◆ Kettle of boiling water.
◆ Basin of cold water.
◆ Two blankets (if patient is sitting up for treatment, wrap well).
◆ Plastic sheeting or newspaper covered with towels to protect bedding (if treatment given in bed).

Procedure:

1. Have the room warm, with no draughts on the patient.

2. Place plastic sheeting, with towel over it, on the floor under the feet.

3. Fill foot-bath with water about 40 °C/104 °F to cover ankles well. (Test with elbow if thermometer is not available.)

4. Place patient's feet in bath and cover with blanket to keep warm.

5. Very carefully add hot water to increase the temperature gradually as tolerated up to 44-46 °C/112-115 °F.

6. Continue treatment ten minutes to half an hour, depending on effect desired.

7. Keep patient's head cool with a cold compress. This can be made from a folded face-flannel wrung out in cold water. It should be applied as needed.

8. When the feet are removed from the hot water pour cold water over them quickly and place them on the towel. Remove the foot-bath. Dry the feet thoroughly, especially between the toes.

Precautions:

✦ In adding hot water, place the feet on one side and pour hot water slowly down inside of bath. Protect the feet by gently stirring water with your hand.

✦ If patient perspires, dry thoroughly with towel.

✦ Do not use hot foot-bath in cases of hardening of the arteries of the feet except under a physician's direction.

✦ If there is a loss of skin sensation burns can occur unless used with due caution.

Indications:

✦ To prevent or shorten a cold.

✦ To relieve a headache.

✦ To stimulate the circulation when the feet are cold.

✦ To relieve pelvic cramps.

✦ To aid relaxation.

Ice or cold pack for sprains*

In the early nineteenth century, Priessnitz, an Austrian peasant lad, discovered the use of cold compresses following a personal injury. We now realise that applications of cold are just as important as applications of heat, provided we use them in the proper way and time.

In the case of a sprained ankle, if ice, or even cold water, is obtainable, treatment should be given at the earliest possible moment. The application of cold will prevent much swelling and will lessen the black-and-blue discolor-ation, which is due to rupturing of the blood vessels. Cold contracts the size of the blood vessels and keeps the blood from oozing out into the torn tissues. If the part is then kept elevated and bandaged, the tissues will be given support, and healing can take place.

An application of heat should not be used at first. Because the blood vessels have been injured, there is swelling, and if more blood is drawn to the part by heating, the swelling increases.

Short applications of cold bring about a stimulation of the circulation and the nervous system, by reaction. *Prolonged* application overcomes the reaction of the body and slows *down* the circulation. Cold also relieves pain. However, a prolonged application should not be left on continuously. It should be removed periodically to allow the body to main-tain its ability to react to changes in temperature.

If possible, the sprained ankle should be put into ice water or under a cold tap for several minutes. This should be repeated every two hours for the first eight to twelve hours. If it is difficult for the patient to put the sprained limb into cold water, an ice bag or an ice pack may be applied, while the limb is kept elevated. If an ice bag is used over a painful joint, the bag must not be more than half filled and the air must be expelled so that it can fit the surface to which it is applied. An ice bag cannot cover the joint entirely. An ice pack is better. See Procedures 1 and 2 for ice pack instructions.

Articles needed:

◆ A light flannel or bandage to wrap the joint.
◆ Two or three large towels.
◆ Piece of plastic sheeting large enough to wrap the joint – or domestic plastic film (plastic bags cut up).
◆ Plastic sheeting to protect the bed.
◆ Finely crushed ice.
◆ Safety pins.

Procedure:

1. Bandage the joint lightly. In order to prevent freezing, ice should not come in direct contact with the skin.
2. Spread the finely crushed ice on a towel, forming a layer about one inch thick. Adjust size as needed for the joint. To make easier application to a large joint, such as the shoulder, it may be necessary to make a small pack with the towel fold-ed in half to put *under* the joint and then put a large pack *over* the joint. Wrap the whole with plastic sheeting or film and pin in place.
3. Protect the bed with plastic sheeting.
4. Continue application for thirty minutes.
5. Remove pack and dry area carefully.
6. Bandage as ordered by the doctor.
7. Repeat procedure every two hours for the first eight to twelve hours.

Precautions:

◆ Observe reaction closely during the applications to avoid injury to tissues by freezing.

◆ Protect bed adequately.

It can often be extremely difficult to know if an injured joint is just strained ligaments of the joint or if a flake of bone has been pulled off, or a hair-line fracture is present. More gross injuries are obvious. If what initially seemed to be a minor sprain is not improving after rest and water treatment for about two days, advice should be sought from medically trained personnel.

Indications:

In case of sprain or torn ligaments: after cold has been used for eight to twelve hours, applications of alternate hot and cold or a contrast bath is beneficial for overcoming stiffness. Massage (light strokes towards the body) may be started as soon as tenderness has lessened. Between treatments it is important to give support by bandaging. Movement should be started as early as possible to prevent stiffness.

Heating compress

By applications of heat to the skin, the blood vessels are dilated and blood is brought to the surface, thereby congestion is relieved. When it is desirable to maintain such a derivative effect, a heating compress may be applied between treatments or overnight.

A heating compress is a cold compress applied to the part and covered by a dry flannel to prevent circulation of air, and to cause an accumulation of body heat. The compress soon warms up and so has the effect of a mild application of heat. If the compress dries out before being removed it has a mild opposite effect.

If the pack is also covered with plastic film, drying is prevented and local sweating will occur. This will also cause relaxation of muscles. When the compress is removed the part should be rubbed with cold water.

Indications:

Heating compresses may be used for a sore throat or in cases of pharyngitis, tonsillitis and quinsy; for the chest in colds, pneumonia, whooping cough and so forth. The heating compress may be applied to knee, ankle, foot, hand or wrist, in joint conditions, or to the abdomen in cases of constipation, certain types of indigestion, and in cases of insomnia. It is important, however, to remember that these treatments do not take the place of recognised medications with antibiotics from a doctor, or seeking medical advice first in problems of abdominal pain.

Heating compress for a sore throat

Articles needed:

✦ Old cotton cloth, two thicknesses about three inches wide and long enough to wrap round the neck twice.

✦ A piece of flannel (single or double, depending upon the weight of the material) about four inches wide, and long enough to wrap round the neck twice. Crepe bandage can be used.

✦ Safety pins.

✦ A piece of bandage (to put over the top of the head to hold the compress up under the lower part of the ear).

Procedure:

1. Wring the cotton cloth from cold water and apply around the neck.

2. Cover well with flannel and fit snugly but not tight enough to be uncomfortable.

3. Pin securely – use bandage over head, from ear to ear, to hold compress in place in cases of tonsillitis.

4. Rub the neck with cold water immediately after removing the compress in the morning.

Precautions:

Considerable water may be left in the throat compress when it is first applied, but it should not drip and it should be dry by morning.

Indications:

◇ Pharyngitis.
◇ Acute laryngitis.
◇ Tonsillitis and quinsy.
◇ Inflammation of eustachian tubes (the tubes leading from the throat to the middle ear).

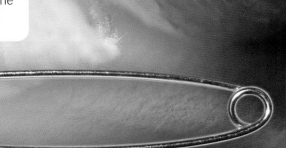

Heating compress to a joint

A heating compress applied to a painful joint prolongs the increased circulation obtained by applications of heat. This helps not only to relieve pain, but also to restore joint motion in chronic rheumatic conditions.

Articles needed:

✦ Old cotton cloth (sheeting will do), two thicknesses, four to six inches wide, and long enough to wrap the joint well.
✦ Piece of flannel or thin blanket material (single or double depending upon the weight of the material) six to eight inches wide and of good length.
✦ Piece of plastic sheeting or domestic plastic film (plastic bags cut up).
✦ Safety pins.
✦ Medication, such as oil of wintergreen (diluted) if required.

Precautions:

✦ The wet compress should be applied so that it is well covered to avoid chilling and to aid in a prompt action.
✦ Take care that the compress is not so tight that the circulation is restricted or joint motion is limited.

Indications:

✦ Chronic rheumatic joint conditions.
✦ Acute painful joints of rheumatic fever.

Procedure:

1. If medication such as oil of wintergreen is to be applied, this should be done just following the application of heat to the part. The cotton compress may be wrung from a solution of the medication.

2. The cotton cloth wrung from cold (tap) water is applied in the manner of a bandage. It is well to begin by placing the width of the bandage on an angle to the extremity so that the bandage will fit better around the joint with as little bulk as possible.

3. The compress is then covered with cling film or plastic bags cut up. This helps to obtain a close application to the skin surface.

4. A dry bandage is then applied and pinned in place.

5. A hot water bottle (not too heavy) may be applied over the outer bandage to prolong the application.

6. The compress may be left on all day or all night, or it may be removed for another application of heat and then re-applied.

7. In some cases the wet compress may be omitted and only the dry flannel used, with medication applied to the skin.

Medicated steam inhalation

With the changeable weather of winter we are exposed to colds on all sides. When one is a victim of the common cold (Coryza), congestion of the membranes of the nose, throat and sinuses occurs. With the cold there is a feeling of stuffiness and some-times excessive drainage. In a 'chest cold' there is often a harsh, dry cough which later 'loosens up'. A steam inhalation is an excellent way of supplying warm, moist air to congested mucous membranes.

Articles needed:

◆ A wide-necked jug or a medical inhaler (Nelson's Inhaler).
◆ Boiling water.
◆ Medication such as:
a. Oil of Eucalyptus – 1 teaspoon to the pint
b. Tincture of Benzoin Co. – 1 teaspoon to the pint
c. Garlic Oil or 2-3 Garlic capsules.
◆ Newspaper or light card to use as cone in jug method.
◆ Large plate or a tray with a towel to provide a non-slip surface and support for the inhalation.

Procedure:

1. Fill jug or inhaler to prescribed or safe level – (care should be exercised to prevent spilling) – usually 1 pint. Add medication prescribed or of choice.
2. Carry to table, bedside table or to the bed of the patient and arrange firm support.
3. If using the jug method, make cone of newspaper or card to direct steam so that the patient can inhale it. If desired, completely cover – drape patient's head with a towel – thereby creating a small steam tent. Remember, some folk, especially some children, do not like being shut in!

Continue inhalation from 20 minutes to half an hour and repeat 3-4 times a day at regular intervals or as indicated by doctor.

Indications:

◇ To relieve inflammation and congestion of the mucous membranes of the upper respiratory tract.

◇ To relieve irritation by moistening the air.

◇ To loosen secretions and to stimulate expectoration.

◇ To relieve coughing.

◇ To prevent excessive dryness of mucous membranes.

When the inhalation is completed, cool sponge face and hands. A bed patient will usually sleep well for a period after this treatment.

Precautions:

◇ Check inhalation often.

◇ Avoid too close contact with steam as this may lead to scalding.

◇ Remember – children will require continuous care.

◇ If, as a result of the cold, the lips or nostrils are sore, smear with a soothing cream or a little Vaseline.

These simple home treatments demonstrate useful ways in which water can be used in dealing with accidents and health problems. The person who can carry out these treatments will be rewarded by seeing the beneficial results that come in such a short time. These are nature's ways of healing. There is healing power in water.

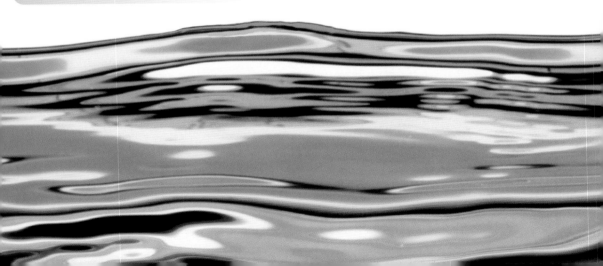

Chapter Twenty-one

First Aid

First aid can be given by anybody, but the simple information given in this chapter can help you to be effective when faced with more serious accidents and emergencies.

No difficult medical terms are used, because they're not necessary and will not make you any better at first aid. It's how you cope and what you do when faced with a crisis that matters.

In order to act correctly, however, you should have clearly in your mind the right course of action to take in a given situation. Just knowing that there are certain things you can do will make you more confident that you can help.

If you read carefully, and visualise yourself acting in the following situations, you will more readily react in the correct way. Even the most simple steps, followed correctly, can save lives.

So, what *is* First Aid?

It is the application of certain principles of treatment at an accident or in the event of sudden illness, using facilities and materials available on the spot. It is treating the casualty until he or she can be seen by a doctor, or taken to hospital where necessary.

Why use First Aid?

Your action may make the difference between life and death for a casualty. You can prevent the condition getting worse. What you do will effect for the good, the person's trauma and long-term recovery.

What should you do as a First Aider?

1. Do not put yourself in danger

Remember, the initial cause of an accident could cause a similar accident – to *you* if you don't assess the danger first. Leave fires to the professionals, and be careful of exposure to harmful chemicals which may have been spilled. Always carry a hazard sign to use in road traffic accidents. If it's a case of drowning, be sure that you are up to the physical challenge before plunging in.

2. Assess the situation

If you are confident of handling things alone, do so. If in any doubt, ask any people around to phone for an ambulance, or help those less injured. If they are not in shock, it will be good for them to have something to do.

3. Find out what is wrong with the casualty

First, protect them from further harm, but do not move them unless they are in danger by remaining where they are.

4. Administer obviously-needed treatment immediately

If there are two or more casualties, quickly but calmly check each to see which needs attention most urgently. Be aware that the one making the most noise is probably least hurt! Your priorities when dealing with any casualty should follow the **ABC** rule.

5. Remain with the casualty until professional medical help arrives.

Talk reassuringly, and listen carefully to anything they might tell you.

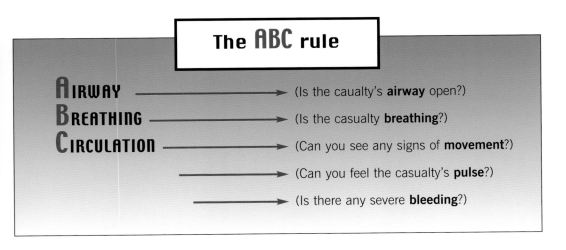

The ABC rule

AIRWAY ⟶ (Is the caualty's **airway** open?)

BREATHING ⟶ (Is the casualty **breathing**?)

CIRCULATION ⟶ (Can you see any signs of **movement**?)

⟶ (Can you feel the casualty's **pulse**?)

⟶ (Is there any severe **bleeding**?)

Assessing the situation
Making an initial diagnosis:
> Find out, if not obvious, how the accident occurred.

> Listen to what casualty might be trying to tell you.

> Use all your senses to gather information: look, speak, listen, feel, and smell.

The Recovery position:

Stage 1

a. Maintain the open airway position

b. If there is time, remove the casualty's spectacles, and any bulky objects from pockets (especially keys!)

c. Straighten the casualty's legs.

d. Tuck the arm nearest to you under the body, with the elbow straight and the palm of the hand upwards.

Stage 2

a. Bring the other arm across the chest, and hold the casualty's hand against the cheek to support the head.

b. Grasp the casualty's leg just above the knee and lift it towards you (so the leg bends at the knee and the foot stays on the floor).

Stage 4

a. Maintain your grasp of the casualty's thigh and pull it towards you.

b. Use your knees, if necessary, to stop the casualty rolling too far.

Stage 5

a. Ajust the upper leg if necessary (hip and knee should be bent at right angles).

b. Draw the casualty's chin forward to clear the tongue from the throat and aid drainage, adjusting the hand under the cheek if necessary.

c. Ajust the back arm so that the casualty is not lying on it.

Artificial Respiration
(Mouth-to-mouth resuscitation)

where casualty has a pulse but is not breathing
To adult or child over age of 1:

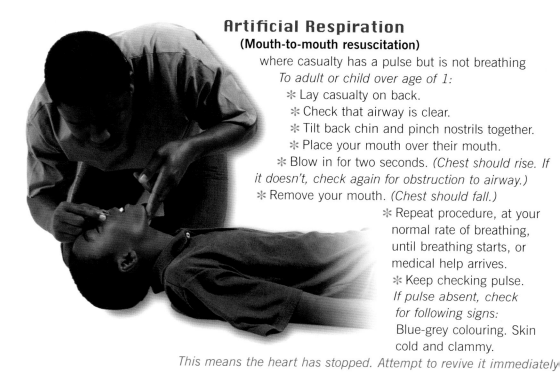

* Lay casualty on back.
* Check that airway is clear.
* Tilt back chin and pinch nostrils together.
* Place your mouth over their mouth.
* Blow in for two seconds. *(Chest should rise. If it doesn't, check again for obstruction to airway.)*
* Remove your mouth. *(Chest should fall.)*
* Repeat procedure, at your normal rate of breathing, until breathing starts, or medical help arrives.
* Keep checking pulse. *If pulse absent, check for following signs:* Blue-grey colouring. Skin cold and clammy.

This means the heart has stopped. Attempt to revive it immediately

Cardiopulmonary resuscitation (CPR)

where casualty is not breathing and there is no pulse
* Lay casualty on his back.
* Kneel at side and over him.
* Place heel of hand over lower breastbone, with other hand on top.
* With arms straight, press down firmly at approximately 100 presses a minute, as follows: after 15 presses, give two breaths through mouth, then another 15 presses and keep repeating.
* Check for pulse after first minute, then every minute until heart starts or help arrives.

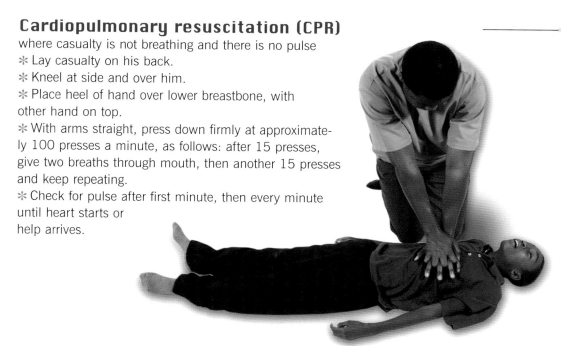

What is Shock?

Shock is the medical condition resulting from insufficient oxygen reaching the tissues because the circulatory system has broken down, either because heart pump fails, or there is not enough blood and other body fluids circulating in body. *Look for* cold clammy skin, weak pulse, faintness, blue lips and difficulty breathing. Lay casualty down with legs raised and cover with warm coat or blanket. Do not give food or fluids. Resuscitation might be necessary. If casualty is unconscious do not leave them.
* Remember: the airway is always the priority.

CPR in children 1-7: Lay child on back. Using only *one* hand, press lower breastbone to third of chest depth for 100 presses as above, giving breath through mouth every five presses. Repeat as above.

CPR in babies under 1 year:
Using only two fingers, press lower breastbone to third of chest depth for 100 compressions as above, giving one breath (through nose and mouth) every five presses. Repeat as above.

Dealing with an unconscious casualty:
Follow the ABC rule:

Airway – clear away anything obstructing the airway. The airway of an unconscious casualty is in danger of being blocked by solids (casualty's tongue, broken teeth, food) and fluids (blood, saliva, vomit).

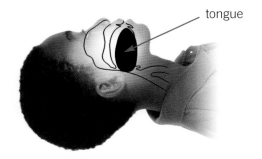

tongue

Breathing –
LOOK for chest movement
LISTEN for sounds of breathing
FEEL for breath on your cheek
LIFT the chin throughout the breathing check to keep airway open
The breathing check should last **10 seconds.**

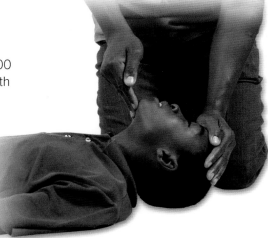

Circulation –

To check that a casualty's heart is beating adequately, you should feel for the carotid pulse in the neck

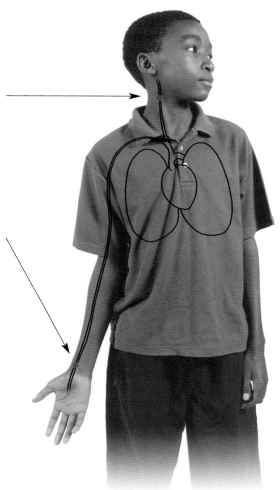

The radial pulse is usually used if your casualty is conscious

Use **2** fingers and feel for **10** seconds. Do **not** use your **thumb**.

Having prioritised and treated any potentially life-threatening conditions, check the casualty for other injuries you cannot see at first glance. Feel for broken bones and bleeding. If there are no obvious injuries, carefully turn the casualty into the recovery position.

BASIC STEPS TO REMEMBER IN CERTAIN EMERGENCY SITUATIONS:

Accidents on the roads: adopt some method of traffic control, then deal with casualties.

Bleeding - controlling heavy loss/wound dressing:
Apply direct pressure.
Raise and support injured limb.
Lay casualty down to treat for shock.
Apply sterile dressing firmly.
 Call an ambulance.
Remember to Protect yourself from infection from casualty's blood.
If blood comes through dressing, do *not* remove it. Apply another dressing on top.

Burns: remove casualty to safety. Cool area affected for at least 10 minutes with cold water. People with severe burns require urgent medical assistance. Give casualty lots to drink, and keep him warm till help arrives.

Chemicals and Poisoning: if *non-corrosive,* take patient to hospital immediately, taking sample of poison with you in safe container. If *corrosive* **do not** make patient vomit, or the poison will burn again on way up.

If resuscitation is necessary, perform only with masking material between your mouth and casualty's. Wash mouth and flood area of affected skin with lots of water. Irrigate away from eyes or other non-affected areas of body.

Remove contaminated clothing, being careful not to get chemical on self. Keep sample of corrosive substance to send to hospital with the casualty.

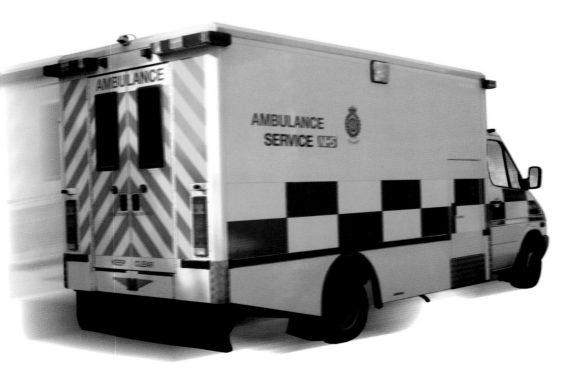

Choking: Pull out any obvious obstruction.If obstruction cannot be seen, get person to bend forward and cough. Slap between shoulder blades. If no success, use the *Heimlich manoeuvre*.

The Heimlich Manoeuvre

→ Stand behind choking person.

→ Place hands over upper abdomen below bottom of breastbone.

→ Link hands with one thumb pushing against abdomen.

→ Pull in sharply and with upward movement five times, then slap back.

→ Repeat if not successful first time.

. . . on child 1-7 years

→ Stand or kneel behind child.

→ Place fist over lower breastbone, other hand on top of fist.

→ Pull firmly in upward direction five times, then slap back.

→ If no success, move hands lower to upper abdomen and try again.

→ Repeat as necessary.

Warning: do not use this manoeuvre on a child under 1 year of age.

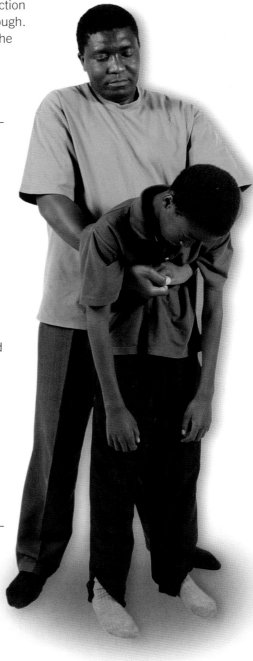

Drowning: First check to see if there is anything you can use to get the person out of the water, e.g. rope, life belt, long piece of wood. Do not enter water if it will endanger your own life. Once recovered from the water, person should be laid on back, head lower than feet to allow water to drain. Check for debris in mouth. Do **ABC** and rescusitate if necessary. Keep person warm until help arrives. Hospitalisation is always recommended afterwards, even if person feels well.

Electrocution: *Before* touching casualty or appliance, ensure that current is turned off. If you can't find source of electrical current, stand on chair or large book and push appliance away from casualty with wooden object. Make sure the surfaces of these are dry. Apply **CPR** if necessary. Treat any burns resulting.

Epileptic fit: Do not restrain patient during convulsion. Move away any objects which could harm. When fit is over, allow person to rest, and they will often sleep. Don't fuss.

Fainting: Patient will be pale and sweaty with slow pulse. If conscious, get them to lie down or sit with head between knees. If unconscious, check their pulse and breathing. Lay them down and raise legs above head until recovered, but for at least ten minutes. Give drink of fruit juice or water. Get help immediately if person does not regain consciousness.

Fractures and breaks:
Leg or arm injuries: support limb (with leg, tie together, with arm, use sling.
Neck injury: Check for severe pain, paralysis, or tingling sensations. Do not let injured person move, and support neck until help arrives. A rolled towel makes a good neck brace.

Fumes: (gas and poisonous) turn off supply if possible; remove casualty. Check breathing as below. Open windows. Resuscitate if necessary.

Heart attack: If person has difficulty breathing, with pain in chest, and lips going blue, lay them down, check pulse and breathing, Do **CPR** if necessary. Get medical help.

Heatstroke and sunburn: Look for nausea with bad headache, confusion, fast pulse and hot skin. Move patient into shade, loosen or wet his clothing or wrap in wet towels. This should help reduce temperature. Resuscitate if necessary. With simple sunburn, cool the skin with water or cooling cream such as calamine. Administer fluids. Seek help if blistering appears.

Hypothermia: patient will feel cold and confused, or may be unconscious. If the cause is near-drowning, remove wet clothes and warm patient gradually with blankets or by holding them close so that your body heat is transferred. If patient is conscious give a warm drink, but never alcohol.

Objects embedded in limb: bandage *around* the object. **Do not attempt to remove.**

Smoke inhalation: Without risking your own safety, remove person from danger.
If moving through smoke, cover your nose and mouth with a wet cloth and keep low as smoke rises.

Suspected fractures:
Do not move patient unless essential for safety of casualty or self.
Support limbs by hand or with splint or sling.
Get casualty to hospital as soon as possible.
Moving a conscious casualty:
Move only if necessary to avoid further harm.

Moving an unconscious casualty:
ABC is more important than not being moved. Steady and support head and trunk, keeping them in alignment throughout procedure.

Dragging injured person: Fold their arms over their chest. Bend your knees and place hands under person's armpits. Pull without jerking.

Supporting walking casualty: Stand on injured side, unless with injured arm, then opposite side. Get person to put their arm across your shoulder. Hold their hand to keep arm in place. Put other arm across casualty's back at waist, gripping clothing. Take small steps.

Dealing with less critical incidents

Bee and wasp stings: Extract sting if possible with sterile needle or tweezers. Apply cold dressing or antihistamine cream. Get help immediately in cases of severe swelling or if person has difficulty breathing.

Corrosive substance in eye: Flood eye with running water for 10-15 minutes. Cover eye with pad and get person to hospital.

Foreign bodies:

In ear: Turn head to one side, shake gently and object might fall out. If not successful, get patient to hospital.

In eye: Do not let person rub eye. Ask them to blink rapidly. Irrigate the eye with water. Sit patient down in good light. Wash your hands, then check patient's eye by getting patient to look up while you gently draw down lower lid. If particle is visible, remove with moistened corner of clean cloth. Do not attempt to dig out embedded object.

Sprains: apply ice pack and see doctor if rest, with ten-minute ice packs does not improve condition.

Index

Picture credits

Science Photo Library 22, 23, 29, 38, 40, 41, 89, 159, 164, 177, 182, 183, 185, 188, 192.